Alternative Conceptions of Civil Society

Alternative Conceptions of Civil Society

EDITED BY

Simone Chambers
and Will Kymlicka

PRINCETON UNIVERSITY PRESS

PRINCETON AND OXFORD

LIBRARY OF CONGRESS CATALOGING-IN-PUBLICATION DATA

Alternative conceptions of civil society / edited by Simone Chambers and Will Kymlicka.
    p.   cm. — (The Ethikon series in comparative ethics)
   Includes bibliographical references and index.
   ISBN 0-691-08795-4 (alk. paper) — ISBN 0-691-08796-2 (pbk. : alk. paper)
   1. Ethics.   2. Social ethics.   3. Pluralism (Social sciences)   I. Chambers, Simone.
II. Kymlicka, Will.   III. Series.
BJ1031 .A48   2002
172—dc21

                                 2001036262

British Library Cataloging-in-Publication Data is available

This book has been composed in Galliard

Printed on acid-free paper. ∞

www.pup.princeton.edu

Printed in the United States of America
10 9 8 7 6 5 4 3 2 1
10 9 8 7 6 5 4 3 2 1
(Pbk.)

Contents

PART IV

PART V

Acknowledgments

THE EDITORS join with Philip Valera, president of the Ethikon Institute; Carole Pateman, series editor; and members of the Ethikon board of trustees in thanking all who contributed to the dialogue project that resulted in this book. We are especially indebted to the Ahmanson Foundation and its trustees, Robert F. Erburu and Lee Walcott, who provided the major support for the project, and to other important donors, including the Carrie Estelle Doheny Foundation, Joan Palevsky, and the Sidney Stern Memorial Trust. In addition to the authors, the project was greatly enhanced by the active participation of other dialogue partners, many of whose ideas have found their way into this book: Jeffrey Alexander; Benedict Ashley, O.P.; James Hanink; Eugene Mornell; Peter Nosco; William O'Neill, S.J.; Carole Pateman; Daniel Philpott; Bernard H. Siegan; Tracy B. Strong; Tu Wei-ming; and Lee Yearley. Special thanks to Sohail Hashmi for help above and beyond the call of duty.

Simone Chambers wishes to thank the University Center for Human Values at Princeton, and especially its director, Amy Gutmann, for providing the time to do much of the editing. We also thank the two anonymous reviewers and Ian Malcolm, our editor at Princeton University Press.

Alternative Conceptions of Civil Society

Alternative Conceptions of Civil Society

Simone Chambers and Will Kymlicka

THIS BOOK is part of an ongoing project by the Ethikon Institute to investigate and compare how various secular and religious traditions organize, understand, and live with ethical pluralism. Previous Ethikon studies have focused on the international dimensions of this question. Given that societies around the world often have distinct and sometimes conflicting ethical beliefs, what rules or principles should govern their interaction? This includes issues of the ethics of war and peace and of migration and boundaries.[1]

In this volume, we shift our attention to ethical pluralism *within* a particular society: how should a society respond to the existence of ethical diversity among its own members? This is a problem that is of central importance for many Western democracies, which are often painfully aware of the fact that they lack any clear consensus on many ethical issues. Indeed, the existence of this sort of pluralism is often part of their very self-conception as "modern" and "democratic" societies.

However, issues of ethical pluralism face all societies. It is, as John Rawls has succinctly pointed out, simply a fact that people have different answers to questions like, What is the good life? What is the source of truth and meaning in the world? What are our obligations to each other? and so on. This fact of pluralism transcends self-consciously "pluralist" societies. Perhaps there is more disagreement in the heterogeneous societies that call themselves pluralist, but even the most homogeneous society will have to decide what is the right way of dealing with dissenting minorities and what are the boundaries of that homogeneity. The conscious endorsement and protection of diversity is one response to the fact of ethical pluralism. But it is not the only response.

So our aim in this volume, and the next two volumes in the series, is to explore how various secular and religious traditions conceptualize and deal with pluralism within societies. This is, of course, a very broad (and somewhat vague) topic, and so we have tried to sharpen the focus by asking authors to describe and explain the concept of *civil society* from the point of view of their respective traditions. Civil society is a useful concept to highlight the question of how we live with ethical pluralism, since it directs attention to the organization of associational life. Because people tend to associate with others who share their values, identity, and beliefs, associational life is the social expression of ethical pluralism. How a particular tradition encourages, tolerates, regulates, or limits such forms of associational life should tell us a great deal, therefore, about how it conceives of ethical pluralism.

We will pursue the topic of civil society in a series of three volumes, of which this is the first. As the first installment, this book is meant to establish some of the broad philosophical and spiritual presuppositions of the way different traditions think of civil society. The second volume will focus on the relationship between government and civil society, and the third will examine in detail some particular examples of ethical pluralism in civil society (such as issues of family and sexuality).

In highlighting the concept of civil society, our hope is to focus attention on the social and political question of how we live with ethical pluralism, as opposed to more metaethical or even metaphysical questions regarding how we might establish truth and right in a world characterized by ethical pluralism. To some extent, such metaphysical questions are unavoidable, and no ethical tradition can be understood without some appreciation of its underlying metaethical beliefs. But our primary aim is to explore the social and political consequences of the metaphysical or metaethical doctrines within each tradition. Thus, many of the chapters discuss fundamental conceptions of cosmology, truth, the human condition, ultimate ends, and moral worth, but these broad themes are intended to underlie and give depth to social and political questions regarding the proper organization of civil society.

Civil society is a much discussed topic within contemporary social science, as well as in normative social theory. One source of this interest is the growing debate surrounding neo-Tocquevillian arguments. Called by Michael Walzer simply the "civil society argument," the neo-Tocquevillian belief is that the strength and stability of liberal democracy depends on a vibrant and healthy sphere of associational participation.While Tocqueville made this argument with regard to early America, many have taken it up as a perspective through which to analyze the strength of liberal democracy in the West, as well as the processes of democratization around the world, from the fall of communism in Eastern and Central Europe, to the rise of democratic regimes in South America, to the challenges in establishing liberal democracy is Africa. While many of the issues raised in this debate are also raised and discussed by the authors, this volume approaches the concept of civil society from a deeper and more fundamental perspective. Indeed, one of the rationales for an Ethikon volume on civil society is that the existing debate is rather narrow and lacks an appreciation for how traditions other than mainstream liberal ones might understand civil society and pose a challenge to liberal views. The concept of civil society is often used unselfconsciously. To be sure, scholars often argue about the boundaries or elements of civil society—for example, whether business corporations or political parties ought to be considered part of civil society or not. However, the debate rarely goes deeper to investigate the concept itself as embedded in traditions of thought. In contrast, our focus is on the conceptual issues that are often presupposed rather than addressed in the contemporary debate. These conceptual issues are essentially tied to traditions of thought that contain comprehensive moral and philosophic visions. Getting to the root of these differences is the task of this first volume.

To facilitate points of contact and comparison between the chapters, we posed a series of guideline questions that all authors were encouraged to address. The first few questions were intended to elicit a description of civil society. Who or what does civil society include? What makes civil society a society and not a simple aggregate? What are the unifying links between its parts? The next series of questions focused on broad normative aspects of civil society. What particular values does civil society offer its members that might be unobtainable in its absence? How and in what way is civil society important? What risks and liabilities, if any, does civil society pose for its members and society at large? The final series of questions looked at the legal, political, and moral organization of civil society. Within civil society, how is responsibility for human well-being properly shared by or distributed among the individual, the family, the state, and private associations? Who is to do what, and by what norms is this to be determined? What is the appropriate balance between individual autonomy, membership constraints, and collective regulation of the common good?

In answering these questions authors were asked to become "representatives" for particular traditions. First, they describe and explain the basic building blocks of their tradition's conception of civil society. Introducing the reader to the core components of a conception was particularly important with regard to the nonsecular and non-Western perspectives that might be unfamiliar to students of civil society. Even in the case of the Christian tradition, which is widely known in the West, such an introduction is necessary because the contemporary debate surrounding civil society is almost entirely dominated by secular views. Being generally familiar with Christianity is not the same thing as being familiar with a Christian conception of civil society. In order to promote the goal of comparison, all contributors, even those representing familiar traditions like liberalism, were asked to begin with the basic building blocks, thereby ensuring that their chapters were addressing similar questions at a similar level of analysis.

Although we asked authors to be representatives of traditions, we did not ask them to be neutral about the debates and controversies within their traditions. Indeed, we encouraged authors to stake out normative positions and defend what they thought to be the most persuasive version of civil society as well as to be critical with regard to inherent problems that might be presented by their tradition. The result is that while the chapters set out the basic components contained in each tradition in an accessible and easily comparative format, each one also makes a unique and sometimes controversial contribution to the debate. Adam Seligman, for example, while outlining the history of the concept, argues quite unexpectedly that there is a deep incoherence with regard to civil society within the liberal tradition. In defending critical theory's reading of civil society, Simone Chambers criticizes that tradition for failing to address the problem of illiberal and antidemocratic groups spreading out into civil society. Suzanne Stone's unique contribution is in articulating a Jewish conception of civil society in the first place. As such a task has rarely been done before, she finds herself taking Jewish social thought into new and uncharted waters. And Hasan Hanafi, a leading Egyptian intellectual, challenges mainstream Islamic doctrine by developing a rights-friendly yet nonliberal conception of Islamic civil society. These are just a few of the ways each chapter makes its own mark. Michael Mosher in his comparative conclusion does a more thorough job in highlighting the distinctive qualities of each chapter.

The main originality of the volume, however, lies in the dialogue that this comparative format promotes. By giving authors a shared and relatively strict mandate, we hope to create a volume that is truly comparative. Such a coordinated mandate is especially important given that the perspectives included are very disparate, spanning divisions between secular and nonsecular, Western and non-Western. This book, like all Ethikon volumes, is committed to pushing ethical debates in new and innovative directions by bringing together views that are not usually found between the same covers. To be successful, however, there must be clear points of contact between the essays that can be identified by the reader. We hope to have enabled such comparisons by employing a shared format and then inviting the reader to see the clear contrasts, similarities, cross-tradition challenges, and irreconcilable differences that emerge from this format. This comparative approach to ethics is an essential part of a full investigation of ethical issues. The critical study of differences and similarities between traditions brings the most significant and distinctive aspects of each tradition into relief. One way to appreciate the size of a redwood is to park a car beside it. Seeing traditions in juxtaposition to one another brings into focus what is unique within a tradition as well as elements that are shared with other traditions. It is particularly difficult to see the full significance of doctrines when one is inside the tradition that has inspired that doctrine. Comparison allows us to see how others might perceive our tradition, and this in turn can open our eyes to aspects that were formerly invisible.

Comparison does not simply create static foils for understanding traditions; it brings traditions into dialogue with one another. Even when the authors themselves do not directly address one another's arguments, by addressing the same questions they create a dialogic format to be exploited by the reader. Such a dialogue can lead to new possibilities, expanded perspectives, and added richness to a tradition. Comparison potentially contains a learning process through which we can improve the way we think about and organize ethical pluralism. Finally, the comparative/dialogic approach to ethical pluralism has a certain self-referential aspect to it. We have asked a group of scholars who themselves could be described as ethically plural to come together and discuss the associational organization of ethical pluralism. This enterprise had some surprising and enlightening results that bring home the unpredictable rewards of comparison.

A number of our contributors pointed out that talking about ethical pluralism in terms of the organization of "civil society" was already to circumscribe the debate, indeed to limit the pluralism of the debate. As a historical phenomenon as well as a theoretical concept, civil society is tied to the rise of liberalism, and some authors argue that the very term *civil society* entails liberal presuppositions. For example, talk of civil society is said by some to presuppose that societies can and should be differentiated into distinct spheres, each of which operates according to its own logic. More specifically, it implies that "civil society" is a different sphere from the state or family, one that operates according to its own logic of voluntary choice, a commitment that in turn is grounded in the value of individual autonomy. Or it is said that civil society operates according to a distinctive logic of undistorted communication grounded in the value of deliberative democracy. These sorts of assumptions about individual autonomy or deliberative democracy are said to reflect a distinctly Western, and perhaps even distinctly liberal, conception of how society should be organized, one that it is not a part of other traditions.

Indeed, many authors from outside the liberal tradition acknowledge that there is no explicit conception of civil society within their own tradition. This implies that to think about ethical pluralism as structured and organized within a civil society framework is to presuppose that we are working within the broad framework of a liberal state. This clearly creates an imbalance between traditions.

Many of the chapters, particularly the five nonsecular perspectives, deepen the debate by opening up a new dimension. Our questions prompted contributors to think about what associational life would look like if governed by their tradition's principles. This raises the intriguing question of whether it makes sense to think about nonliberal or even nonpluralist civil society or whether this is a contradiction in terms. What role, if any, the idea of civil society can play within nonliberal traditions is discussed at some length by several of our contributors.

One way to understand the complexity of the answers to our questions is to note that for each tradition the question of associational life arises in different contexts. To oversimplify, we could distinguish two sorts of contexts:

(*a*) situations in which adherents of a particular tradition form a clear majority within a society, and so have the power to establish and regulate civil society based upon their own ethical principles. In such a society, there might be a wide consensus on certain principles of civil society, and yet there will still likely be conflicts arising from the associational claims of reformist or dissident movements within the tradition. What are the mechanisms for expressing and accommodating these internal forms of dissent and diversity, and what are the limits to their freedom? There will also likely be conflicts arising from the associational claims of minority groups who fall outside the tradition entirely. How much room for associational life does each tradition provide to minorities who exist within civil society, but fall outside the ethical tradition?

(*b*) situations in which members of a particular tradition are in a clear minority within a larger society in which the rules are established by some other ethical tradition. Consider orthodox Jewish minorities within a Western liberal state. In such a society, members of the minority tradition cannot establish the ground rules of civil society, but will presumably demand the sorts of associational life and associational rights that are required to be able to pursue their particular beliefs and values.

These are obviously very different contexts for thinking about civil society, and raise different challenges for the various traditions. Consider the case of Islam. On the one hand, we can ask about civil society in the context of predominantly Islamic states, and then the challenge would be to evaluate the associational claims of reformist groups within Islam and the claims of non-Islamic groups, such as the Copts in Egypt, the Baha'i in Iran, or the Christians in Pakistan. On the other hand, we can also ask about the associational claims of Muslims when they form a minority, as in India, Britain, or the United States. What sorts of claims do they make against the state regarding legal recognition of their family law, funding of Muslim schools, accommodation of Muslim religious holidays, or respect for Muslim dietary restrictions in public institutions?

The same sorts of questions can be asked of all the other traditions. The importance of these two contexts varies in each tradition. Prior to the establishment of Israel, for example, the idea of a predominantly Jewish state was either a milleniums-old historical memory or a Messianic hope for the future. For most of the last two thousand years, therefore, the pressing challenge facing Jews was to establish and protect their associational life as a minority within non-Jewish states. For Muslims, by contrast, with a long and continuous history of statehood, the historical challenge has been how to regulate their own civil society and to deal with non-Islamic minorities. It is only recently that there have been large numbers of Muslims as minorities within Western states who have had to face the question of how they relate to a non-Muslim government. The situation of Christians is different yet again. Like Muslims, they historically have dominated their own states, governed in accordance with explicitly Christian norms. Yet in recent years they have accepted the principle of secularism in politics, and so now increasingly see themselves as but one group—perhaps even a relatively powerless and disadvantaged group—within liberal, secular civil societies. These differences in history are reflected in the sorts of questions each tradition asks about civil society, and the answers it gives.

The way in which we have organized the volume reflects some of the issues raised above. In particular we sought a balance between secular and nonsecular perspectives. The secular perspectives include libertarianism, liberal egalitarianism, critical theory, and feminism; the religious perspectives include Christianity, Judaism, Islam, and Confucianism. Needless to say, this is not an exhaustive survey of all the world's ethical traditions: this would not be possible in a single volume. One can easily imagine several additional perspectives that could be considered, both secular (e.g., conservatism) and religious (e.g., Hinduism). But we hope that the traditions examined in this volume give an indication of the scope of, and need for, an intercultural dialogue on civil society.

We have placed the secular traditions first because they are the most familiar and often contain positions against which nonsecular views argue. The book begins with a historical overview of the origins of the concept of civil society that sketches its essentially liberal roots. Adam Seligman introduces the reader to "the idea and ideal of civil society" through its emergence in late-seventeenth- and eighteenth-century European thought. As he notes, part of the liberal ideal of civil society at the time was that it would provide a space for the expression of individual and group differences, and hence an arena of freedom. But another equally important part of the ideal was that civil society would somehow ensure the harmonious integration of these differences, and provide the site for reconciling the competing pulls of individuality and community, public and private. While emphasizing the liberal roots of the concept of civil society, Seligman argues that it occupies an uneasy place even within liberalism, since there is little theoretical basis within liberalism for this hope of harmonious integration. Indeed, he argues that by the time of Marx and Hegel, the original basis for this optimistic assumption—namely, the Enlightenment belief in the innate moral sympathies of human beings—was effectively demolished.

Hence, Seligman argues, while *civil society* remains a catchword for liberals, and embodies a hope that individuality and sociability can be reconciled, it is no longer backed up by any coherent theory or principles.

The subsequent two contributions can be seen as taking up Seligman's challenge, trying to show that there is a coherent liberal reading of civil society. Michael Walzer defends a left-liberal or liberal egalitarian understanding, while Loren Lomasky explores what right-wing liberals or libertarians might say about civil society. Although coming out of the same tradition, these two chapters form one of the starker contrasts of the book. Walzer's egalitarian perspective leads him to defend a strongly positive theory of the state, while Lomasky insists on a minimal state. Walzer's civil society is one in which the opportunities afforded by voluntary association are guaranteed by the state, whereas for Lomasky civil society thrives by default, that is, by the state withdrawing in favor of maximum liberty for individuals to "direct their affairs as they see fit." The differences between these two chapters remind us that there is no one liberal conception of civil society. Despite these internal disagreements about how to characterize civil society, the link between liberalism and civil society remains a strong one, and in one way or another this link forms a backdrop to all the other contributions.

The next section contains internal critiques of the Western liberal tradition. Anne Phillips's essay on feminism and civil society and Simone Chambers's discussion of a critical theory of civil society again form a stark contrast while developing similar critiques of liberalism. While Phillips begins by admitting that civil society has played a "minimal part in the feminist division of the world," Chambers notes that civil society has been a central concept within critical theory from its inception. Both authors nevertheless defend a similar normative goal—an egalitarian and democratized civil society that can serve as a site of progressive politics. As Phillips notes, "[P]rograms for radical change have to capture people's hearts and minds and cannot depend just on directives from the state." Civil society is a place where we can experiment with new ideas and new ways of life; this in turn can lead to transformation. Chambers is also interested in transformatory politics. For her, civil society is the social basis of a democratic public sphere through which a culture of inequality can be dismantled.

From there the book moves ever farther from liberal assumptions but ever closer to a comprehensive comparative perspective. Like feminism and critical theory, the chapters on Christianity and natural law are in critical dialogue with liberalism. Of particular critical interest here is the rise of individualism, secularism, and materialism associated with the liberal tradition. Michael Banner, while acknowledging that the history of Christian social thought is anything but monolithic, nevertheless sees a potentially common Christian approach to civil society in the twin doctrines of sociality and subsidiarity. The former describes "the natural sociability of men," while the latter invokes the value of human accountability by insisting that responsibility is "to remain at the lowest level from state to individual provided that its remaining there is compatible with the common good." In his discussion of natural law, Michael Pakaluk takes up the issue of subsidiarity in more detail and places it within a strongly teleological tradition. Civil society is considered from the point of view of human ends and the laws and norms that will promote those ends.

The final three traditions represented in this volume pose the most radical challenge to liberalism and offer, certainly for a North American audience, the most innovative views of civil society. As the authors note, the Judaic, Islamic, and Confucian traditions do not contain a theory of civil society in the modern liberal sense. Nevertheless, they each offer a rich tradition of social thought from which to answer all the questions asked about associational life, and to paint a picture of a civil society governed in a very different way from a liberal civil society. Suzanne Stone notes that the Jewish tradition has little to contribute to the traditional "civil society versus the state" debate that has preoccupied liberals. However, if civil society is understood as concerned "with the conditions for establishing bonds of social solidarity between diverse members of society and shaping rights of association to promote bonds, then Judaism has much to contribute to the discussion." Hasan Hanafi offers a view of Islamic civil society that, although not liberal, contains a strong endorsement of human rights. He introduces a comparison with liberalism that points to the ways in which traditions can learn from each other in dialogue: Islam needs a universal declaration of human rights to complement the traditional Islamic declaration of human duties; the West needs a universal declaration of human duties to complete its commitment to human rights. In his discussion of Confucianism, Richard Madsen also uses liberalism as a contrast. Particularly important is the distinction between voluntary and nonvoluntary associations. While many liberals see voluntary association at the heart of civil society, Madsen sees the fundamental building blocks of a Confucian-inspired civil society as nonoptional institutions. The point of departure is the most nonvoluntary human institution, the family. The goal is to expand family virtues beyond the home.

In his concluding essay, Michael Mosher provides an engaging comparison of the various conceptions of civil society developed in the volume, and draws out some surprising areas of convergence and disagreement between the various traditions. He suggests that all of the traditions, in their own ways, are prone to underestimating the chaotic and messy pluralism of associational life, and succumb to the temptation to reinterpret or misinterpret the nature of associational life to fit their preconceived norms. This brings us back full circle to Seligman's introductory essay, which expresses similar skepticism about whether any ethical tradition has the resources to develop a satisfactory ideal of civil society. This may seem like a pessimistic conclusion, but the limits of existing approaches only highlight the need for further dialogue among the different ethical traditions that characterize our pluralistic world.

NOTES

1. Previous Ethikon projects include Brian Barry and Robert Goodin, eds., *Free Movement: Ethical Issues in the Transnational Migration of Peoples and Money* (University Park: Penn State University Press, 1992); Chris Brown, ed., *Political Restructuring in Europe: Ethical Perspectives* (London: Routledge, 1993); Terry Nardin, ed., *The Ethics of War and Peace: Religious and Secular Perspectives* (Princeton: Princeton University Press, 1996); David Mapel and Terry Nardin, eds., *International Society: Diverse Ethical Perspectives* (Princeton: Princeton University Press, 1998); and David Miller and Sohail Hashmi, eds., *Boundaries and Justice: Diverse Ethical Perspectives* (Princeton: Princeton University Press, forthcoming).

PART I

CHAPTER 1

Civil Society as Idea and Ideal

Adam B. Seligman

THERE CAN BY NOW be little doubt that the idea of civil society has become over the past decade a much used, perhaps even overused, concept. Indeed, and just as the slogan arose in Eastern Europe in the 1980s as a cudgel to batter the totalitarian State, it has emerged in the 1990s in Western Europe and in the United States by critics of the existing political order to press home their claims. Interestingly (and in a way that should be a warning to us all), the idea of civil society is used by political groups and thinkers on both the right and the left, and though in Europe in general it is most often the province of the left, in the United States it has been appropriated by both groups to advance their political agenda.

Thus, for right-of-center thinkers as well as for libertarian followers of Friedrich von Hayek, the quest for civil society is taken to mean a mandate to deconstruct many of the powers of the State and replace them with intermediary institutions based on social voluntarism. For many liberals, civil society is identified with social movements, also existing beyond the State. And while many of the former refuse to recognize that voluntary organizations can be of a particularly nasty nature and based on primordial or ascriptive principles of membership and participation that put to shame the very foundations of any idea of civil society, the latter are blind to the fact that the Achilles' heel of any social movement is its institutionalization, which—one way or the other—must be through the State and its legal (and coercive) apparatus. In the meantime, both communitarians and liberals continue to assimilate the idea of civil society to their own terms, invest it with their own meanings, and make of it what they will. Right, left, and center, North, South, East, and West—civil society is identified with everything from multiparty systems and the rights of citizenship to individual voluntarism and the spirit of community.[1]

To some extent these contradictory usages are rooted in the concept itself; the early-modern idea of civil society emerged in the eighteenth century as a means of overcoming the newly perceived tension between public and private realms. In fact, what stood at the core of all attempts to articulate a notion of civil society in that period, and since, has been the problematic relation between the private and the public; the individual and the social; public ethics and individual interests; and individual passions, and public concerns. More pointedly, the question of civil society was, and still is, how individual interests could be pursued in the social arena and, similarly, the social good in the individual or private sphere. What is ultimately at stake in this question is, moreover, the proper mode of *normatively* constituting the existence of society—whether in terms of private individuals or in the existence of a shared public sphere.

If constitutive of civil society is some sense of a shared public (as I believe all would agree), so is the very existence of the private. It is after all the very existence of a free and equal citizenry—of that autonomous, agentic individual, of the private subject—that makes civil society possible at all. The public space of interaction is a public space only insofar as it is distinguished from those social actors who enter it as private individuals. Where there is no private sphere, there is, concomitantly, no public one—both must exist for sense to be made of either one. As the following essays make clear, the issue of public and private realms (and interests) continues to define the different conceptions of civil society, from contemporary feminist perspective to more classically liberal ones and, of course, to those still more indebted to the different religious and natural law traditions where more premodern ideas of community and communal obligations hold sway. The very plethora of uses made of the concept would, however, seem to dictate a brief historical overview of the early-modern emergence and use of the concept, to which this chapter is devoted.

John Locke and the Scottish Enlightenment

Much as it has done today, the idea of civil society as normative ideal emerged in the later-seventeenth and eighteenth centuries as the result of a crisis in social order and a breakdown of existing paradigms of the idea of order. The general crises of the seventeenth century—the commercialization of land, labor, and capital, the growth of market economies, the age of discoveries, and the English and later North American and continental revolutions—all brought into question the existing models of social order and of authority. Whereas traditionally the foundations or matrix of social order was seen to reside in some entity external to the social world—God, King, or even the givenness of traditional norms and behavior itself—these principles of order became increasingly questioned by the end of the seventeenth century. By the eighteenth century, people began more and more to turn inward, to the workings of society itself, to explain the existence of the social order. The execution and, more importantly, the trial of Charles I in 1649 (which put the King firmly under the laws of the Realm); the incipient market economy and the Physiocratic doctrine of the economic as a self-regulating arena; the discovery of diverse traditions and models of organizing social life in non-European lands; as well as the later, eighteenth-century image of a clockworker God all brought into question the idea of the source of social order as external to society.

The image of civil society as an ethical model for conceiving the workings of the social order emerged from within this major and radical reorientation of European social thought in the seventeenth and eighteenth centuries. As such, it represents a critical new attempt to argue the moral sources of the social order from within the human world and without recourse to an external or transcendent referent. This challenge and, with it, that of squaring the newly emerging interests of increasingly autonomous individuals with some vision of the public good provided the theoretical and ethical ground for the idea of civil society.

Of major significance in the early-modern reorientation of social thought was the work of John Locke. Locke is, in this context, very much a transitional figure—building on the tradition of individual rights (so central to the civil society tradition) through a "liberal" reading of Hugo Grotius and other medieval political theorists, but, as John Dunn pointedly reminds us, rooting these rights in a religious vision.[2] For Locke, in the *Second Treatise*, civil society is still coterminus with the political realm in toto, and there does not yet exist that latter differentiation of civil society from the State that we find in late-eighteenth- and nineteenth-century thought. Civil society is that realm of political association instituted among men when they take leave of the "state of nature" and enter into a commonwealth.[3] Political or civil society is, for John Locke, that arena where the "inconveniences" and insufficiencies of the state of nature are rectified through the mutuality of contract and consent.[4]

Without entering too much into an analysis of the *Second Treatise*, we can say that what is of central importance to our argument is the ontological status of the rights and privileges that Locke posits as the basis of civil society. These of course draw on the traditions of natural law, but also on a specific Christian, if not Calvinist, reading of man's relation with God. The normative status of civil or political society for Locke turns on the state of nature, that "state all men are naturally in, and that is a state of perfect freedom to order their actions and dispose of their possessions and persons as they think fit within the bounds of the law of nature, without asking leave, or depending upon the will of any other man."[5] This state of liberty (though "not of license") is, however, itself rooted in a theological matrix—rooted in fact in the medieval Christian tradition of right reason and Christian Revelation. Moreover, and as Locke makes clear, the very limits on liberty (as for instance in the prohibitions on suicide or self-enslavement) as well as the sources of this liberty are rooted in a certain set of theological presuppositions. "For men being all the workmanship of one omnipotent and infinitely wise Maker—all servants of one sovereign Master, sent into the world by His order, and about His business—they are His property, whose workmanship they are."[6]

Locke was positing not a historical reality of equality and freedom as the bases of civil society, but a theological axiom whose ontological status was not given to empirical evidence or questioning.[7] He posits an ethical and inherently Christian ideal that need not bear any relation to the given historical reality (and inequality) of seventeenth-century English society or, indeed, of any other society. Locke's concern (on the substantive and not polemical level) was to find a point beyond the status and property differences in society, beyond what John Dunn termed "the tangle of seventeenth century social deference," where the moral integrity and autonomy of the individual (male) social actor could be validated and so could serve as the basis for a vision of social order. This ground was to be found only in a set of theological principles that were in fact a natural theology of a uniquely Calvinist variant.[8] The individual is, as quoted above, God's workmanship, even His property. Man's existence is still rooted in what Charles Taylor termed, in a different context, an ontic-logics[9]—that is to say, in a cosmic scheme where the existence of man's calling as well as his reason are validated in terms of a specific soteriology.

If with John Locke the supporting struts of civil society are those of an unproblematic and rationalized theology where God's will and right reason still work in a coordinate state (resonant of the Calvinist unity of nature and grace), by the mid-eighteenth century the conjectural basis of the social order had become more problematic. In the writings of Francis Hutcheson, Adam Ferguson, and Adam Smith, a new appreciation of the problematic existence of individuals in society appears that was absent from the thought of Locke. To a great extent the developing idea of civil society is—within the Scottish Enlightenment—an attempt to find or, rather, posit a synthesis between a number of developing oppositions that were increasingly being felt in social life. These oppositions—between the individual and the social, the private and the public, egotism and altruism, as well as between a life governed by reason and one governed by the passions—have in fact become constitutive of our existence in the modern world.

Not surprisingly, the attempt to return to the eighteenth-century idea of civil society is today an attempt to readmit that synthesis of private and public, individual and social, egotistical and altruistic sources of action that such an ideal represents. Prior to any synthesis, however, lies the very awareness of conflict. And, to be sure, the developing economy of market relations in the eighteenth century problematized social existence in new ways. The freeing of labor and of capital developed together with a new awareness of individuals acting out their private interests in the public realm. By the middle of the eighteenth century it became increasingly difficult to square the traditional image of the individual as bounded by and validated within the network of social relations with that of the autonomous social actor pursuing his (not yet her) individual interests in the public realm. The very grounding of new forms of social action and motivation based on self-interest (indeed, on the very concept of the self) made it imperative to posit a new moral order that would accommodate and in a sense "hold" the development of interpersonal relations based not on a shared vision of cosmic order, but on the principle of rational self-interest.

The first expression of this need and the problems it implied in any attempt to "think" society as something over and above its individual parts can be found in the central and growing realization that man is motivated by two divergent and contradictory principles: altruism and egoism. Alasdair MacIntyre has claimed that, following Malebranche, Shaftesbury (who was Locke's pupil) was the first of the moral philosophers to have understood this defining contradiction in human nature and motivation.[10] Its appreciation, however, played a salient role for all of the thinkers of the Scottish Enlightenment and continued into the end of the nineteenth century, where we can find it, redefined in more sociological and what were then assumed to be scientific principles, in the work of Emile Durkheim. It was, moreover, the cognizance of this distinction and the need to overcome it, to posit some unitary framework for ethical action (that could no longer by based on God's dictates), that led eighteenth-century thinkers to the idea of moral affections and natural sympathy, which in turn served as the basis for the idea of civil society.

Moral sentiment, by which "men are united by instinct, that they act in society from affections of kindness and friendship," was for the thinkers of the Scottish Enlightenment an axiomatic property of the human mind.[11] On the epistemological level it is an attempt to ground the existence of the social order in an intimately human propensity of innate mutuality. With society no longer conceived in the hierarchic and holistic terms of medieval orders but of discrete individuals, a new bond between its particulars had to be found. This takes the form with Adam Smith, for example, of *The Theory of Moral Sentiments,* which argues that the moral basis of individual existence is the need for recognition and consideration on the part of others. "To be observed, to be attended to, to be taken notice of with sympathy, complacency and approbation" are for Smith the driving forces of "all the toil and bustle of the world . . . the end of avarice and ambition, of the pursuit of wealth."[12] Thus, and as tellingly pointed out by A. O. Hirschman, economic activity itself is rooted, in *The Theory of Moral Sentiments,* in the noneconomic needs for sympathy and appreciation.[13] It is for Adam Smith our interest in "being the object of attention and approbation" that leads to the complex of activity that defines economic life.

What is central to this perspective is the idea of the arena of exchange (which is that of civil society) as rooted in a sphere of values predicated on the mutuality of individual recognition. This stress on mutuality and recognition runs through all the writings of the Scottish Enlightenment on civil society and serves to underpin that "propensity to exchange" that is at the heart of market transactions.

Preceding Adam Smith, we can find Adam Ferguson asserting that "[t]he mighty advantages of property and fortune, when stripped of the recommendations they derive from vanity, or the more serious regards to independence and power, only mean a provision that is made for animal enjoyment; and if our solicitude on this subject were removed, not only the toils of the mechanic, but the studies of the learned, would cease; every department of public business would become unnecessary; every senate-house would be shut up and every palace deserted."[14]

Vanity here is crucial and plays the same role as Smith's "attention and approbation." It builds on the social nature of our existence and on our individual validation in and through the eyes of others. The public arena of exchange and interaction—the realm of civil society—is not simply a "neutral" space of market exchange where already fully constituted individuals meet to exchange property and develop commerce, manufacture, or the arts. It is itself an ethical arena in which the individual is constituted in his individuality through the very act of exchange with others. Vanity is that which links us to the social whole as we become who we are through the other's perception of us (a sort of "Meadian" social self *avant la lettre*).

What is novel in the thought of the Scottish Enlightenment is of course not the mere positing of shared social space as an ethical arena. This had always existed within the political and philosophical traditions of Western civilization. What was new in the eighteenth century was the very terms in which that ethically validated and validating social space could be conceived. Not yet totally throwing loose its moorings in a Godly benevolence, it nevertheless came to be characterized by increasing innerworldliness— that is to say, by human attributes that themselves had to support a vision of the social good.

Indeed, as the Deism of the eighteenth century no longer accepted a model of human, this-worldly activity framed in theological terms, it had no recourse but to posit in its stead a new philosophical anthropology. In fact, this move or turn inward to a natural, inworldly, and ultimately human source of social order can be seen by a brief comparison of the opening chapters of Locke's *Second Treatise* and of Adam Ferguson's *Essay on Civil Society*. Both begin with the "State of Nature." But whereas for Locke this state of nature is, following Hooker, based on the common subordination of humans to God, for Ferguson, it is nothing more than a short course in natural history with no reference, or indeed need of reference, to a divine being. Ontology has, as it were, been replaced with epistemology.

By positing the sources of natural benevolence within the human world, the distinction between public and private lives attained a saliency, indeed a recognition, it had never had before, which in fact brings us to the heart of the image of civil society as a moral vision. What made the classic vision of civil society unique was its positing of the social space of human inter-action as a moral sphere—that is, not simply as a neutral arena of ex-change—where moral attributes were derived from the nature of man him-self. What was unique was precisely the coupling of a vision of society with that moral field implied by the term *civil society* while, at the same time, rooting this field in an innerworldly logic and not in a transcendent real-ity. This, as history has shown, was a fragile synthesis that could not sup-port either the expansion of capitalism or the growth of rationality. It rested on a particular view of the relations between men's passions and their in-terests and of the crucible of civil space where a synthesis between them could be achieved.

What the idea of civil society meant to the thinkers of the Scottish En-lightenment was primarily a realm of solidarity held together by the force of moral sentiments and natural affections. These forces provided a "moral grid" that severely attenuated any attempt to think of rational self-interest in terms of either disengaged reason (i.e., reason or interests freed from the "passions") or of the self freed from the eye of the other. We have seen above how for Smith himself the very focus and motivating force of eco-nomic activity, of the hustle and bustle of worldly affairs, was the search for recognition on the part of others. The need for respect and approval, man's very *amour de soi,* rested on the praise of others. Therefore, the individual self could never, in this reading, be totally disengaged from society, nor could reasoned self-interest be abstracted from those passions which, through the moral sentiment, rooted man in society.

It was these passions that set men over the animals and the basic life of material substance and which "reserved for man to consult, to persuade, to oppose, to kindle in the society of his fellow-creatures, and to lose the sense of his personal interest or safety, in the ardor of his friendships and his oppositions."[15] This vision of sociability and mutual recognition rested, moreover—and this was its Achilles' heel—on a particular under-standing of reason that, while embracing the concept of interest, went far beyond any utilitarianism. Indeed, the idea was of a reason that was itself an element of the natural affections. Reason and rationality in thinkers such as the Third Earl of Shaftsbury brought us, through our innate benevolence, to an understanding and so a love of the whole—of the uni-versal. Natural affections, which bound societies together (a type of social solidarity), emerged from a happy confluence of Reason and benevolence that allowed us to put the good of the whole above the good of the parts and so the public or social good above our individual interests. Reason in its universal sense (that is, as part of the passions) takes us beyond particular interests to affirm the universal good where the particular and the universal, the private and the public, are united within one field of meanings. This unity of Reason and moral sentiment was not to stand the test of time, however, and would in fact begin to unravel already in the thought of David Hume.

HUME AND KANT

The challenge posited by Hume to that tradition of thought that saw civil society as ethical model or ideal was disarmingly simple. He simply tore asunder the unity of Reason and moral sentiment upon which the model rested. Hume's distinction between "is" and "ought," upon which was based what Alasdair MacIntyre has appropriately termed his "subversion from within" of the Scottish Enlightenment, was, as well, an outright attack on the tradition of moral sentiment and universal benevolence upon which the idea of civil society rested.[16] In terms most germane to our own problematic, of the moral basis of the social order, the most succinct formulas of the above, taken from *A Treatise on Human Nature*, has it that "[s]ince morals, therefore, have an influence on the actions and affections, it follows, that they cannot be derived from reason; and that because reason alone, as we have already prov'd, can never have any such influence. Morals excite passions, and produce or prevent actions. Reason of itself is utterly impotent in this particular. The rules of morality, therefore, are not conclusions of our Reason."[17] Thus, for Hume, "the ultimate ends of human action can never . . . be accounted for by reason, but recommend themselves entirely to the sentiment and affections of mankind."[18] A strict "boundary" in Hume's phrase is posited between what is *ascertained* by reason and what the *motives* are for human action, which can only be understood in terms of sentiment. The fragile concomitance of both upon which the unity of the individual and society, private and public, had been seen to rest no longer holds. Reason has no place in a psychology of human motivation—which is solely relegated to the passions, which, in turn, have no privileged knowledge—indeed, none at all—of universal truths.

However, if the working of Reason can only bring us to universal truths that are beyond the field of morality or virtue, how can a representative vision of the social good be posited? How, in this reading, can society be conceived as a normative order? It was Hume's answer to these questions that had such a strong impact on later liberal theory; in fact, Hume abstained from positing the social order in terms of any morally substantive good.

The universal good was nothing beyond the calculus of individual or particular good, and the public good was supported solely by the workings of private interests.

The role of Reason in the Humean idea of society was fixed within this calculus—allowing the individual to ascertain his own benefit as deriving from following certain universally applicable rules of conduct. In itself, Reason has no other role and certainly no autonomous moral validity. Of these rules, the three fundamental ones for the workings of society are the stability of possessions, their transfer by consent, and the performance of promises.[19] These, as Hume emphasizes, are "artifices" of society—necessary for its workings, but not rooted in any historical, mythical, logical, or transcendental status. ("In the state of nature, or that imaginary state, which preceded society, there be neither justice nor injustice.")[20] Foreshadowing Hegel, Hume well realized that "justice," as well as the rules governing the exchange of property and indeed the whole edifice of civil society (of which the obligations to fulfill promises and thus secure a realm of continued human interaction was central), "takes its rise from human conventions." They are decidedly not to be found in any set of natural principles—cosmic, transcendental, or otherwise.[21] Moreover—and crucially, in terms of the death toll of the Scottish Enlightenment—men, in the Humean reading, would follow the rules of justice not because they represented some universal, constitutive good, but simply to maximize their self-interest. In the social reality as Hume conceived it, characterized by people's "selfishness and limited generosity" joined with the scarcity of goods "in comparison with the wants and desires of men," men's only recourse to realize their *own* interests was to follow universally validated rules of justice.[22]

It is this proposition, Hume asserts, and not a "regard of public interest or a strong extensive benevolence," that leads us to follow the rules of justice.[23] Not only is moral sentiment here distinguished from the *rules* of justice, but the *sense* of justice, which is historically contingent and takes different forms in different societies, is divorced from Reason. It is founded, Hume argues, not on any set of "eternal, immutable and universally obligatory relations between ideas," but solely on our "impressions." In this reading what is *deemed* moral has no foundation in Reason, as the latter is indeed uncoupled from any moral sentiment. And while it is reasoned self-interest that leads us to follow the rules of justice, justice itself has no more than an instrumental value and no autonomous standing beyond those particular interests that are served by following its dictates (those three rules quoted above).

With Hume the distinction between justice and virtue, between a public sphere based on the workings of self-interest (in conformity to law) and a strictly private sphere of moral action (predicated on such consideration as those of friendship, for example), is presented in its starkest form. It was this distinction and its attendant dilemmas that the Scottish Enlightenment and the whole civil society tradition attempted to avoid. The ensuing dilemma—of how to posit a prescriptive and not just descriptive model of the social order, given this distinction between abstract and general rules of justice on the one hand and the particular desiderata (of either rational self-interest or such other-regarding sentiments as friendship) on the other—has defined the modern period from Hume onward. Its theoretical challenge was first addressed by Kant, who, despite his theoretical innovations, remained very much within a Humean problematic.

With Kant a number of themes that had been central—if still somewhat latent—in the thought of the Scottish moralists achieve a new recognition. The problems of the relation between the particular/individual and the universal/social and, with this, of the proper mode of representing social life, which were inherent in the civil society tradition, take on a new rigor. It was, in fact, only in the writings of Immanuel Kant that the above-noted problems, of properly representing the public and private spheres (as well as the relation between this and the idea of Reason), were first fully articulated.

In certain respects Kant continued (and of course substantially deepened) the thought of the Scottish philosophers, making the themes of freedom and equality central edifices of his philosophical anthropology. Similarly, and of equal if not greater importance, he united these ideas with the progressive workings of a universal Reason through which individual rights (to civic freedom and political equality) were articulated. Reason supplied that ideal (or model, *Urbild*) through which our judgment is guided by the moral law.[24] Right (*Recht*, embracing both personal "rights" and the very notion of justice) is ensured through the autonomous and agentic individual subject following the dictates of a Reason that, in its very universality, bridges the distinction between private and public, individual and social. As mankind comes into his own, that autonomy, freedom, and equality of each individual (which must be assured in the juridical community of citizens) itself engenders—through a universal reason—the workings of the moral law.

Kant's famous strictures on never using any individual as a means cut to the heart of the civil society debate. They provide a new, more analytic formulation of the realm of moral sentiment and natural sympathy upon which the Scottish philosophers constructed their idea of civil society. In Kant however, this injunction is not founded on any "natural" endowment but—and this is precisely its critical importance—on following the strictures of reason itself. For Kant reason, more concretely practical reason, was realized in the juridical community of citizens and as such represented the crowning achievement of human freedom in the modern world.[25] Reason and equality were thus firmly united in the representative vision posited by Kant of the social or political order.[26]

Moreover and central to the whole Kantian conception of practical reason was the existence of a shared public arena where the workings of reason were substantiated.[27] As Hannah Arendt has made clear, the category of the "public" was central for the Kantian synthesis of reason, equality, and freedom.[28] It was for Kant within the public arena of critical discourse that reason and equality, and with them the preconditions for the "kingdom of ends," were validated.[29]

On one level, Kant's notion of publicness would appear as a more fully developed and more highly theorized concept than that mutuality inherent in the Scottish Enlightenment idea of natural sympathy. With Kant a labile and subjective idea takes a rigor and objective form in and through its unity with Reason. Similarly, with Kant a new, more rigorous vision of social differentiation began to develop. The State is no longer viewed as coterminus with civil society because the publicness of rational debate and critique is seen (and indeed emphasized) as the province of civil society in its distinction from the State.

In Kant's objections to the absolutist state, this role of a critical citizenry freed from civil constraint is salient. The very legitimation of constitutional rule rests on the idea that its laws would be such that had all the (rational) citizenry debated them, they would have arrived at the same conclusion.[30] Kant, thus, would appear to overcome (through his very synthesis of Reason with the public realm) that distinction between individual (interests) and social (good) with which the moralists of the Scottish Enlightenment wrestled.

This synthesis however, contained the critical distinction between the juridical and the ethical that was to prove so important for further theoretical attempts to articulate an ethical vision of societal representation. The public arena was for Kant the sphere of right (*Recht*), of mutual and rational consent to the individual and collective will (*Willkur*) of others.[31] It was not, however, the realm of the ethical, which was reserved for the private workings of inner life.[32]

In Kant's writings the (private) sphere of morality and ethics is thus divorced from the representative vision of society as juridical community. The public arena as the realm validating the juridical equality of citizens is thus invested with value, while concomitantly remaining removed from the realm of the ethical. Kant then, more than anything else, absolutized that distinction noted above by Hume, rather than overcame it. This solution (and distinction) to the dilemma of how to represent the public good, still critical in the discourse of liberal political theory—in debates over a politics of right versus a politics of the Good—perpetrated rather than resolved the tension between public and private realms. By distinguishing right or duty from ethics and reserving the later for the private realm, Kantian theory left unresolved the critical issue of ethical representation and of the status of the public sphere: Did it embody a shared vision of the Good, or was it circumscribed to the guarantee of individual "rights" only (issues that appear in some contributions to this volume, such as those by Walzer and Lomasky)?

HEGEL AND MARX

It was this separation of the juridical from the ethical that gave rise to the Hegelian critique of Kant. Hegel's criticism and development of Kant's philosophy turned, precisely, on this point—the divorce of public right from private morality and so the mediated and incomplete realization of reason this entailed.[33] Leaving morality as a "regulative principle" only, and one not fully integrated into the domain of Right (that is of Law), meant, in Hegel's reading of Kant, the abdication of morality from its proper place in the ethical representation of society. Marx, as is well known, followed in Hegel's footsteps in attempting to unite the private realm, now conceived of as individual interests (rather than simply private moralities) residing in civil society, with the public realm (of political concerns). As opposed to Hegel, he posited this unity as a prescriptive for future development and not as embodied in the actually existent state. What unites both thinkers, however, is a concern with the proper integration of the ethical realm (hitherto conceived of as private) within the public arena.

With Hegel and Marx we come in fact to the end of the civil society tradition as a normative model of social life. Both, in different ways, seek to overcome that distinction between public legality and private morality, between juridical community and ethical life, that was first posited by David Hume and "absolutized" by Immanuel Kant. For both Hegel and Marx this distinction was a fatal flaw in the idea of civil society, and both sought to provide the theoretical means for a reconstruction of civil society as idea and praxis. In their different reconstructions, however, the very distinction of the idea of civil society as it had been articulated in the eighteenth century was overcome and transformed. However great the difference between Hegelian and Marxist models of civil society, they can (both) be understood only in terms of an attempt to reintegrate the two realms of legality and morality that stood at the core of the original normative idea of civil society. In doing so, both thinkers stressed the shared, collective nature of morality, its sources in group interests and, most critically with Marx, in the relative position of these groups within the relations of production. Both nevertheless sought, in different ways, to realize that model of civil society as an ethical vision for which the ideas of moral affections and natural sympathy were no longer sufficient. The difference between both thinkers was of course in the realm where this ethical vision was real-

ized and the contradictory injunctions of public law and private morality—
that is, of the contradictory nature of civil society—finally overcome.

While Hegel clearly distinguishes civil society from the State and provides an acute analysis of the workings of particular interests within civil society, civil society is not, in itself, that realm of ethical realization. As he
makes clear, civil society as such is the realm where the Idea of Freedom is
only present in its "abstract moment," as an "inner necessity."[34] "It is the
system of the ethical order, split into its extremes and lost." The hetero-
geneity of interests and classes which make up civil society are, in Hegel's
thought ultimately self-defeating—so long as they remain within *that* "moment" where universality is not concretely (but only abstractly) realized.
Hegel's whole analysis of civil society turns in fact on the overcoming of
the contradictory desiderata of particular interests (those of different strata,
classes, occupational groups, and so on), and so the realization of ethical
life through its embodiment in a universal framework that begins *but* does
not end with the sphere of civil society.

Rather, as is well known, the true overcoming of particularity, of the individual interests of burghers, Corporations, or Estates (which comprise
civil society) is achieved only in the realm of the State proper (and more
concretely the universal interests represented by the class of civil servants)
which is the sole representative of the universal idea.

Thus, interestingly enough, one way of reading Hegel is to see in his
writing an attempt to maintain the reciprocity and mutuality of the classic
civil society tradition while placing it on a firmer foundation than that of
innate and natural sentiments. Indeed, he artfully shows how civil society
is itself the object of historical development and not a predetermined natural state. Moreover, his new synthesis seeks to sidestep the critical Kantian (and Humean) distinction between legality and morality, which left the
latter beyond the realm of concrete ethical action in the world. In squaring this circle and overcoming the dichotomies of both the Scottish Enlightenment and Kantian theory, Hegel, however also "overcame" the very
autonomy of the concept of civil society—positing its very realization in
the State.

If Hegel "resolves" civil society into the existent and ethical (universal)
entity of the State, Marx, it can be said, resolves it into itself. It is a resolution, however, that will be achieved only in the future negation of the existent distinction between civil society and the State and a future unity of
human existence within which true freedom will be achieved. Following
Hegel, Marx rejected all "myths and fantasies" of the eighteenth century
on the natural origin of civil society.[35] He was, however, aware, as they
were, of the abiding contradiction of modern existence between the philosophically posited autonomous and isolated individual and his (and with
Marx and Engels we begin to have her) social existence. For Marx, the

eighteenth century, that epoch of civil society, produced both the isolated individual as well as the most highly developed forms of their social relations. This dichotomous reality stands in contrast to that view of a "society of free competition," where "the individual *seems* detached from the ties of nature." Marx's castigation of the eighteenth-century philosophy of the Scottish Enlightenment stems from its penchant to resolve both aspects of modern existence into a mythical and abstracted reading of human nature.

The division of human existence into disparate realms of civil society and the State, or political life, was for Marx the defining characteristic of modernity as a civilization, and belied any attempt to posit the autonomous, individual pole of this dichotomy in terms of true human nature. Marx rejected both the anthropological naïveté of the eighteenth century as well as the abstract idealism of Hegelian thought. He saw the very emergence of civil society as identical with the political emancipation of the eighteenth century and not as in any way preceding it (ontologically or historically). The emergence as well as differentiation of both resulted ultimately from the overthrow of the unified feudal order where "the vital functions and conditions of life of civil society remained . . . political."[36] In feudalism the components of civil society were not individuals as such, but estates, corporations, guilds, and privileged groups. These were the participatory actors in a public sphere. The destruction of feudalism "abolished the political character of civil society" and at the same time broke up civil society into its individual components—setting up on the other side the realm of political community as "the *general* concern of the nation, ideally independent of those *particular* elements of civil life."[37] Consequently, "a person's distinct activity and distinct situation in life were reduced to a merely individual significance. They no longer constituted the general relation of the individual to the state as a whole."[38] Existence in civil society thus became one of conflicting individual interests devoid of that communal mutuality that was relegated to the political province proper. This atomization of society—conceived of as "the emancipation of civil society from politics"—is at the same time a removal of those "bonds which restrained the egoistic spirit of civil society," that is, that mutual responsibility that was part and parcel of feudal ties and obligations and that was based on the relative "holistic" model of the social order represented by feudalism.[39]

Marx is, as we can see here, fundamentally concerned with the same set of problems that led his philosophical forerunners one hundred years earlier to their own idea of civil society. With them, however, the very idea of civil society was a solution to the problem of how to posit a social whole beyond the particular interests that define individual existence. With Marx (here following Hegel) civil society is itself that realm of conflict between particular interests that must be somehow overcome in another (ethical) unity. However, and whereas this conflict was for Hegel overcome in the State, for Marx the State was itself subservient to the conflicting forces of civil society. Their resolution was only to be in the future, when true human history would begin.

CONCLUSION

From the eighteenth century through the nineteenth, what was of major concern to all social philosophers was the possibility (that is to say, the normative possibility) of positing a unified vision of the social order that, at the same time, recognized the legal, moral, and economic autonomy of its component parts. The idea of civil society emerged at the beginning of this period as just such a solution. Its fundamental premises, rooted in a theological anthropology and combined with a naive belief in the congruence of reason and sentiment, were critically undone within a short sixty years— as the writings of Hume and Kant testify. The problem first addressed by Hutcheson, Shaftsbury, and Ferguson—of the proper relations between the individual and society, between the public and private realms—remained, however, as the defining problem of social thought.

The writings of Hegel and of Marx, however, attest to the continuity (of sorts) of the civil society paradigm into the nineteenth century. In their own work however, its viability as a normative concept and model of social representation disappears. In Hegel it disappears into the universal state, in Marx in the future reunification of civil and political society. "Only" Marx asserts at the end of *On the Jewish Question,*

> [W]hen the real, individual man re-absorbs in himself the abstract citizen, and as an individual human being has become a species-being in his everyday life, in his particular work, and in his particular situation, only when man has recognized and organized his "forces propres" as social forces, and consequently no longer separates social power from himself in the shape of political power, only then will human emancipation have been accomplished.[40]

With this, the classic idea of civil society comes to an end. Its shadow, however, continually remained in the background of both liberal and socialist theory and politics into the twentieth century. In liberalism, the idea of the morally (and economically) autonomous individual, which served as the basis of the idea of civil society, remained as the fundamental premise of political life. However, the loss of the early-eighteenth-century notion of natural sympathy and moral sentiments made it increasingly difficult to root this individual in a community and so present a coherent vision of society beyond its individual members.

The contemporary condition characterized by a questioning of many of the core assumptions that have guided postwar social life (on the boundaries of public and private realms, the role of the State and corporate groups in the making of social policy, the nature of work, the family, gender roles, etc.) has led contemporary social theorists to return to the original Scottish Enlightenment idea of civil society as a possible resolution of contemporary impasses. Posited as a panacea, the idea of civil society has reappeared among writers across the political spectrum, in many different countries, and the term itself has taken on many different meanings. And though our concern here has been more with the original idea of civil society as formulated in the Scottish Enlightenment, it would do well to briefly note some of these usages—if only to highlight their distinction from the classical meaning of civil society.

There are at least two broad uses of the term in current social and political practice; usages whose differences become especially salient when we compare the thoughts of those writing in such cities as Bucharest, Budapest, Vilna, and Prague to those writing in Princeton, Chicago, Toronto, or Boston. What characterizes the demand for a "return" to civil society for those living "East of the Elbe" is most essentially a call for the institutionalization of those principles of citizenship upon which modern liberal, democratic polities in the West are based. In this sense, for many in East Central Europe, civil society is but a different term used to characterize those institutional features that are taken to define democratic regimes, and that are based on the principles of civic, political, and social citizenship first adumbrated by T. H. Marshall in midcentury.[41]

Indeed, I would hazard the guess that the use of the term *civil society* instead of *democracy* in Eastern Europe to describe the organizational features of social life that we identify with civil society is to be found less in any additional analytic weight carried by the idea of civil society and more simply in the fact that *civil society* as a term was neutral and uncorrupted by forty years of State propaganda, whereas the term *democracy*—as in People's Democracy—was heavily tainted by the past and as a political slogan was not as unencumbered as *civil society*. In a sense, then, what civil society means to writers in contemporary East Central Europe are the formal, legal, and institutional venues through which the individual as an autonomous moral agent can act out his and her needs and desires in the social and political spheres.

This is in contrast to the situation in the West, where the idea of civil society invokes a greater stress on community, on the "reestablishment" of some public (and perforce communal) space to mediate somewhat what are seen as the adverse effects of the ideology of individualism—at least in the United States. Thus we may think of Edward Shils's dictum that civil society is the "conscience collective" of society or of the recent writings of Michael Walzer and Charles Taylor, which stress the "associational" character of civil society as, in true Hegelian fashion, a realm of community existing "between" the family and the state.[42] This reading of civil society in the contemporary West is perhaps best summed up by Daniel Bell, who noted that "the demand for a return to civil society is the demand for a return to a manageable scale of social life," one that "emphasizes voluntary association, churches and communities, arguing that decisions should be made locally and should not be controlled by the state and its bureaucracies."[43] Interestingly, we find this concern not only among authors most identified with the "communitarian" perspective in American politics, but also among such as Seyla Benhabib, Jean Cohen, Andrew Arato, and others who, from their own emphasis on individual rights and fulfillment (as drawing on what has come to be considered the critical tradition in political theory), offer similar critiques.[44] In all, we find a concern for defining civil society (and indeed citizenship) in terms of some set of highly generalized and universalistic moral bonds obtaining between social actors and that, in turn, are seen as providing the preconditions for that reading of civil society as a self-regulating community existing between individuals yet distinct from their existence as citizens of the nation-state.

The problem with this reading, however, is what it ignores, and what it ignores is precisely the problem of liberal-individualist ideology: that is, of how to constitute a sense of community among and between social actors who are conceived of in terms of autonomous individuals. In slightly different but similar terms it ignores Weber's problem of the iron cage of increasing rationality which, while furthering the workings of a universal Reason, also cut at the basis of a shared communality. Community or communality is always particular. And not surprisingly most of the more popular cries for a reconstituted sense of civil society in the West stress precisely this need to reassert a sense of shared communality in the face of what is perceived as an individualism devoid of communal referents. The more the relations between individuals are defined by abstract, legalistic and formal criteria, the less the public realm can be defined by a shared solidarity based on concrete ties of history, ideas, love, care, and friendship. As the public space of interaction is increasingly defined by the workings of an abstract, what Max Weber would term "instrumental," rationality, the less the concrete concerns for mutuality and trust are realized (or perhaps seen to be realized) in the public realm. One consequence of this is the increased difficulty of re-presenting social life in terms of the public sphere and (most salient perhaps in the United States), the positing of sometimes private, sometimes simply particular entities and interests as public concerns—as in fact defining the public good. In fact, I would hazard the claim that much of the emphases of multiculturalism, on the maintenance of (often ethnic, but always particular) group solidarities in contrast with the prior ideology of the "melting pot" (based of course on the ideology of the individual as moral absolute) are part of this dynamic. However, just as the idea of civil society could not provide a coherent synthesis of the wills and conflicting desiderata of the individual actors with which the Scotish moralists were concerned, so it also fails to synthesize a public good out of the discrete yet more group-based demands of a multicultural citizenry. Whether in the case of ultra-Orthodox Jews, Chicana Lesbians, Christian Evangelicals, or Japanese philatelists, the universalization of particular claims to represent the public and its good(s) remains intractable. Indeed, as a shared public sphere recedes from the affective grasp of the citizenry (through its very formalization and increased institutionalization), the particular and often the private is posited in its stead as an alternative mode of symbolizing society. The renaissance of arguments based on a "republican" conception of citizenship by Sandel, MacIntyre, and others is of course rooted in the self-same dynamic as these, somewhat less theoretically principled, developments.[45] What both are, in the final analysis, challenging is precisely the idea of a political sphere predicated solely on the politics of rights rather than on a shared vision of the collective Good. The inherent particularism of these collectivist or group-based ideas of the Good inevitably, however, come up against the universalist claims of individual rights in ways that none have yet managed to synthesize. The two poles of the civil society dilemma, seek a resolution in contemporary society that has not been possible since the mid-eighteenth century.

The perduring question of how individual interests can be pursued in the social arena and, similarly, the social good in individual or private life thus continues to be a subject of public debate in Western as well as Eastern Central Europe. The idea of civil society that touches on and embraces elements of both community and individualism can however no longer serve as a point of synthesis between these conflicting ideas—for civil society is at the same time that realm of "natural affections and sociability" recognized by Adam Smith as well as that arena where man "acts as a private individual, regards other men as means, degrades himself into a means and becomes a plaything of alien powers"—in Marx's famous characterization of market relations.[46] It is the realm of "rights" but also of property, of civility but also of economic exploitation. It rests on both the legally free individual, but also on the community of said individuals. Apart from the State, it is nevertheless regulated by Law. It is a public realm, yet one constituted by private individuals.

All these different resonances are contained in the idea of civil society as they reflect the contradictions of modern existence—in the seventeenth century and today. Whether the concept of civil society itself as either analytic idea or normative ideal can bring us any further toward their resolution is, however, open to serious question.

FURTHER READING

Jean Cohen. *Class and Civil Society*. Cambridge: MIT Press, 1982.

John Hall, ed. *Civil Society: Theory, History, Comparison*. Cambridge: Polity Press, 1995.

Chris Hann and Elizabeth Dunn, eds. *Civil Society: Challenging Western Models*. London: Routledge, 1996.

Robert Hefner, ed. *Democratic Civility: The History and Cross-Cultural Possibility of a Modern Political Ideal*. New Brunswick, N.J.: Transaction Press, 1998.

John Keane, ed. *Civil Society and the State*. London: Verso, 1988.

Augustus Norton, ed. *Civil Society in the Middle-East*. Leiden: E. J. Brill, 1995.

Adam B. Seligman. *The Idea of Civil Society*. Princeton: Princeton University Press, 1995.

NOTES

Portions of this chapter are reprinted from Chapter 1 of *The Idea of Civil Society*, by Adam Seligman. Copyright 1992 by Adam Seligman. Reprinted with permission of The Free Press, a Division of Simon & Schuster, Inc.

1. Daniel Bell, "American Exceptionalism Revisited: The Role of Civil Society," *Public Culture*, no. 95 (1989): 38–56; Edward Shils, "Was Is eine Civil Society?" in *Europa und die Civil Society*, ed. K. Michelski (Stuttgart: Kult Cola, 1991), pp. 13–52; Vladimir Tismaneau, *Reinventing Politics: Eastern Europe after Communism* (New York: Free Press, 1992); Amitai Etzioni, *The Spirit of Community* (New York: Crown Publishers, 1993).

2. Richard Tuck, *Natural Rights Theories* (Cambridge: Cambridge University Press, 1979), pp. 3, 6, 79, 172–73; John Dunn, *The Political Theory of John Locke* (Cambridge: Harvard University Press, 1969).

3. John Locke, *Two Treatises of Government*, ed. Peter Laslett (Cambridge: Cambridge University Press, 1960), p. 325.

4. Locke, *Two Treatises*, p. 334.

5. Locke, *Two Treatises*, p. 269.

6. Locke, *Two Treatises*, p. 271.

7. Dunn, *Political Theory*, p. 103.

8. Dunn, *Political Theory*, p. 260

9. Charles Taylor, *Sources of the Self: The Making of Modern Identity* (Cambridge: Harvard University Press, 1989).

10. Alasdair MacIntyre, *Whose Justice, Which Rationality* (Notre Dame, Ind.: University of Notre Dame Press, 1988), p. 268.

11. Adam Ferguson, *An Essay on the History of Civil Society*, 5th ed., ed. T. Cadell (London, 1782), p. 57.

12. Adam Smith, *Theory of Moral Sentiments* (Indianapolis, Ind.: Liberty Classics, 1982), p. 50.

13. Albert O. Hirschman, *The Passions and the Interests* (Princeton: Princeton University Press, 1979), p. 109.

14. Ferguson, *Civil Society*, p. 52.

15. Ferguson, *Civil Society*, p. 365.

16. MacIntyre, *Whose Justice,* pp. 281–325.

17. David Hume, *A Treatise on Human Nature* (New York: Macmillan, 1948), p. 33.

18. David Hume, *An Enquiry Concerning the Principles of Morals,* in *Hume's Ethical Writings,* ed. A. MacIntyre (Notre Dame, Ind.: Notre Dame University Press, 1965), p. 131.

19. Hume, *Human Nature,* pp. 55–69.

20. Hume, *Human Nature,* p. 69, 63.

21. Hume, *Human Nature,* p. 65.

22. Hume, *Human Nature,* p. 63.

23. Hume, *Human Nature,* p. 64.

24. Susan Meld Shell, *The Rights of Reason* (Toronto: University of Toronto Press, 1980), p. 83.

25. Immanuel Kant, "Idea for a Universal History from a Cosmopollitan Point of View" (1784), trans. L. Beck, in *Immanuel Kant on History,* ed. L. Beck (New York: Bobbs-Merrill, 1963), pp. 11–16.

26. See Kant, "Universal History," as well as his *Anthropology from A Pragmatic Point of View,* trans. M. Gregor (1791; reprint, The Hague: Nijoff, 1974); and *On the Old Saw "That What May Be Right in Theory Wont Work in Practice,"* trans. E. B. Ashton (Philadelphia: University of Pennsylvania Press, 1974).

27. John Laursen, "The Subversive Kant: The Vocabulary of Public and Publicity," *Political Theory* 14, no. 4 (November 1986): 584–603.

28. Hannah Arendt, *Lectures on Kant's Political Philosophy* (Chicago: University of Chicago Press, 1982), p. 60.

29. Immanuel Kant, *What Is Enlightenment?* (1784), trans. L. Beck, in Beck, *Kant on History,* pp. 3–10.

30. John Rundell, *Origins of Modernity* (Madison: University of Wisconsin Press, 1987), p. 28.

31. Immanuel Kant, *The Metaphysical Elements of Justice,* pt. 1 of *The Metaphysics of Morals,* trans. J. Ladd (1794; reprint, New York: Bobbs-Merill, 1965), pp. 237–38.

32. Shell, *Rights of Reason,* p. 123.

33. Rundell, *Origins,* pp. 35–55.

34. G. W. F. Hegel, *The Philosophy of Right,* trans. T. Knox (1821; reprint, Oxford: Oxford University Press, 1952), p. 123.

35. Karl Marx, *Preface and Introduction to A Contribution to The Critique of Political Economy* (Peking: Foreign Languages Press, 1976), p. 10.

36. Karl Marx, *On the Jewish Question,* in K. Marx and F. Engels, *Collective Works* (Moscow: Progress Publishers, 1975), 3:165.

37. Marx, *Jewish Question,* 3:166.

38. Marx, *Jewish Question,* p. 166.

39. Marx, *Jewish Question,* p. 166.

40. Marx, *Jewish Question,* p. 168.

41. T. H. Marshall, *Class, Citizenship, and Social Development* (Westport, Conn.: Greenwood Press, 1973).

42. Charles Taylor, "Modes of Civil Society," *Public Culture* 3, no. 1 (Fall 1990): 95–118; Edward Shils, "The Virtues of Civil Society," *Government and Op-*

position 26, no. 2 (Winter 1991): 3–20; Michael Waltzer, "The Idea of Civil Society," *Dissent* (Spring 1991): 293–304; Bell, "American Exceptionalism Revisited," pp. 38–56.

43. Bell, "American Exceptionalism Revisited," p. 56.

44. See Seyla Benhabib, *Critique, Norm, and Utopia* (New York: Columbia University Press, 1986), pp. 278–353; Jean Cohen and Andrew Arato, *Civil Society and Social Theory* (Cambridge: MIT Press, 1992); Jean Cohen, *Class and Civil Society* (Cambridge: MIT Press, 1982).

45. See Michael Sandel, *Democracy's Discontent: America in Search of a Public Philosophy* (Cambridge: Harvard University Press, 1996).

46. Marx, *Jewish Question,* p. 154.

CHAPTER 2

Equality and Civil Society

Michael Walzer

THE ARGUMENT OF this chapter is probably better described as the defense of a political position than as the exposition of a coherent or well-established tradition. But the position I mean to defend can be located within a broad current of thought that has its sources in nineteenth-century Europe. It reflects the politics of the non-Marxist secular left, whose adherents seek greater political, social, and economic equality. They differ from Marxists in believing that civil and political liberties are neither a capitalist sham nor a temporarily necessary evil, but rather are fundamental to human freedom and dignity. Unlike Christian or utopian socialists, they do not see the achievement of equality as a salvational project or as the end of history (in either of the senses of the word *end*). Their goal is greater equality, not perfect equality, and they (mostly) do not imagine that progress toward that goal will be uncontested or that the partial successes that might be won will bring an ethically unified society. Rather, they assume that citizens of a free and democratic state will have diverse and conflicting conceptions of the good, and will use their freedom to pursue diverse and conflicting goals.

This political tendency goes under different names in different countries. In Italy, for example, its protagonists currently think of themselves as democratic leftists—though their politics has an earlier history, best represented by Carlo Rosselli's book *Liberal Socialism* (1930; English translation, 1994). In Northern and Central Europe, it is called social democracy, even though social democrats came to liberalism only gradually, as they shed their commitment to scientific Marxism and revolutionary transformation; the crucial text is Eduard Bernstein's *Evolutionary Socialism* (1899; English translation, 1909). In Great Britain, laborite politics has always been strongly egalitarian and mostly liberal as well: L. T. Hobhouse (*Liberalism*, 1911); T. H. Marshall (*Citizenship and Social Class*, 1949); and R. H. Tawney (*Equality*, 1931) (Tawney would probably have called himself a Christian socialist, but he belongs with the others) are representative figures. In North America, this same politics is likely to be called liberal egalitarianism; among contemporaries it is probably best represented by John Rawls (*A Theory of Justice*, 1971) and Ronald Dworkin (*Taking Rights Seriously*, 1977). But these different designations reflect differences in context more than in doctrine (though there would certainly be doctrinal dis-agreements among the people I have named). It is, for example, the weak-ness of left politics and the historical phobia against anything called "so-cialist" that lead egalitarian writers in the United States to identify themselves as liberals rather than as socialists with liberal convictions. Al-though I am myself a displaced social democrat, I shall write here, without misgivings, as a liberal egalitarian, and in the first person.

THE INCLUSIVENESS OF CIVIL SOCIETY

There is no liberal theory of civil society that is distinct from the theory of voluntary association. Because the two pretty much coincide, a liberal ac-count of civil society would include all social groups that are or can be un-derstood as voluntary and noncoercive, thus excepting only the family, whose members are not volunteers, and the state, which, even if its legiti-macy rests on the consent of its members, wields coercive power over them.[1] Between these two, autonomous individuals form a multitude of associations and freely move from one group to another or from activist membership to peripheral passivity, and back again, as they choose (I will want very soon to qualify this description, but it will do for now). They are motivated by interest or conviction or by cultural or religious identity; they pursue wealth (in partnerships and companies), or power (in parties and movements), or salvation (in churches and gathered congregations); or they aim to advance some particular good (in interest groups or trade unions), or to deliver some general benefit (in philanthropies and founda-tions), or to ward off some general evil (in organizations for the preven-tion of this or that). Civil society makes room for all these aims and includes all the resulting associations, by virtue of their free and consensual charac-ter. This means that it reaches to politics and economics as well as to the multitude of social activities distinct from these two.

This is an extended definition; there are theorists who would exclude whatever goes on in the marketplace (and sometimes also in the political arena) from their account of civil society, perhaps because they do not think of such goings-on as "civil." But I see no good reason for the exclusion. If unions, for example, are to be included, as they standardly are, then why not the companies with which they are regularly engaged in negotiations over money and job security? To be sure, giant corporations sometimes ex-ercise statelike, coercive, or near-coercive powers, but that seems a better reason for reforming and restraining the corporations than for excluding them from our definition of civil society.[2]

In fact, however, this extended definition is not extended enough to serve the purposes of an egalitarian theory; the most disturbing inequali-ties of contemporary society mark off groups that probably are not best described as "free and consensual." Race, religion, nationality, and gender are all unchosen designations, and the hierarchical rankings within and among them are never deliberated or agreed on. Of course, associations for the advancement of some racial interest, or for collective self-defense, or for a particular form of national/cultural expression will be included in any account of civil society, since their members must join up; no one is born a member of the NAACP or the Anti-Defamation League or the National Organization for Women. But I would be inclined to say that civil society also includes the more inchoate groupings that these associations claim to represent, into which people are indeed born, which they leave only with difficulty (if at all), and which many, but not all, of them would acknowledge if asked to "identify themselves." Race, religion, nationality, and gender are the crucial reference points of the contemporary politics of identity and recognition, which is probably best worked out—this will be my argument below—within the associational world. But the working out will require some revision of the liberal theory of civil society . . . and a little help from the state.

THE UNITY OR COHERENCE OF CIVIL SOCIETY

However we conceive them, all the groups that constitute civil society occupy a common terrain, across which individuals are (relatively, not absolutely) free to move. Because of this freedom, many men and women are members of different associations, often of many different associations. Multiple and overlapping memberships help to tie all the groups (or, perhaps better, all their individual members) together, creating something larger and more encompassing than any of them. This larger entity is still a particular grouping—namely, the civil society of a country, defined (but again, not absolutely) by its state boundaries. Some groups extend across those boundaries, like the Catholic Church, or the Socialist International, or new social movements like the environmentalists and feminists, but these are likely to have local "branches" that take on the characteristics of a particular civil society. So Irish and French Catholics, say, are characteristically different from each other, as are French and German socialists.

If there were a Sartrean "series" of groups, an unlinked set of associations, without overlap, without any coming and going, no movement of members from one to another, minimal conversation across the boundaries, we probably would not call this a civil society.[3] And if there were a rule, even an implicit and unenforceable rule, that each person "belonged" to only one association or one set of associations, because of his or her social class, say, or religious or racial or gender identity, the resulting society would not be "civil" in the liberal sense. Membership would be a trap, even if it were still, formally, a choice. It is not that this society would be a simple aggregation: so many class organizations or faith communities, say, with no connections of any sort among them. More likely, exclusive memberships would breed fairly intense forms of hostility, connection-through-conflict, so that "civility" either would not exist at all or would always be at risk. A recent study of the Weimar Republic suggests that the tendency of its various class-based or religious groups to claim the full attention and all the associational time and energy of their members, leaving no room for multiple memberships, was one of the causes (or was it only a symptom?) of the troubles to come. What the sociologist Lewis Coser calls "greedy institutions," which tolerate no rivals for the loyalty of their members, may exist within civil society, but they are its enemies.[4]

Of course, individuals are free, if they please, to devote all their time and energy to a single group—as many of them do, even choosing groups that do not demand that kind of devotion. But in an open society, without rigid class hierarchies or systematic racial, religious, or sexual segregation, most people will not do that. Historically, it seems fair to say, liberalism has made for plurality and for divided time and energy. This is another reason why the boundaries of civil society are likely to be provided by the boundaries of the liberal state, which establishes, so to speak, the chief playing field, though not the only one, for associational commitment.

THE VALUES OF CIVIL SOCIETY

Civil society is (ideally) a realm of free choice, community, and participation.[5] The first of these is sometimes said to be unimaginable in its absence (though that proposition might make the early history of civil society hard to figure out). In fact, I can easily imagine individuals choosing spouses, say, and also jobs or professions in a world without any, or at least without much, associational pluralism. But any more extended version of free choice would not be available. Civil society makes it possible to choose not only among possible individual lives but also among patterns of economic cooperation, political ideologies, and complex "forms of life"—and then, so to speak, to keep on choosing. Within civil society, individuals can come and go (though they mostly stay); they can join and leave a great variety of groups. Within these groups, they establish (stronger or weaker) ties with fellow members and devote (more or less) time and energy to everyday organizational work, collective celebrations, committee meetings, fundraising and recruitment, and so on.

Similar ties and activities are also available, obviously, in the democratic state, where citizens are members of the political community, invited to join with their fellows in "giving the law to themselves." But what Aristotle called the "friendship" of citizens is highly attenuated in the modern state, and participation is reduced, for most of the citizen/friends, to the bare minimum of voting at election time. The actual experience of solidarity and cooperation with other people, and the acquisition of the different kinds of competence associated with cooperative work—this takes place largely in the groups that make up civil society. These groups have sometimes been described as "schools for citizens," as if their value were only preparatory and instrumental.[6] They can indeed serve as schools, and most studies of political participation suggest that there really is a link between engagement in state politics, on the one hand, and in civil society, on the other, though the causal direction of this link is uncertain. Active men and women tend to be active everywhere.[7] But it is probably also true for most of them that their most satisfying engagements, where they are most likely to work closely with other people, achieve something of value, and recognize themselves in the achievement, take place in their churches, unions, movements, or mutual aid organizations—in civil society, that is, and not in the state.

Something else happens in civil society, which is also of value, though many participants are slow to recognize the value. Because it is a realm of difference and fragmentation, civil society, even in the absence of "greedy institutions," is always a realm of conflict—of competing "causes," interest groups, companies, parties, even churches and philanthropies. The competition is sometimes for power and influence, sometimes for money, sometimes for members; sometimes it reflects programmatic disagreement, sometimes only personal rivalry. But there is no avoiding it, and it may well be that the most important thing people learn in civil society is how to live with the many different forms of social conflict.[8]

The living is easier if there is no single, dominant, all-encompassing conflict between exclusive groups—and that is probably a necessary condition for the existence of civil society. Under ordinary conditions of conflict and competition, what participants experience is sometimes painful, sometimes exhilarating, and also, often, tedious and dull—victory or defeat, usually on a small scale, and the long days in between, and then victory or defeat again, for the conflicts are permanent and no outcome is final. But there are many conflicts, and the same people are differently involved in this one and that one; ideally, no one is always triumphant or always defeated. The protagonists may begin with some religious or political vision of a fully coherent civil society, but they come slowly to recognize that the purposes they support, the beliefs they hold, are not and will never be universally supported or held; they are forced to reckon with, and perhaps eventually to understand, the opposition of the others (but the "others" are not always the same people). Civil society is a school indeed—for competitive coexistence and toleration, which is to say, for civility. Of course, it is also, simultaneously, a school for hostility and sometimes for zeal. But these latter passions work to shut down civil society, and insofar as they fail in this aim, their protagonists find that they have no choice but to live with men and women who differ from them but whom they cannot finally defeat. So toleration may win out in the end, if only by exhausting its enemies.

Exhaustion, however, depends on the democratic state, which has to hold the ring and make sure that the conflicts within civil society are never permanently won by any single group and that the norms of civility, at least in some minimalist version, are maintained throughout. At the same time, the democratic state depends on a civil society in which pluralism and toleration are the rule, for the associational world is a kind of "home" for oppositional tendencies and a guarantee that there will always be alternatives to any political establishment. All the different interest groups, schools of thought, religious congregations, associations for mutual aid, even if they imagine themselves apolitical and in fact take no part in everyday political debate, serve nonetheless as sources of ideas and even of activists for some possible future politics. Without these sources, democracy has only a surface, more or less plausible, but no depth.

THE RISKS AND LIABILITIES OF CIVIL SOCIETY

Whether or not it includes market associations, civil society reflects and is likely to reinforce and augment the effects of inequality. This is so because every organized group is also a mobilization of resources: the more resources its members bring with them, the stronger the group. The stronger the group, the more it is able to enhance the impact of the resources it collects. Hence it is a general rule of civil society that its strongest members get stronger.[9] The weaker and poorer members are either unable to organize at all—they are excluded or marginalized—or they form groups that reflect their weakness and poverty. Of course, these same groups can also serve, to some degree, to make their members slightly less weak and poor. Only infrequently, however, is a larger achievement possible. Numbers are a potent resource in a democracy, and civil society provides space for mass mobilizations of different kinds that, in certain historical junctures, can reshape the established hierarchies of wealth and power. But these mobilizations are rare, in part because they are likely to require, before they can succeed, the assistance of the democratic state (as the American labor movement, for example, needed the Wagner Act and the National Labor Relations Board).

In the absence of such assistance, the greatest danger of civil society is often realized: namely, exclusion from it. The danger is that the benefits of association will be captured by middle- and upper-class citizens, who already possess the time and money necessary to form strong organizations and the education and skill necessary to run them effectively. Sometimes, when this happens, lower-class citizens are simply reduced to anonymity and silence; they become invisible men and women. But there is another possible outcome, more relevant to the self-consciously multicultural character of contemporary civil society, where the crucial divisions reflect not only class difference but also racial, ethnic, and gender difference, and where these two (partly) coincide. This is the politics of identity and recognition, which I take to be (though it is not always or necessarily) the politics of civil society's dispossessed.[10]

Men and women who cannot mobilize resources for a successful defense of their interests or for a satisfying enactment of their cultural values live not only with a sense of deprivation but also with a sense of disrespect. We commonly think of status and reputation as attributes of individuals, perhaps also of families, and we imagine competition in civil society as having some other aim, material or ideological in character. But when the members of excluded or marginalized groups are oppressed because of their membership, their standing in the world is a collective, not an individual, issue. They stand or fall together. This collective condition might suggest the need for a redistributive politics aimed at providing resources and opportunities to individuals—so as to liberate them from identities or, at least, from conditions that they have not chosen. But, for very good moral and psychological reasons, it regularly leads first to a political defense of the devalued identities, articulated in a collective demand for respect: an acting out (with plural pronouns) of the old American insistence on equality: "Call me mister!"[11]

Identity politics is only sometimes aimed directly at the state—as when a subordinated group with an established territorial base demands autonomy or secession. When the groups are dispersed, as they commonly are in immigrant societies and, increasingly, in nation-states, the acting out of the demand for respect takes place mostly in civil society (the public schools are the crucial exception here, but I will leave them aside in order to focus on associational life more generally). Identity politics greatly intensifies the normal conflicts of civil society, for it makes racial, ethnic, and gender difference an issue at every point where it is experienced—in everyday encounters and conversations, in the competition of groups, in the self-government and internal life of "integrated" associations. Hate speech and "political correctness" are controversial first of all in civil society, even when the state is asked to deal with them. I doubt that anyone has been collecting statistics here, but I would guess that questions of group representation arise at least as often in civil associations as in the civil service of the state, and probably in ways that involve more people. The demand for public acknowledgment of the existence, achievements, and needs of minority groups is probably made more often in companies, unions, churches, parties, philanthropic organizations, professional associations, and so on, than in more offical settings. It is more often as workers or believers or neighbors than as citizens that men and women search for ways to take pride in who they are. The pathologies of the search are experienced as distortions of everyday life more than of citizenship; the benefits, if and when they come, are associational more than political.

The problems of inequality have to be dealt with in civil society, which is a realm of inequality. But it is not easy to say how this can be done. Before turning to possible practical answers to this question, however, there is a theoretical problem that I need to address. Identity politics in modern pluralist societies—so I have argued—is most importantly and most problematically the politics of weak groups, whose members are poor and (relatively) powerless. So it would seem—and so I will argue—that the best way to respect them is to address their collective (as well as their individual) weakness. But this indirect approach avoids the question whether they have a right to recognition and respect *as members* and whether it is necessary, or possible, to enforce this right directly. I am skeptical about the standing of the right (though not about its negative version: the right to be protected against group defamation and degradation) and more skeptical about the likely effectiveness of its enforcement. We might require, say, state-sponsored celebrations of the common history and culture of this or that group: holidays, media programs, museum exhibits, and so on. Such celebrations are, obviously, easy to disregard or mock, but perhaps, even if they do not promote respect, they are in themselves respectful. And then there is no reason why they should not be a feature of the everyday life of a multicultural society. Still, promoting respect is what we should aim at, and this is best achieved indirectly, by promoting the conditions that make for respect, that is, by dealing with the problems of group weakness. Strong groups command respect without having to ask for it.

The Distribution of Responsibility

Two different arguments about how we might best deal with the problems of inequality have emerged in recent debates—in uncomfortable and largely useless polarization. The first is the work of neoconservative intellectuals, but it reflects something close to a classical liberalism. It holds that "we" should not do anything; individual men and women must take responsibility for their own lives—not only individually but also in (voluntary) association, pooling resources, bringing their numbers to bear, acting on their own behalf. The second argument is liberal egalitarian or social democratic; its protagonists commonly call for state action aimed at a redistribution of resources, sometimes through the tax system, sometimes through education, job training, reverse discrimination, and so on. Taken together, both arguments are right; in isolation, both are wrong. The distribution of responsibility is a pluralist business.

It will help us think about this pluralism if we consider the economic base of civil society. This is, I think, a necessary and also a natural egalitarian enterprise. Equality is largely a commitment of the left, and most leftists are inclined to materialist modes of thought. So let us see what analytical advantage this materialism offers. Thus far, I have described associations as mobilizing the resources of their members. That is indeed the standard description, but it misses a great deal; it misses, for example, half or more of the money that is actually dispensed by many associations. This money comes from the state, but it comes in a great variety of ways, often in disguise. It comes, for example, in the form of tax exemptions for philanthropic gifts and "nonprofit" organizations (exemptions that leave no record in the budgets of the organizations that spend the money, though without them there would be far less money to spend). It comes in the form of subsidies and subventions, "matching grants" and low-interest loans, services provided by the state (including regulatory services), and "entitlements" paid on behalf of individuals to privately run health and welfare services (often organized by religious communities).[12] In a famous speech, President George Bush once spoke of voluntary associations as "points of light" in American society, as if government by contrast was a realm of darkness. In fact, there would be very little light if the state did not organize and maintain the electricity networks and subsidize the costs of fuel.

In principle this state funding ought to have equalizing effects on civil society, but it will have these effects only if they are part of its design—for the inequalities of associational life are also inequalities of political power and competence and therefore of access to tax money. Some people in some groups know better than others how to get the money—partly because of the people they know, the "networks" in which they are located; partly because of the things they know about how the system works. So it is not enough simply to tell people to organize and go to work, though that is no doubt a good thing to tell them. It is also necessary to make sure that the assistance the state provides to associational life is directed first of all toward the weakest associations.

I am inclined to think that if these associations, which are largely those of minority groups, were significantly strengthened and enabled to provide services for their members—not only of a material but also of a cultural sort—the pathologies of identity politics (extremist claims, expressions of group hatred, narrow chauvinism) would mostly disappear, resurfacing now and again on the political margins. A strong associational life is an achievement in which people will take pride, and which will command respect in the larger world, even if it requires state help (since everyone gets state help). But this is not yet a program, only a hope, since state help comes to those who demand it, and effective demand requires organization, and some groups are (still) more capable than others of organizing them-selves. . . . It is much less difficult to describe a principle of egalitarian as-sistance—help the weakest groups first—than to imagine the process through which this principle might be realized.

And, of course, there are other principles that also have to be realized—criteria in addition to group weakness that citizens and state officials ought to invoke in deciding which groups to help. Not every organization of the weak should be subsidized or assisted by the liberal state. Claims on tax money are legitimate only if they come from organizations that enable their members to act out their cultural, religious, ethnic, racial, or gender par-ticularity in a citizenly way. That means in a way that is fully compatible with similar enactments by other citizens—and with the practice of citi-zenship itself. The formula is standard for liberals, and no doubt requires interpretation, but it has wide applicability.

Whatever the principles at stake, it is worth insisting on the entangled and pluralist character of responsibility. There is no simple set of norms that determine who is responsible to do what. If we imagine men and women as individuals, parents, members of associations, and citizens of the state, there will be things that they ought to do in each of those roles, but ex-actly what the required activities are will depend on their immediate cir-cumstances, on the opportunites open to them, and, as always, on the re-sources they command. Within the relationship that I have been stressing, between civil society and the state, we cannot say much more than that cit-izens should work to expand and properly direct state assistance; members should work to expand the services provided by their own groups. Though citizenship is the more general role, there is no hierarchy here, for the cit-izen, outside of his or her associations, is a lonely and insubstantial figure, without political influence.

The relation between state and civil society is of a kind that used to be called "dialectical," which means that it bears some resemblence to the chicken and the egg. No significant move toward greater equality has ever been made without state action, but states do not act in egalitarian ways unless they are pressed to do so by mobilizations that can take place only in civil society—and that already represent a move toward greater equal-ity. The mobilization of Black Baptists in the American civil rights move-ment of the early 1960s is a useful example. If we were to tell that story, looking for some pattern of causation the way historians do, where would we begin? With Supreme Court decisions and presidential orders or with bus boycotts and student sit-ins? In Washington, D.C., or Montgomery, Alabama, or Raleigh, North Carolina? In a lawyer's office or a church base-ment? Even after the fact, we cannot easily assign causal responsibility, let alone know in advance where to start the process. The politics of civil so-ciety is necessarily experimental.

INDIVIDUAL AUTONOMY AND STATE INTERVENTION

Indeed, civil society itself is an experiment or a long series of experiments, in the sense that everything about it is tentative and subject to revision. But no one is in charge of the experiments. Any entrepreneur, ideologist, or prophet, any man or woman with a project, can try to form an association. On the liberal understanding, all associations are self-organizing (though the state may regulate the process, as in the case of corporations and labor unions). In the absence of political or military coercion, groups spontaneously appear and disappear. But there is at any given moment an actually existing civil society, even if it is changing as we watch, and the question for liberal egalitarian theorists is how to relate to this associational world—which is sure to include illiberal and nonegalitarian groups.

Religious believers and political militants tend to pose the question differently: How would we organize civil society (if we had the chance)? Or, what would civil society look like if everyone shared our faith or ideology? But those cannot be my questions here. I assume a civil society that already includes the Atheists' Association, the Rosicrucians, the various Masonic Lodges, the Trotskyists, the California Monarchist Society, the National Organization for Women, General Motors, B'nai Brith, the Animal Rights League, Pentacostal sects, the Amish, the United Auto Workers, the Catholic Church, the Elks and the Lions, the Nation of Islam, and so on, and on. This is what John Rawls calls the "fact of pluralism," and this "fact" extends to cultural and moral as well as organizational diversity. So we commonly encounter organizations that reject the deepest values of the (liberal egalitarian) state that frames and protects those same organizations—and of the wide-ranging and disorganized civil society in which they find a place.

In principle, liberal civil society is created by autonomous individuals, but in practice many of its associations are unfriendly to autonomy. More than this, many of the groups that coexist in civil society, that seek recognition and respect within it, though they appeal to liberal and democratic norms, are not themselves liberal or democratic. Inequality in civil society does not exist only between or among groups but also within them, in the form of charismatic leadership, hierarchical organization, elite dominance, and gender discrimination. So if we are concerned with individual autonomy, the question we have to ask is not, how do we express this value? but rather, how do we defend it under conditions of group autonomy and of hierarchical subordination in so many groups? Or, given the "fact of pluralism," what sorts of subordination, and what sorts of subordinating practices, are we prepared to tolerate in the civil society of a democratic state? Answering these questions (again) is not easy; nor is there one answer for all occasions and all associations. We require democratic elections in trade unions, for example, but not in churches. I suppose that there are good reasons for this difference—which have to do with our ideas about religious freedom, also with the relative oldness of churches and newness of unions, and with the role of the state in union organization. On the other hand, we have barred polygamy among the Mormans, despite its biblical precedents and religious character.

The principle at stake here probably has a twofold, social and political, character: first, associational policies and practices that radically curtail the life chances of members ought to be resisted by the (liberal egalitarian) state; and, second, policies and practices that limit the rights or deny the responsibilities of citizenship should be similarly resisted. The harder question is posed by the first of these: what constitutes "radical" curtailment? Or, more fundamentally, what range of life chances is required by the idea of individual autonomy? That last question goes to the heart of liberal theory, but it does not invite a single answer for all times and places. Nor is it clear that autonomy in a given time and place requires equal access to every locally available life chance. In fact, many sorts of restrictions, whether desirable or not from the standpoint of liberal theory, are compatible with the existence, even the flourishing, of autonomous individuals. But which sorts?

It may be easier at this point to turn to the criteria suggested by the second, the political, aspect of the principle at stake: the rights and responsibilities of citizens. What is at issue, after all, is state intervention, and liberal democratic states may do better if they avoid philosophical disputes about the meaning of autonomy and focus on the requirements of citizenship. The policy of the Catholic Church that bars the priesthood to women, for example, even though it will be opposed by liberal egalitarians, does not qualify on these grounds as a reason for state intervention. It is not only that no one has a right to be a priest, but also that citizens do not need to have access to the priesthood in order to function well in democratic politics. But a refusal to educate Catholic (or Hasidic or Amish or Native American) women would qualify, not only because it curtails their life chances but also because it denies them the skills and knowledge that we judge to be necessary for citizenship. Here we do not have to refer to individual autonomy but only to mutual dependency: these women are going to be citizens of our country, they are going to vote in our elections, and so we all have an interest in their education.[13]

But how can problems like these ever arise in a civil society formed by voluntary association? If we imagine a perfect civil society (which is something like a perfect market), there would be no curtailments of opportunity or denials of rights—for individuals would simply not join, or would quickly leave, associations in which they were discriminated against or systematically subordinated. And so there would be no need for state intervention. But there is in fact no such thing as a perfect civil society (just as there is no such thing as a perfect market). One of the important insights of egalitarian (as opposed to classical) liberalism, and of social democracy more generally, is that the social world cannot be adequately explained as the work of autonomous individuals. Many of the supposedly voluntary associations of civil society are in fact involuntary—or, at least, their voluntary character is compromised in a variety of ways. Individuals do not join, for example, but are enrolled by their parents, and their membership is tied up with their familial loyalty and their racial, religious, or ethnic identity, so that even if they are formally free to leave, they do not feel free, and any attempt to distance themselves is likely to be painful. Moreover, not all autonomous individuals are prepared to defend their autonomy, or are able to defend it, when there are high costs involved in the defense. For these reasons, there will always be local hierarchies and even local tyrannies within liberal democratic states, and so we will always need a theory, however loosely structured, that tells us when to intervene and when not.

It is an interesting question whether the aim of intervention should be to overcome or simply to limit the involuntariness of associational life: should we be moving toward the ideal of a perfect civil society? But involuntary and semivoluntary association is a necessary feature of social and cultural reproduction, and a likely feature of the moral character and mental attitudes that we aim to reproduce. We can imagine a kind of absolute freedom, like that claimed by the seventeenth-century English radical Robert Everard when he told Oliver Cromwell that "whatsoever hopes or obligations I should be bound unto, if afterwards God should reveal himself, I would break it speedily, if it were a hundred a day." But it is not so easy to imagine a civil society inhabited and sustained over time by people like Everard. Cromwell's response seems entirely justified: that engagements should not be broken whenever someone imagines his personal scruples to be warnings from God.[14] When we educate our children to be members of some particular group or association, we commonly mean to teach them a stronger loyalty than Everard here acknowledges. We want them to understand the burdens of membership as well as the rights of dissent and withdrawal.

So state intervention should not aim at a perfect civil society, but rather at partial and temporary remedies to the complex imperfections of actual associations. The postmodernist account of self-fashioning individuals, which represents a kind of liberal perfectionism (not so different from Everard's radical Protestantism), would be more attractive than it is if human beings arrived in the world like colonists in a new country.[15] Since they arrive as infants, in need of socialization, in need of love, attention, and nurturance, and since none of these can be provided in neutral ways that leave their future options entirely open, we had best make our peace with one or another compromised version of individual autonomy (we can argue about the different versions). And then we will have to deal with the anomalies of "civil" subordination (which are something like the anomalies of market coercion).

CONCLUSION

From the arguments of the last four sections, and from the understanding of civil society that they reflect, there follows a strongly positive theory of the state. This above all distinguishes liberal egalitarianism from classical liberalism, which has its origin in a rebellion not only against organized religion but also against what we might think of as organized politics. The classical argument is that autonomous individuals always and everywhere need to be protected against state officials. Egalitarians, by contrast, though they accept the need for constitutional limits on what those officials can do, are ready at the same time to recognize the usefulness of the power they exercise and to give them (some) room to exercise it—for three reasons: first, because the state is necessary to enforce the norms of civility and regulate the conflicts that arise within civil society; second, because the state is necessary to remedy the inequalities produced by the associational strength of different groups, some of which are highly successful, some far less so, in mobilizing resources and providing services for their members; and third, because the state is necessary to set limits on the forms of inequality that arise within the different associations. A decent civil society requires state action.

I do not mean to deny that civility must sometimes stand in opposition to the state, as in Eastern Europe in the last years of communist rule. But this will be a difficult stance, the terrain of civility narrowly circumscribed, the movement of individuals constrained. Civil society in these circumstances takes on a romantic character: life and work within it is something like an underground activity; its oppositional values lead to a voluntary repression of internal conflicts, generating fierce loyalties and utopian aspirations—above all, the aspiration for the replacement of the state by pure associationalism (George Konrad's "antipolitics," a response to the communist restoration in Hungary after the failed revolution of 1956, is a useful and attractive example).[16] But the collapse of the unfriendly state quickly reveals the need for a friendly state, that is, for regulation, redistribution, and (sometimes) intervention. If we reject the theory of a perfect civil society, we can be sure that the state will never wither away.

Political friendliness, of course, can never be guarranteed; the three necessary forms of state action invite abuse; even states that have foresworn totalitarian ambition are still power-driven and (often) corrupt. If there is no perfectly self-sufficient civil society, so there is no perfectly serviceable state. I have focused here on the ways in which civil society requires, and will always require, a strong state. I could also have written about how this same civil society must always defend itself against state power—and also about how the inequalities of associational life make this defense problematic. But that would require another essay, for another time.

FURTHER READING

Jean Cohen and Andrew Arato. *Civil Society and Political Theory.* Cambridge: MIT Press, 1992.

Amy Gutmann, ed. *Freedom of Association.* Princeton: Princeton University Press, 1998.

Susan Moller Okin. *Is Multiculturalism Bad for Women?* Princeton: Princeton University Press, 1999.

Anne Phillips. *Democracy and Difference.* University Park: Penn State University Press, 1993.

Nancy L. Rosenblum. *Membership and Morals: The Personal Uses of Pluralism in America.* Princeton: Princeton University Press, 1998.

Adam Seligman. *The Idea of Civil Society.* New York: Free Press, 1992.

NOTES

1. In modern societies, of course, marriage itself is a voluntary association, even if it entangles the partners with relatives they have not chosen and responsibilities they may not yet understand. And people do walk away from their families. For these reasons, and also for the feminist reasons suggested by Anne Phillips in her essay in this volume, it might be better to include families in our account of civil society. On balance, I think that the special intimacies of familial life set it apart, but I argue below for including familylike groups—ethnic and religious communities.

2. For a useful but perhaps too complicated account of the relation of civil society to "economic society," see Jean L. Cohen and Andrew Arato, *Civil Society and Political Theory* (Cambridge: MIT Press, 1992), pp. 75–77, 416–18.

3. For an account of Sartre's idea of seriality, more accessible than his own, see R. D. Laing and D. G. Cooper, *Reason and Violence: A Decade of Sartre's Philosophy, 1950–1960* (New York: Pantheon, 1971), pp. 120–28. A serial group is a "plurality of solitudes."

4. Sheri Berman, "Civil Society and the Collapse of the Weimar Republic," *World Politics,* April 1997; Lewis A. Coser, *Greedy Institutions: Patterns of Undivided Commitment* (New York: Free Press, 1974).

5. See Cohen and Arato, *Civil Society,* chap. 8 on "discourse ethics" for a theoretically specific account of the values of civil society—a stronger account than I can endorse given the argument above about the inclusiveness of civil society; cf. the essay by Simone Chambers in this volume.

6. The classic version of this argument can be found in A. D. Lindsay, *The Modern Democratic State* (London: Oxford University Press, 1943), chap. 10. Lindsay,

however, is more ready than some later theorists to recognize the intrinsic as well as instrumental value of associational life (especially of the "small religious society," in which, he says, democracy began).

7. See Gabriel A. Almond and Sidney Verba, *The Civic Culture: Political Attitudes and Democracy in Five Nations* (Boston: Little, Brown, 1963)—the pioneering study, much imitated and mostly confirmed in the years since its publication.

8. On the positive value of conflict, see Lewis A. Coser, *The Functions of Social Conflict* (Glencoe, Ill.: Free Press, 1956).

9. But I have found little recognition of this rule in the recent literature on civil society—e.g., Cohen and Arato, *Civil Society;* Adam Seligman, *The Idea of Civil Society,* (New York: Free Press, 1992); John Keane, *Democracy and Civil Society* (London: Verso, 1988). Feminist writers, however, are likely to understand the rule well enough. See, for example, Carole Pateman, "The Fraternal Social Contract," in *Civil Society and the State,* ed. John Keane (London: Verso, 1988), pp. 101–27; and Anne Phillips in this volume.

10. See Charles Taylor, "The Politics of Recognition," in *Multiculturalism: Examining the Politics of Recognition,* ed. Amy Gutmann (Princeton: Princeton University Press, 1994).

11. I have discussed this political demand in "Multiculturalism and the Politics of Interest," in David Biale, Michael Galchinsky, and Susannah Heschel, eds., *Insider/Outsider: American Jews and Multiculturalism* (Berkeley and Los Angeles: University of California Press, 1998), pp. 88–98. "Call me mister!" is originally a response to the use of "boy" in addressing black men; it obviously has feminist versions, perhaps not so succinct.

12. For an account of the uses of tax money by religious organizations, see Dean M. Kelley, *Public Funding of Social Services Related to Religious Bodies* (New York: Institute of Human Relations, American Jewish Committee Task Force on Sectarian Social Services and Public Funding, 1990).

13. On the possible conflict between individual autonomy and group rights, see Will Kymlicka, "The Good, the Bad, and the Intolerable: Minority Group Rights," *Dissent* (Summer 1996); for the best extended treatment of these issues, and an argument somewhat different from that suggested here, see Kymlicka, *Multicultural Citizenship: A Liberal Theory of Minority Rights* (Oxford: Oxford University Press, 1995).

14. A. S. P. Woodhouse, ed., pt. 1 of "The Putney Debates," *Puritanism and Liberty* (London: Dent and Sons, 1938), p. 34. I discuss this exchange in *Obligations: Essays on Disobedience, War, and Citizenship* (Cambridge: Harvard University Press, 1970), pp. 196–97.

15. Or, in Julia Kristeva's words, if individuals determined their identities "through lucidity rather than fate." See Kristeva, *Nations without Nationalism,* trans. Leon S. Roudiez (New York: Columbia University Press, 1993), p. 35.

16. George Konrad, *Antipolitics: An Essay,* trans. Richard E. Allen (New York: Harcourt Brace Jovanovich, 1984).

CHAPTER 3

Classical Liberalism and Civil Society

Loren E. Lomasky

I

CLASSICAL LIBERALISM is the theory of the minimal state, the primary function of which is to vindicate individual rights by protecting against aggressors internal and external. But it also is a minimal philosophy. Liberalism offers an account of political justice.[1] It holds out no comprehensive catalog of the virtues, refrains from endorsing any specific conception of the good life, supplies no depiction of the delights of intimate association or communal solidarity. Its range of prescriptions can be summarized as: Respect the rights of others. Beyond that, liberalism does not tell people what to do. These silences do not bespeak lack of interest in broader moral concerns, but rather are a strict consequence of liberalism's commitment to decentralizing questions of choice and value to individuals acting in their private capacity. A "liberalism" that purports to speak authoritatively on these matters will have forfeited its claim to the title. Nonetheless, commentators have frequently (mis)interpreted this restraint as expressing a particular conception of human nature or desirable interpersonal relations. Characters in the traditional liberal drama are described as "atomistic"[2] practitioners of "possessive individualism."[3] An influential critique of John Rawls's *A Theory of Justice* faults the contractors in the Rawlsian original position as "unencumbered selves" pathologically detached from the local moral environments and affections that are necessary to confer on individual lives meaning and a sense of purposeful activity.[4]

This is not the place to confront these stereotypes, except in passing. Rather, the preceding observations are a prologue to confessing liberalism's lack of attention to the concept of *civil society* in its contemporary signification. I say "contemporary signification" because the literature of liberalism uses *civil society* as the counterpart to the anarchy of the state of nature. Whether via explicit contract, hypothetical contract, or some other means, civil society is that which is created through egress from the natural, prepolitical condition. This meaning of *civil society* bears no connection to the sense in which it signifies the realm of voluntary association that stands between individuals (and, perhaps, their families) and the state. Indeed, the usages are contraries. It would, therefore, be unrewarding to inspect liberal employments of the term as a synonym for political order. To the best of my knowledge, though, it has no other place within the discourse of classical liberalism. The discussion of this essay, then, has to be constructed inferentially rather via setting software search functions to churn their way through prominent liberal texts.

The roots of the modern discussion of civil society go back to Hegel, but its current prominence stems from its invocation during the latter years of Soviet hegemony in Eastern Europe to refer to the web of private associations that invigorate a normal, healthily functioning society but that are constricted to the edge of oblivion under totalitarianism. Civil society so understood is uncontroversial; outside of venues such as North Korea, there is no other side to the debate. Since then, however, civil society has increasingly come to be understood not simply as a realm of voluntary association, but also as excluding market interactions. Underlying this metamorphosis is a perception of individuals squeezed between the Scylla of the state and the Charybdis of corporations, both of which are roughly comparable in their gigantism and concomitant capacity to oppress.[5] Against these overbearing forces of domination, organizations such as trade unions, churches, philanthropic and eleemosynary societies, neighborhood associations, friends of the environment, and citizen advocacy groups of every type are the indicated remedy. They are intermediates that in some measure serve to even out the size disparity between individual citizens and the Department of Defense/IBM.

To the extent that civil society so understood is implicitly hostile to the market or that it equates the domination potential of corporations with that of the state, then liberals will be suspicious of civil society and vice versa. Indeed, such suspicions may seem inevitable. Is not the liberal order virtually indistinguishable from a market order, the patron saint of both being Adam Smith? If capitalism is to be unfettered by any controls that, as the saying goes, put people above profits, then will we not find ourselves the vassals of corporate suzerains only marginally more hospitable than the commissars to the full flourishing of human beings in all their dimensions?

A forerunner of these contemporary misgivings is seen in an influential description of the triumph of the market order as "having left no other nexus between man and man than naked self-interest, than callous 'cash payment.' . . . It has resolved personal worth into exchange value, and in place of the numberless indefeasible chartered freedoms, has set up that single, unconscionable freedom—Free Trade. . . . All that is solid melts into air, all that is holy is profaned."[6] If something along these lines is correct, if liberalism does stand first and foremost for the freedom incessantly to buy, sell, accumulate, and invest, and if the realm of the economic inexorably expands to drive out other, more benign forms of human association, then liberalism does indeed yield implications concerning the normative status of civil society, albeit not implications that liberals will be pleased to acknowledge.

As plot outlines go, this one is not without promise. It has conflict, identifiable heroes and villains, suspense, and, under alternative endings, displays itself as either tragedy or comedy. But as with many stories, full appreciation presupposes willing suspension of disbelief. And with this story there is much to disbelieve. First, an equation of corporate and governmental oppressiveness is spurious. Second, liberal orders do not privilege market relations over other forms of voluntary association. Third, expanding markets do not entail the diminishment of nonmarket entities; the relationship is not zero-sum. Fourth, although liberalism does indeed conduce to the breaking down of some significant, meaning-conferring bonds among persons, so too does a vital civil society. They are correspondingly conducive to the generation of new bonds. Whether such destructive creation is desirable serves as the basis of another story with opposed protagonists. That, though, is the story of the controversy between liberals and conservatives. If it should seem as a corollary of this essay that it is liberalism rather than conservatism that is the natural ally of civil society, that would not be an unwelcome result.

II

That individual human beings are the fundamental bearers of moral status is a postulate of liberalism. Their natural condition is one of liberty and equality.[7] More precisely, it is with respect to their liberty that they are equal. It is evident, says liberal forerunner John Locke, "that Creatures of the same species and rank promiscuously born to all the same advantages of Nature, and the use of the same faculties, should also be equal one amongst another without Subordination or Subjection."[8] Although that natural condition is stateless, it is not lawless. Human beings live under a natural law which, although ultimately authorized by God, is accessible independently of special revelation to all unimpaired adults via their rational faculties. What reason prescribes to them is peace and the preservation of all mankind. Respect for persons' natural rights to life, liberty, and property is the primary instrumentality through which this is achieved. These basic rights are understood by Locke and the ensuing liberal tradition as negative: that is, as rights not to suffer interference in one's peaceful pursuits rather than as entitlements to assistance.[9] Whatever one's ends or attachments may be, one must not pursue them in a manner that transgresses the rights of others. What one owes everyone in virtue of their status as rights holders is noninterference. Crucially, that is *all* that is owed.

A quick reading of this position supports the characterization of atomistic individualism. Lockean persons are minisovereigns, normatively separated one from another, free to go about their private businesses provided only that they refrain from bumping against others. The quick reading, though, is too quick. It confuses liberalism's strictures of minimal moral acceptability with an account of recommended forms of human sociality. For Locke and his liberal successors, if individuals are atoms, then—the occasional specimen of helium or xenon aside—they are atoms regularly prone to bind themselves to others in molecular formations of greater or lesser stability. No less for liberals than for Aristotelians and communitarians, human beings are social animals. If these theories diverge, it is with regard to the liberal postulate that communities are constituted by individuals and not vice versa. A life apart from a nexus of associations may be stultifyingly miserable, but it is up to individuals to decide with which societies they will affiliate. This holds true even for relationships originally unchosen, such as the primal unit of the family, as well as ethnos and nationality. Although these afilliations are not established *ab initio* through acts of choice, their centrality or lack of same in one's ongoing projects is a determination that devolves on individuals, not the discretion of collectives in which they find themselves. Most people will find their lives enriched through family or communal ties, but some will not; the latter are at liberty to detach themselves from these associations and seek others that are more fulfilling.

The one association, if it can be called that, from which one is not free to divorce oneself is the universal association with all other human beings. That is the proper domain for construing the rationale of the Lockean law of nature. One is obliged to respect the rights of everyone, no matter how little regard in which one holds them and the ends that move them. Because the demands consequent on rights are both universal and mandatory, it follows that a rationally sustainable order of rights will be sharply restricted in the scope of its demands so as to be minimally intrusive on individuals' prerogatives in deciding how they will construct their lives. A general requirement of noninterference, as opposed to precepts of beneficence and mutual support, is the least implicative standard of social coexistence. That is why it is especially suitable as the moral basis for the universal association—and why it is unsuitable for expressing the range of moral ties that bind people to each other in voluntary affiliations characterized by shared affections and commitments. If liberals did maintain that for the latter as well as the former the only moral considerations that apply are people's rights, then their theory would indeed be obtusely atomistic. But it does not and so it is not.

Although we do not live in the natural condition, neither do we live entirely beyond its parameters. Hobbes takes the establishment of political order to be the nullification of the rights of the state of nature,[10] but Locke and the liberal tradition instead take it to be their vindication. The state of nature may be law-governed, but its interpretation and enforcement are precarious. Because of partiality toward oneself and loved ones and antipathy toward those of opposed interests, the task of upholding rights in anarchy is burdened by manifold "inconveniences."[11] From these the social contract is the recommended means of egress. The transition from anarchy to political society brings a legislature that can specify in a clear and determinate form persons' rights and duties under the law of nature, an executive to give effect to legislated ordinances, and a judiciary to rule on alleged violations. Through these institutional structures justice is more expeditiously served, but in all essentials it is the same justice that governs relationships among individuals in the state of nature. Most relevant for present purposes is that the political order is to be impersonal, neither privileging some rights-respecting personal projects above others nor enshrining any preferred conception of so-called social justice or civically virtuous fraternity as the object of official state policy.[12] The state is to leave people at liberty to associate or dissociate as they choose, to transact among themselves either on a pecuniary or cash-free basis, and to pursue whichever forms of civility they see fit to follow—just so long, of course, as they refrain from violating rights in the process.

III

Where into the sort of liberal order described above does civil society fit? In one sense, nowhere. Beyond insisting on a regime of rights, liberalism simply does not prescribe concerning intermediaries between individuals and the state. That is liberal neutrality under one of its guises. But in another sense, though, implicit in liberalism is a profound appreciation of civil society, although not of any particular version in which it may present itself. By paring down the realm of the strictly obligatory to a minimum, a liberal order affords maximum latitude to voluntary association. One is not obliged to assume the station and associated duties of caste, community, socioeconomic class, religion, nationality, or kinship group. It is undeniably the case that such unchosen affiliations confer on most individuals handholds to satisfying and worthwhile lives, and liberal principles preclude interfering with people's choices to remain content within their confines. (There is no "forcing to be free" within classical liberalism; welfare liberalism allows much more scope for prodding people into what the illuminati take to be more authentically autonomous modes of life.) But it is also undeniably the case that for many individuals the status to which they are born is unsatisfying and inimical to their good as they see it. Therefore, liberal principles similarly preclude interfering with people's capacity to exercise the exit option.

This is part of what is meant by liberalism's friendliness to civil society.

A liberal society differentially privileges voluntary association over involuntary association. Indeed, all associations (other than the universal association of rights holders) are at least passively voluntary insofar as one's continued (though not initial) allegiance is discretionary. Severing deeply rooted ties may be imprudent and psychologically onerous, but it is permissible. Noninterference is mandatory; remembering to send Mother's Day cards is optional. Indeed, some critics maintain that this very partiality for voluntary forms of association evinces a deep inconsistency in liberal theory. Insofar as liberal principles refuse to afford protection to collectives against defection by their members, they do not display neutrality between voluntary and nonvoluntary modes of association.[13] This may be what Marx has in mind when he claims that bourgeois society dissolves what is solid, profanes all that is holy. In any event, the critique is misplaced. Liberal neutrality is not neutrality concerning *everything;* that would not be neutrality, but rather vapid mindlessness. Rather, it is specifically a refusal to take sides between rights-respecting types of activity. A liberal is not committed to neutrality between rapists and rape victims; neither is liberalism committed to neutrality between organizations that conscript their members and those that secure allegiance voluntarily. And of course it is individuals, not collectives, that are the primary moral unit within liberal theory. Associations do not possess a right to life that defection by members impermissibly jeopardizes.

So much can be read off the surface of liberal theory. More speculatively, there is a deep rationale underlying a regime of rights that can be understood in terms of the value of voluntary associations from the perspective of those who have enrolled themselves. Liberals take rights very seriously; they are the heavy artillery of the moral arsenal. Rights engender maximally weighty claims with which transactors *must* comply. For one viewing from outside the liberal church, this insistence on respect for rights will seem somewhat mysterious, if not bordering on fanaticism. Rights block the realization of otherwise alluring social ends—for example, those of a redistributive nature intended to advance overall welfare or equality. They also impede paternalistic interventions designed to prevent individuals from doing harm to themselves.[14] The occasional misanthrope or ayatollah aside, no one would be comfortable with a regime in which state officials are entirely unchecked in their benevolent designs by individual rights. However, only classical liberals rule out as a matter of principle all intrusions into the protected moral space of competent individuals. One can, to be sure, embrace the inviolability of persons as a dogma, neither requiring nor admitting of justification. But a dogmatic liberalism is an unpersuasive liberalism. Assuming, then, that there is some basis to the liberal credo, on what can the near-absolute bindingness of rights be grounded?[15]

It is no secret that liberal theorists differ among themselves with regard to the foundations of basic rights. Locke sees them as stemming from God's ownership of all creation, Kant as implied by the universal prescriptivism of the Categorical Imperative, Mill as validated by considerations of utility. And there are more. But one plausible route to the underpinnings of rights is to focus on the way they function in the lives of the individuals who bear them. Each person stands in a unique relationship to those particular ends that are distinctively her own. Without gainsaying the relevance to morality of an impartial point of view from which one recognizes oneself to be merely one person among others, practical reason also allows— I would go further and say "requires"—partiality on the part of the agent toward those projects which she has made her own. I have discussed the logic of individuated practical reason at length elsewhere and will not attempt to reprise the argument here.[16] Skipping directly to the conclusion: rights are to be understood as establishing for individuals zones of limited sovereignty within which they enjoy an immunity from demands on their moral attention and thus are free to direct themselves by their *own* moral lights rather than hitch their wagon to whatever happens to be in fashion or subscribed to by majorities. So important is the permission to be partial that it is allowed to override even very strong claims lodged from an impartialistic perspective. That is, there are many things that people *ought to do* that they may not be *compelled to do*. To phrase this in a way that will seem paradoxical to nonliberals, individuals have a robust right to do what is wrong.

Why should the personal, partialistic perspective be allowed to take precedence over the impersonal, impartialistic perspective? The most plausible strategy for framing an answer will be to underscore the necessity of self-directedness for lives that will be perceived from the inside to be worthwhile and meaningful. It is, then, a short step from the predominance of the voluntary to the importance of voluntary associations—that is, to a rich civil society. It is theoretically possible for a liberal to have a taste for a collection of Garbos who want above all else to be alone, but that would be most uncommon. Among the fundamental liberal rights is freedom of association, and there is every expectation that in the normal course of events it will regularly be invoked. That is why a characterization of liberal atomism is so thoroughly misleading. Privacy too will be prized by liberals, but this should not be understood as being in tension with liberal sociality. These are two sides of the coin of the overridingness of the voluntary.

I fear that the preceding discussion may seem unduly saccharine: just leave people alone and thereby allow them to live happily ever after. Would that that were so. Unfortunately, leaving people alone does not guarantee either in individual cases nor for aggregates results approaching the well-being optimum. That is why I believe it to be ill advised for liberal advocates to place all their bets with consequentialistic chips. Sometimes redistributionist measures of the welfare state really *do* eliminate more misery than they engender; sometimes paternalistic interventions really *do* keep individuals from damaging their own interests.[17] Few classical liberals would disagree with the proposition that on balance the welfare state's interventions do far more harm than good, including serious harms to intended beneficiaries;[18] nonetheless, an instrumental justification of liberal rights is both superficial and subject to forays by "reforms" that advertise themselves as *this time* having gotten the hang of actually helping. Liberals who make aggregate measures the primary criteria for acceptance of social rules are playing the other camp's game. As noted above, rights enter the moral arsenal as the device uniquely responsive to personal value. They legitimize and safeguard the judgments that issue from an individual's attachments to his own particular projects. Rights are to be respected not because they always/usually procure the greatest happiness for the greatest number, but because they afford individuals the moral space within which they can direct themselves according to their own conceptions of the good.

But not all self-direction is accurate direction. Economists may suppose within the confines of their models that agents are all perfect maximizers of their own well-being, but outside of those models that is distinctly not so. Due to excessive passions, inattentiveness, lethargy, illogicality, and intermittent bouts of stupidity we wander off the true path or, indeed, never quite manage to put ourselves on it. People make miseries of their lives through addicting themselves to harmful chemicals, betting on sure things that somehow finish seventh, marrying too impetuously, divorcing too impetuously, swallowing arterial plaque in the form of cheeseburgers, following their messiah to an out-of-the-way homestead in Waco. Had they chosen otherwise, their lives would have gone better. More arguably, had they not been afforded the prerogative to direct their choices along these detrimental lines, their lives would have gone better. A regime of maximum feasible liberty is friendlier than any other to life enhancing choice making, but it is similarly hospitable to cul-de-sacs and poison pills. A liberal order can be viewed as the standing wager that people who guide their own projects rather than consign these to the putative wisdom of technocrats, benevolent despots, and philosopher-kings will do better than their more coddled cousins. And like any genuine wager, it is one that can be lost.

Classical liberalism historically has shown itself willing to assume that risk. In the seventeenth century it would have seemed to most people a rash leap into folly to suppose that a society could hold itself together without a common religion to bind them into one ecclesiastical polity. In the eighteenth century there existed widespread skepticism concerning the desirability of an economic order in which entry and exit were not controlled by the crown and in which goods would be allowed to cross borders with minimal constraint. Nineteenth-century liberals offended against the received wisdom when they argued that the emancipation of women from their domestic role would not imperil the stability of the household and drown society in vice. And in the twentieth century, and now in the twenty-first, the majority hoots at the suggestion that we might wind down a war against drugs that has proven itself to be both unwinnable and extraordinarily profligate in the direct and collateral damages it causes; that employment contracts might be entered into on whatever terms to which the parties consent; that people might employ their own criteria concerning which foods and pharmaceuticals they will ingest; that an official state school system is no more necessary or desirable than an official state religion; and so on. In contrast, competing political philosophies such as welfare liberalism, conservatism, and social democracy show themselves to be considerably more risk-averse in their insistence on qualitatively and quantitatively more substantial direction from above.

Some may suspect that the preceding paragraph stacks the deck by listing only those wagers that have already shown themselves to be winners for liberalism (not including contemporary ones on which the moral bookmakers are still giving odds). By way of defense I note that the preceding four centuries have been a conspicuous winning streak for liberalism. The point is not that liberalism has been on a roll but that it (logically) could have been otherwise, and that many intelligent, well-informed observers at the time did indeed expect things to proceed otherwise. Marx, for example, announced the implosion of capitalistic economies to be imminent, and academics in the 1960s took seriously Khrushchev's boast that his society would bury ours. Many contemporary conservatives argue that feminist liberalization, removal of prayer from the schools, and tolerance of homosexual relationships are, even as we speak, leading us down paths to social disintegration. We may believe them to be mistaken, but they are not jousting against truisms. Liberalism's risks have shown and will, I believe, continue to show themselves to be well judged, but that is not because they are contrived.

Civil society is no less chancy. Across a wide swath of the political spectrum there exists consensus that a variety of structures intermediate between individuals and the state is necessary for the health of the polity. There exists no such consensus concerning the means through which those intermediate structures are most successfully nurtured.. Might it not be the case that absent the deliberate application of political means to their sustenance, individuals will find themselves progressively more dissociated one from another, will secure entertainment while sitting alone in front of their wide-screen TVs and pursue companionship in chatrooms on the Internet? Is there cause for concern as attendance at PTA, Rotary, and chess club meetings plummets? What does it say about the health of the body politic that even on those occasions when individuals can be induced to leave the wired-in comforts of their homes for a few hours at the Bowlarama, they will increasingly eschew leagues and instead bowl alone?[19] One line of interpretation has it that these are the predictable fruits of a liberal non-interventionism that, in its apotheosis as unfettered individualism, takes it to be a matter of principle to refrain from opposing the centrifugal forces that fracture social bonds. Even if atomism is not implicit in the very foundations of liberalism, a desiccated collection of atoms is its long-term progeny.

Those espousing this viewpoint tend to issue calls of one sort or another for civic renewal.[20] Typically these entail the creation of new public programs, typically those programs are to be funded from tax revenues, and typically those employed to design and manage these programs will be drawn from the same class of intellectuals who had proclaimed the urgency of these measures. This is not the place to hold such proposed remedies up to critical inspection; the primary intent of this essay is explication of liberalism's conception of civil society, not its defense. (To be sure, these tend to converge when explication involves exposing misconceptions and inaccurate stereotypes.) Instead, two brief observations: First, the existence of the civil society debate itself constitutes evidence that a laissez-faire attitude toward voluntary associations is by no means vacuously uncontroversial. Rather, it is to take a disputable—and disputed—stance on the question of whether voluntary associations when left to their own devices can adequately generate and regenerate themselves or whether guidance from above is required. Second, the diagnosis of an atrophied civil society cuts in both directions. Perhaps it is not the prevalence of liberal ideology that best explains developments inimical to a vibrant civil society, but rather the overriding of liberal strictures by an omnivorous public realm. Functions that formerly were mostly the domain of communal and charitable institutions have increasingly been taken over by the state. Ethnic and neighborhood groups used to self-insure against unemployment and the death of a breadwinner, provide subventions for support of the indigent aged, float small loans to respond to emergencies, and provide both pecuniary and spiritual support to the "worthy poor." Now these mutual aid societies have gone the way of the dodo, and charity is increasingly supplanted by welfare state programs. One need not be an unrequited nostalgist for "good old days," which in various respects were not so good at all, to observe that whatever benefits the expansion of the welfare state has conveyed, those benefits have not come free of associated costs. Among these are supplanting of the voluntary by the nonvoluntary. Those costs may or, as I am inclined to believe, may not have been worth incurring, but the point beyond dispute is that in at least this one regard it is welfare liberalism rather than classical liberalism that has done more damage to the infrastructure of civil society.

IV

Critics of classical liberalism may accept the charge that an expanding state realm narrows the space within which civil society can flourish. They are apt to respond, however, that this restriction is more benign, more manageable, and more limited in magnitude than constrictions originating from the other direction: the hegemony of corporate capitalism and its associated cash nexus. If in our private lives we are to be precariously situated between two gargantuas in the shadows of which we are dwarfed, then at least let them be opposed gargantuas. Insofar as the ministrations of the protective state neutralize in some measure the cold discipline of capitalism, then its interventions may on balance be more enabling than constraining: when flower power ruled the streets of San Francisco, this was known as capitalism with a human face.

Recall Marx's imprecations against the solvents unleashed by the ascendancy of the bourgeoisie. This is an early version of the call to arms against dehumanizing market forces, the most recent incarnation of which are warnings about the specter of globalization. To be sure, Marx and his epigones did not demonstrate themselves to be friends of civil society—their comradeship took a rather different form—but perhaps charity demands that the benefit of the doubt be accorded to those who alleged a parity between the oppressiveness of big corporations and the oppressiveness of big government when both were young. Enough time has passed to render that excuse stale. But whether in its early or late incarnations, the parity-of-oppression analysis is flawed for at least three fundamental reasons.

First, the comparison is immediately undercut by the simple observation that the putative oppression exercised by corporations cannot belong to the same genus as that exercised by states. Both are "powerful," but their powers takes radically different forms. States and their component parts exercise authority through coercive means. Possession of a monopoly on legitimate exercise of coercion is, indeed, the Weberian definition of the state. Corporations do not enjoy a prerogative of unleashing force against those who decline to purchase their wares or labor in their employ. Rather, whatever power they possess is a power of persuasion. They induce consumers to purchase by offering goods and services that in the subjective valuation of those consumers are more valuable than the money spent to secure those items. Similarly, employee services are procured by offering a wage that is more highly valued than alternative uses of the hours forgone. Nor is this sham persuasion, the sort that godfathers employ when they dangle offers that can't be refused. The business of business takes place in a highly competitive environment in which someone who is not persuaded to shop from/work for GM can take her dollars/labor to Ford or Chrysler or—thanks to the benefits of globalization—Volkswagen, Honda, Toyota, and a handful of other purveyors. Or she can choose to ride a bicycle. That corporations neither enjoy a monopoly nor have instruments of coercion at their disposal distinguishes them in the most obvious way from governmental instrumentalities.[21] Grammar to the side, *state* is a doggedly singular noun while *corporation* is capaciously plural.

A second and related point is that market structures and the transactions that take place within their ambit are not something *other* than civil society; they *are* voluntarily association in one of its many forms. Corporate stockholders, whether individuals or institutions, have chosen to join their savings alongside those of willing others to undertake activities they believe will make their lives go better. Shopping is not the passive transformation of income into means of subsistence by cogs of the capitalist order, but rather a calculated manifestation of self-direction along avenues that one judges to be personally enhancing. Purchasing manifests individuality. It also typically is undertaken as an expression of sociability; as the father of two teenage daughters, I can speak with some authority on this matter. Nor is labor the alienation of one's species-being in the fetishistic practice of transforming one kind of commodity into others. The profession one selects, the trade-offs one makes between its pursuit and other employments of one's energies, the ends one serves through one's work: these too are manifestations of individuality through voluntary arrangements with willing others. If one chooses to "buy American" or not to work for companies that employ child labor in Southeastern Asian countries—or if one declines to limit one's consumption or labor in these ways—that is to take a moral stance. These are the free actions of free men and women in a way that "contributing" to Social Security or giving up cigarette smoking because the government has imposed punitive taxes are not. To be sure, there are important differences between market transactions and other forms of civil association, but that does not make the former any less a component of civil society than is singing in the Salvation Army choir or signing up for league bowling.

Third, I turn now to a consideration of those important differences. To spend an evening bowling with one's friends because one cherishes their company and wishes to join with them in a team activity is more edifying than charging them an hourly rate for one's kegler services. It does not follow that cash transactions are less creditable than those fraternally motivated. Rather, each is perfectly appropriate in its proper domain.

It was argued in section II that rights are to be understood not as the be-all and end-all of liberal morality, but rather as standards of peaceful interaction for members of the universal association. They are equipped to serve this function because they abstract away from particular affections and attachments so as to provide articles of justice claimed from everyone and owed to everyone. For less inclusive, more intimate groups, supplementation by other moral standards is requisite. Similarly, the cash nexus is the standard for economic interaction among the diverse participants in a vast (now global) market order. A market order is not, however, *only* a market order. Rather, it peacefully coexists with a diverse number and variety of less inclusive, more intimate groups. These include friends, families, neighborhoods, clubs, educational and philanthropic organizations, and the whole myriad of associations that constitute civil society. For these, the operative rule is not simply cash on the barrelhead. That is why it is odious for one friend to charge another for her time and companionship; it is culpably to misidentify something as what it is not. The precisely opposite mistake, however, is to apply patterns of intimacy and concern to transactions in which one is properly indifferent to the identity of the parties to whom one is thereby related. "Treat persons always as ends in themselves rather than as mere means."[22] Yes, but simply to acknowledge and respect the rights to life, liberty, and property of one's transactors is sufficient to certify their status as ends in themselves.

In revivals of Thornton Wilder's *Our Town* as well as in the currently fashionable philosophy of communitarianism there is a tendency to wax nostalgic over an era of tightly knit communities in which everyone knew everyone else, and all relationships were tinged with the personal. Perhaps in the eclipse of such modes of life we have lost something valuable. Or perhaps we have been released from stifling incursions on privacy and autonomy. Or perhaps both. In any event, for nearly all of us, the community of engagement and intimacy is no longer our home, certainly not our only home. We are plugged into international information systems, depend for our livelihoods and entertainments on people who are thoroughly anonymous to us, benefit from enormous welfare gains brought about through increasing economies of scale consequent on an unfathomably intricate division of labor. That is the condition of modernity. Whether one celebrates or bemoans its ascendancy, the question important for practice is: What are to be the terms of interaction within the national and international megalopolis?

Marx answered this question with the bright idea of a centrally controlling dictatorship of the proletariat. Even then better proposals were on offer. Today we know with as high a degree of certainty as the human sciences afford that the singularly adequate regulative standard for large-scale economic systems is the price mechanism.[23] Money prices serve two crucial functions without which economies will founder. First, they convey information. Offers to buy and sell at a particular price inform transactors of effective demand for the good or service in question. Second, and equally important, prices conceal information. When buyer pays seller one hundred dollars for a carton of widgets, the only information conveyed is the willingness of the other party to transact at that price. Seller need not know whether buyer is an upstanding pillar of the community or something of a rogue; whether buyer is Christian, Jew, Druid, or none of the above; what buyer intends to do with the widgets once they are obtained; whether widget possession will truly enhance the life of buyer or instead lead him down the winding road to abject widget dependency. Nor need buyer trouble his mind concerning seller's personality and motivations. They simply come to terms at the striking price.

Some will object that economic activity so understood depersonalizes individuals. That claim is true. Exchange abstracts away all features of the transactors other than their liberty to transform one set of property holdings into another. There are two things to be said about such depersonalization. First, it is a necessary thing. Persons are endlessly rich and complex entities. If a precondition for exchange were "getting to really know" the opposite party, then economic relations would bog down in an epistemic morass. Prices abstract away from the personal goo. But second, such depersonalization is a good thing. It is protective of privacy. If one had to bare one's soul to buy a newspaper or rent a video, then modern economies would indeed be ghastly panopticons. Moreover, depersonalization undercuts invidious grounds of discrimination. If people regularly buy from the vendor who offers the best goods at the best price, then whether that vendor is of the same religion or race or sexual preferences as oneself becomes immaterial. This is not to maintain, of course, that a capitalistic economy is immune from the perversities of prejudice, but it is to note that these all-too-common failings are meliorated by an impersonal price system. Compared with allocation via ties of consanguinity or political clout, capitalism is very much an equal-opportunity supplier.

This may seem efficient but also dreary, lifeless. If capitalistic means of production achieve their enormous efficiencies only by driving intimacy out of human relations, then perhaps the price of a market order is itself too steep. But if this is the mordant reflection that prompts critics of capitalism, they can release their apprehensions; the components of civil society that operate via a cash nexus are thoroughly compatible with the existence of other modes of voluntary association not pecuniarily based. Specifically, those that presuppose shared ideals or strands of affection cannot operate via monetary bids and offers. That is because the information abstracted away by prices is crucial for the sustenance of these more personal relationships. Just as basic rights do not exhaust for liberals the domain of morality but only provide the most inclusive standards of interaction, so too does the cash nexus not dominate liberal civil society, but rather is the basis for transaction where more committal and revealing relationship patterns are either not feasible or undesirable. By countenancing whichever voluntary associative choices individuals make, a liberal order is equally hospitable to both market and nonmarket arrangements.

As Adam Smith well knew, commercial society may be dynamically expansive, but it is not ubiquitous.[24] Rather, it is interlaced with a myriad of noncommercial formations and affiliations. The succeeding two centuries of capitalistic development have not altered that fact. Nor is knowledge of it confined to a coterie of academic specialists. Ordinary men and women are able to preserve the separation in their common practice. Hiring labor is not like giving one's daughter her allowance; those who occupy both roles rarely confuse them. Americans are workers and consumers, but they are also joiners, volunteers, even league bowlers. For the most part, institutional structures spontaneously evolve to mark off the relevant distinctions. Sometimes governments employ legal sanctions to do likewise. For example, statutory prohibitions of prostitution and the sale of transplantable bodily organs express the conviction that the cash nexus is an inappropriate basis for relations of sexual intimacy or conveyances of the gift of life. That sentiment is not in itself discreditable. Unfortunately, when instantiated in law, it counterproductively tends to obliterate the sorts of distinction it intends to preserve. Sex for love and sex for cash are quite different activities that for some five thousand years have shown themselves quite able comfortably to coexist. Transplantation boasts a considerably shorter history, but there is no reason to suppose that donations from love and sales in pursuit of economic interest cannot coexist equally successfully.[25] By attempting to force all sexual activity and all organ transfers into the same Procrustean bed,[26] prohibitionists themselves undermine the distinction between pecuniary and nonpecuniary bases of civil association.

To conclude briefly: Liberal theory traditionally has paid scant attention to civil society. Nor has it much attended to love, beauty, athletic prowess, the wonderful palate-caressing properties of a classic Burgundy, poetry or, for that matter, metaphysics. Silence concerning the latter group should not be interpreted as hostility; neither should it be so interpreted with regard to civil society. Liberalism commends none of these, but it affords a place to all. If individuals acting in their private capacity should decide that the presence of any of these ingredients makes life go better than does its absence, then they are at liberty to act accordingly. With regard to items of potential value, liberalism is disinterested, not uninterested.

But although liberal theory does not speak explicitly of civil society, congeniality to it is implied at the most foundational level. That level is the inviolability of individuals' moral space within which they enjoy an extensive liberty to direct their affairs as they themselves see fit. By minimizing the scope of the mandatory, liberalism maximizes the domain of the voluntary.

That, of course, includes voluntary association. Liberalism takes no sides concerning which forms of voluntary association are to be preferred over others; all such questions are devolved down to the level of the concerned individuals. Unless demonstrated otherwise, there is a presumption that there is no fixed upper bound to the number of flowers that can simultaneously bloom. There exists no presumption, however, that once one has bloomed, it must be preserved forever in some sort of museum of species of sociality. Groups will wax and wane in response to the desires of the individuals who enter into them or defect. There exists no guarantee that the result either in the individual case or for aggregates will be auspicious. That is why a liberal order is the continuing wager that men and women let alone to direct their own affairs is the fitting and proper basis for human society.

NOTES

1. Semantic shifts have rendered the term *liberal* slippery. The minimally interventionistic state of classical liberal theory has over the years taken on functions undreamed of by its philosophical forebears. The closest equivalent to the original meaning now in common usage is *libertarian*, but the proper scope of libertarian doctrine is a matter of intense debate among its votaries. *Classical liberalism* is accurate but ponderous. In what follows I shall employ *liberal* and its cognates with primary reference to the tradition that reigned from Locke through Mill. Where clarity requires a more finely honed distinction between the earlier and later stages of the semantic divide I shall employ, respectively, *classical liberalism* and *welfare liberalism*.

2. See Charles Taylor, "Atomisim," in *Communitarianism and Individualism,* ed. Shlomo Avineri and Avner de-Shilit (New York: Oxford University Press, 1992), pps. 29–50.

3. C. B. McPherson, *The Political Theory of Possessive Individualism* (Oxford: Clarendon Press, 1962).

4. Michael Sandel, *Liberalism and the Limits of Justice* (Cambridge: Cambridge University Press, 1982).

5. See Benjamin Barber, "An American Civic Forum: Civil Society between Market Individuals and the Political Community," *Social Philosophy and Policy* 13 (Winter 1996): 269–83.

6. Karl Marx and Friedrich Engels, *The Communist Manifesto,* ed. Harold Laski (New York: Random House, 1967), pp. 135–36.

7. Traditionally this condition has been described as the *state of nature.* Although liberal theorists differ importantly in their understandings of the state of nature, for all of them its primary significance is as a normative baseline rather than as some bygone historical epoch.

8. John Locke, *Second Treatise of Government,* ed. Peter Laslett (Cambridge: Cambridge University Press, 1960) sec. 4.

9. Secondarily Locke endorses a title to charitable provision for those who nonculpably fall below a level of resources necessary to sustain life and self-directed ac-

tivity. Most of the liberal tradition follows Locke in justifying the existence of a background social safety net. In welfare liberal theories both the scope and prominence of this apparatus is markedly expanded. For elaboration of this point see Loren Lomasky, "Justice to Charity," *Social Philosophy and Policy* 12 (Summer 1995): 32–53.

10. With the significant exception of the right to do whatever one must to defend oneself from attack on one's life.

11. Locke, *Second Treatise*, sec. 13.

12. It is with regard to this restriction that welfare liberalism diverges most prominently from classical liberalism.

13. See, for example, Joseph Raz's critique of liberal neutrality in *The Morality of Freedom* (Oxford: Clarendon Press, 1986).

14. It goes without saying that this is not true of liberal welfare states that routinely effect transfers from the rich to the poor, the poor to the rich, and from one middle-class special interest group to another, and that are comparably busy with putting helmets on reluctant motorcyclists, deciding which pharmaceuticals patients will be allowed to ingest, and "helping" individuals give up smoking cigarettes by imposing punitive taxes on the noxious weed.

15. I discuss the near absoluteness of rights in "Rights without Stilts," *Harvard Journal of Law and Public Policy* 12 (Summer 1989): 775–812.

16. See Loren E. Lomasky, *Persons, Rights, and the Moral Community* (New York: Oxford University Press, 1987), esp. chap. 2.

17. For example, although it is very likely that Food and Drug Administration edicts cost more lives than they save, it is also likely that laws requiring motorists to wear seatbelts on balance decrease death and serious injury.

18. E.g., rent control laws generate shortages of rental units; minimum wage laws turn the working poor into the unemployed poor; and so on.

19. See Robert Putnam, "Bowling Alone: America's Declining Social Capital," *Journal of Democracy* 6 (January 1995): 64–78. Although at first blush the demographics of bowling may seem to have only the most tenuous connection to concerns of social stability, in fact this essay has prompted a burgeoning literature discussing whether the alleged phenomenon is real and, if so, what implications ought to be drawn. See also David Brooks, "Civil Society and Its Discontents," *Weekly Standard* (February 5, 1996), pp. 18–21; and Michael Sandel, "America's Search for a New Public Philosophy," *Atlantic Monthly* (March 1996), pp. 57–74, for complementary reports from distant points of the political spectrum on the liberalism-induced pathologies of American civil society.

20. If I may be allowed an autobiographical excursion, for reasons still not entirely clear to me I was appointed four years ago to the Scholars Panel of the National Commission on Civic Renewal, cochaired by William Bennett and Sam Nunn. Among panel members, the liberal etiology of civil decay was a popular theme.

21. "Obvious" is, admittedly, my personal gloss on the contrast. For many critics of markets it is far from obvious. They characterize as "coercive offers" consumption or employment proposals that induce individuals to transact because they represent the most highly valued opportunities open to them. Presumably this is taken to constitute coercion, because not to accept the offer is to acquiesce to a

lower level of well-being than can be achieved by its acceptance. I confess that I am unable to find any plausibility in this position—as, I am sure, those who advance such views are unable to find any plausibility in mine. Perhaps we are confronted here with the moral equivalent of color blindness. But whose?

22. Paraphrase of the third form of the Kantian Categorical Imperative.

23. The post-1989 collapse of the Soviet empire is but the latest piece of evidence confirming the proposition.

24. That is why the so-called Adam Smith problem of scholars endeavoring to render consistent the views expressed in *The Theory of Moral Sentiments* with those of *The Wealth of Nations* are challenging what is mostly a phantom.

25. I have explored these cases in Loren E. Lomasky, "Gift Relations, Sexual Relations and Liberty," *Philosophical Quarterly* 33 (July 1983): 250–58.

26. No double entendre intended.

PART II

CHAPTER 4

Does Feminism Need a Conception of Civil Society?

Anne Phillips

THE DIVERSITY OF FEMINISM is a commonplace of contemporary comment, something so well established that many book titles now opt for the pluralistic feminisms rather than feminism per se. It is still possible to generate positions acceptable to any brand of feminism: it is hard to imagine a feminist who would object to the claim that women are subordinated to or disadvantaged relative to men, and that something should be done to change this. Beyond this, there are enormous differences. Some of these are expressed in the various traditions to which feminists look for inspiration and potential alliance: this might be liberalism or socialism, nowadays it might be postmodernism or critical theory, more rarely but not impossibly it might be one of the religious traditions. This produces one kind of hyphenated identity (what Catharine MacKinnon has disparaged as "modified" feminism),[1] but there are also the more experiential differences that have generated distinctively "black" or "Third World" feminisms. Within and beyond all such sources of divergence, feminists continue to position themselves differently on a number of recurrent issues. One theme much discussed in recent decades is whether women should be claiming equality with men (which might suggest they accept the superiority of "male" practices and goals) or pursuing a world better attuned to the values of female culture (which might suggest the two sexes really are "naturally" different and distinct). Though recent literature tends to converge on the idea that we need both equality *and* difference, there is still considerable disagreement about this.

The version of feminism I develop here involves a particularly strong egalitarianism that others will see as exaggerated or simpleminded or both, and I make no claim about this as "the" feminist perspective. This frames my analysis of what feminism can do with a conception of civil society, but my perception of what feminism has so far done is intended to be more universal. Despite other disagreements, there has been a consistency in feminist appropriations of "civil society," the main unifying feature being that the concept plays a minimal part in the feminist division of the world. Feminists do use the phrase: they use it when discussing women's confinement to the family and exclusion from the public activities of the wider world; they use it in discussions of women's citizenship. But while the distinction between public and private spheres has been central to (any) feminist analysis, feminists have remained—in Jodi Dean's phrase—"oddly silent" on the subject of civil society.[2] Civil society is not a significant organizing category for feminists, and rarely figures in the feminist taxonomy.

The explanation lies partly in what other traditions have included in the category and what, by implication or design, they have left out. Civil society is often presented in terms that make it seem a place where women are not: this is most apparent when it is presented in contrast to the sphere of nature, or as a middle term between family and state. Early social contract theorists employed civil society (usually synonymously with "political society") as a way of marking the transition from a state of nature to one regulated by "man-made" obligations and laws, and in the contrast they drew between a natural state and a civil society, women turned out to be more visible, and more nearly men's equals, in the first. Carole Pateman has described the extraordinary contortions such theorists went through so as to get women sufficiently into civil society to be bound by its laws yet sufficiently out of it to be subordinated to men; and many have shared her perception that the story of civil society is a story of "masculine political birth."[3] At a later stage, Hegel employed the concept to generate a tripartite distinction between family, civil society, and state, and was even more explicit than his predecessors in placing women in an earlier, "more primitive," stage. Hegel saw man as having his "actual substantive life" in the state, in labor, and in struggle with the external world (these last two being part of what goes on in civil society), and woman as having "her substantive destiny" in the family,[4] and this highly gendered understanding of civil society is by no means unique. "Civil" often implies a contrast with natural or familial. "Woman" still suggests an association with nature or family. It is hardly surprising that civil society so often conjures up a masculine realm.

And yet feminists did not stop talking about the state just because so few women exercised political power—if this were the policy, there would be all too many things on which feminists would choose to remain silent. The exclusion of women from either theory or reality of civil society does not of itself explain the lack of interest in the category, and the odd silence becomes even odder when we consider the way recent theorists have employed the term. In the course of the last twenty years, civil society has come to be used to refer to those intermediate associations (churches, unions, clubs, campaigning organizations) that exist between the individual and the state. This usage was given particular prominence by a wave of global democratization spreading across East/Central Europe, Latin America, and Africa, but has also entered into discussion of the longer-established democracies and the strength or weakness of their civic engagement.[5] Women are often said to be especially active in voluntary or neighborhood organization (they have certainly been more active here than in the higher echelons of the state), and a definition of civil society that highlights this space of social interaction would then seem peculiarly woman-friendly. Indeed, contemporary theorists often seem to go out of their way to list refuges for battered women or societies for promoting female advancement as illustrations of what civil society is about. If there is a gender-loading in the current usage, it might be said to favor women rather than men.

A long history links feminism to practices of local democracy, the roots of which lie in women's status as an outsider group. Caught within family circumstances that they have experienced as confinement rather than haven, and denied access to most of the corridors of state power, many women have looked to their involvement within churches, housing associations, campaign groups, and local branches of political parties as the main way of changing their own (and other people's) lives. They have looked, that is, to what many now regard as the bulwark of civil society: those intermediate, nonstate, nonfamily associations that link citizens in some active collective engagement and are, in principle, open to anyone who chooses to belong. Civil society, in this sense, was hugely important to the development of nineteenth-century feminism, which drew many of its activists from the philanthropic and reform associations that proliferated through the century and gave women their first experience of public life. Both historically and today, civil society can be said to be peculiarly important to the feminist project.

So why so little talk of civil society? The key difficulty is that even when the category has been made more welcoming towards women, the problems that generate it still derive from a nonfeminist agenda. What makes civil society/state a useful way of dividing up the world is usually some thesis about the coerciveness of state power or the amoral fragmentation of market relations. Feminists will have views on both these topics, but they approach them from a different direction. To contemporary ears, "civil society" resonates with thoughts about whether democracies can survive without a dense network of voluntary organizations, whether people need forms of association that are not regulated by either market or government, or whether the tyranny of the state can be tempered by self-governing and independent-minded groups of people who act (in John Keane's phrase) as "a permanent thorn in the side of political power."[6] The appropriate balance of power between civil society and state figures large in this. But the key boundary for feminists has lain elsewhere, in the relationship between the private sphere (understood as the sphere of the familial and domestic) and the public sphere (understood as including what other traditions have demarcated as civil society *or* state). Focusing as it does on the dichotomy between (all) the public and the (really) private, feminism has been less interested in where to draw the line between civil society and state.

Two things then happen. The first is that feminists adopt a broad definition of civil society, spanning virtually everything that is not located in the domestic sphere.[7] In the standard contrast between civil society and state, there is a reading of the relationship between private and public that takes this away from what most feminists have understood by the private. Domestic life drops from view, and all the discussion of public versus private is diverted to what—from most women's point of view—is already a public realm. Political theorists talk endlessly about the appropriate relationship between state, market, and private association, worry away at what they regard as excessive state regulation, or (from the other side) become increasingly agitated about the decline of a specifically "political" sphere. They rarely seem to notice that all this boundary maintenance takes place within what is already, from the perspective of domestic life, a pretty public world.

For feminists, by contrast, the domestic subordination of women looms large, generating a certain impatience with the finer details of who or what goes into civil society. Other traditions may encourage a careful delineation of distinctions between state, economy, and intermediate associations or may generate strong views on where the institutions of the market fit. Feminism is more inclined to blur these distinctions. Where civil society gets a mention (this is not, as I have noted, too often), it is typically as that from which women are excluded. It can then stand in variously for labor markets, old boys' networks, political organizations, as well as for state power. Some of this does become too casual—a kind of returning of the compliment to those who became so obsessed with the civil society/state distinction that they failed to noticed the further separation between the domestic sphere and the rest. But it also reflects what has been an important theme in feminist thinking: the idea that conceptual frameworks are deeply flawed by the way they have dealt with gender and that most require fundamental revision.

The second thing that happens in feminist thinking is that civil society expands to include family as well. When feminists refer to the familial and domestic as the "really" private sphere, they do not mean it exists behind closed doors, is shrouded in mystery, or detached from everything that goes on in "public" life. On the contrary, most argue that the practices nurtured in the private sphere exert a profound influence on the way men and women relate in the worlds of work or politics or scientific endeavor—and that the priorities established in these worlds exert a profound influence on the way "private" lives are lived. To take the most obvious illustration, the fact that it is women rather than men who tend to bring up the children has enormous consequences on the kind of people we become, the structure of the labor market, and who ends up with state power. Conversely, the conditioning of domestic patterns by a complex of educational, employment, cultural, and political forces sets limits to what individuals can do to change their domestic patterns. When feminism focuses on the private sphere, it is not just to say that the activities and relationships of this sphere are as important as what goes on elsewhere. The point, rather, is to highlight the intersection of private life with public existence, and demonstrate that the familial or domestic are not so separate from all the rest. This has the effect of making the category of civil society even broader. If the first move was for feminists to treat civil society as more or less synonymous with the public sphere (making less than other traditions of distinctions between civil society and state, making more of the distinction between the family and both of these), the second has been to put the family right in there as well.[8] Because they regard familial/domestic relationships as inextricably intertwined with the way people organize and relate in the wider society, feminists are more inclined to treat the family as part of civil society rather than as a separate entity. This generates an even more inclusive definition of civil society.

This final stage also reflects what has been a characteristically feminist take on social relationships. Feminists have long been wary of the doctrine of separate spheres, and not only because they see this generating an ideology that has constrained and confined generations of women. A feminist looks around the world and sees much the same patterns repeating themselves in every sphere of existence, whether this be family, market, civil society, or the institutions of the state. In the starker contrasts suggested by some other traditions, we are encouraged to believe that human relationship are ordered very differently in different parts of our lives. Most versions of feminism have doubted whether the differences are really so great.

Consider the much-touted idea that it is inappropriate to insist on rights or equality inside the family because the family is ordered through generosity and love. Consider the parallel notion that the market is indifferent to sexual difference because it treats people only in their capacity as producers and consumers. A number of feminists have queried the first as obscuring the coercive (sometimes brutally coercive) nature of familial relationships, and playing down the importance of justice and equality in regulating relationships between wives and husbands as well as the relationship between parents and children.[9] Others have queried the second as historically inaccurate, arguing that it ignores the networking and clubbish behavior through which dominant groups maintain their control. When feminists try to make sense of the wage differentials that persist between men and women, or of the evolution of a family wage system that defined men as breadwinners and women as dependents, they are more inclined than other economists or historians to stress the norms and practices that arise from the interactions of social groups. Explaining the outcomes through the anonymous workings of the market seems distinctly implausible, and feminists often draw attention to the active intervention by particular groups of employers or workers and the way this contributed to women's exclusion from certain categories of work. My point here is not that feminism is committed to a conspiracy theory of the world. The point, rather, is that the reworking of relationships between public and private— the insistence that these are not separate spheres, that each profoundly shapes the other, that the boundaries are permeable, and often enough wrongly drawn—makes feminism less inclined than some other traditions to accept the distinctiveness of different spheres.

This has important implications for the perception of civil society. Those who describe the family as a unit based on love, or the market as linking people "behind their backs," or bureaucracy as the implementation of impartial rules may well come to regard civil society as more "social" than any of these: less intense than the family, less anonymous than the market, and crucial to social cohesion. Those unconvinced by the descriptions are less likely to conceive of civil society as so very different from everything else. We might want to say that people are linked in civil society through their shared membership of particular organizations, and linked in some sense by voluntary choice. But "membership of the club" also characterizes activities within state or market, while the choice element in civil society cannot be regarded as entirely free. People exist in civil society already as women and men, and their positioning in sexual hierarchies will have a considerable effect on the kind of organizations they are most likely to join as well as their propensity to join any. We do not find women in the Masonic League; we do not find men in the Mother's Union. But we also do not find the sexes evenly distributed among associations that are supposed to be open to all. Civil society remains gendered and exclusionary, neither an aggregate nor really a society, or not if "society" implies that all of us belong.

The Attractions of Civil Society

The above suggests that feminism neither needs nor wants a conception of civil society, but this would be far too abrupt. If we take civil society in its characteristically modern meaning—as a way of referring to the terrain of voluntary associations that exist between economy and state—there are two reasons why feminism should nonetheless be attracted to the politics associated with this. The first is that a feminist perspective is radically pluralist, and that pluralism flourishes more readily in the associations of civil society than in either family or state. The second is that some of the associations that spring up in civil society have a looseness, even an indeterminacy, that makes them particularly hospitable to feminist politics. Feminism is always in some sense about transformation, about articulating previously unheard voices, exposing previously unchallenged bias, and rewriting political agendas. Because it is so often about bringing something new into existence (not, that is, just about pursuing long-established interests and claims), it can be said to have a particular affiliation with some of the less regimented of civil society's groups.

The background to both points is that it is difficult to state in advance what "women" need or want, and that this indeterminacy affects the kind of politics in which feminism best thrives. Sexual difference runs deep in human identity and is not something we can temporarily suspend. We can decide not to reveal our religious or political beliefs; we may even be able to conceal our class and ethnic origins; but few of us can conceal whether we are women or men. This affects the way others view us. It also affects the way we view ourselves. Our sense of ourselves as women and men has been built up through so many circumstances and in so many layers that we can rarely separate out those aspects of our personality that are just "us" from those that express historical practice and cultural conventions. This is not to say people are doomed to repeat whatever they learned in an early socialization, or that sexual identity is so pervasive/invasive that no one can hope to change it. But imagining a world without sexual hierarchy— and imagining what kind of people we might become in such a world—is an awesome task. One consequence is that feminism is by definition exploratory: it is experimental, implies listening to many different voices, and exploring as yet untried possibilities. This is a pluralist politics rather than one that seeks "the" solution from on high.

If there is to be a contest between civil society and the state—a sense in which societies can choose to have a bit more of one and a bit less of the other—feminism is then more likely to situate itself on the side of the first. (I shall qualify this in the next section, for nothing is ever so simple.) In a vibrant civil society, there will be as many organizations as there is energy to go around, and even if most of these continue to be dominated by men, the very multiplication of alternatives opens up opportunities for contesting dominant conventions and promoting radical change. This is part of the argument Nancy Fraser develops against what she sees as the state-centric emphasis that envisages people participating within a single, overarching public sphere. Arguing for a multiplicity of "subaltern counter-publics" in which subordinated social groups can "invent and circulate" their counterdiscourses, Fraser offers, as "perhaps the most striking example," the case of late-twentieth-century U.S. feminism, "with its variegated array of journals, bookstores, publishing companies, film and video distribution networks, lecture series, research centers, academic programs, conferences, conventions, festivals, and local meeting places."[10] Those on the margins of existing public life need the openness and inventiveness of this plethora of associations if they are to have much chance of developing their alternative scenarios and ideas. Jürgen Habermas makes a similar point— and also illustrates it with examples from feminist politics—when he argues that democracies need the "wild," "anarchic" opinion formation that occurs in civil society in order to stretch the boundaries and unsettle the traditions of the existing political agenda.[11] If all action takes place within the legislature—that public place, par excellence, where representatives of the citizenry can deliberate and reach their decisions—there is less chance for those most radically questioning the prevailing consensus to influence the public agenda.

The other point about associations in civil society is that as voluntary associations, they belong to nobody but their members. This means that even those with no particular pretensions toward democracy will be vulnerable to internal pressure. As one exemplification of this, Jodi Dean cites the dramatic changes, including the ordination of women, that have occurred within a number of churches. Churches are hierarchical associations (they take their lead from God), and not really amenable to equality legislation; despite this, some have embarked on revolutionary changes respecting women's position, pressed on by internal processes of discussion, reflection, and critique.[12] For associations that additionally pride themselves on reflecting their members' views, there are even more opportunities for contesting sexism or male bias. The further practical point is that the many associations that are locally based—the housing cooperative, the association of black parents, the group formed to protect a historic local building—are more accessible to women than the grander avenues that lead to state power.

In 1970s Britain, feminists often expressed a preference for the self-financing, self-regulating community nursery over the local authority nursery subsidized by local taxation. The former was usually housed in makeshift accommodation, and often depended on a fragile rota of voluntary workers, but because it was under the control of parents and workers, it was felt to offer favorable conditions for developing nonsexist ways of caring for children and engaging with parents' preferences and needs. In this, as in many other instances, feminists expressed reservations about centralized state power, talked of the risks of co-option and betrayal, and presented state institutions as actively patriarchal or peculiarly unresponsive to human need. There are disagreements about this (this is one place where one needs to talk of feminisms rather than feminism), and many have felt that the antistatism of the contemporary women's movement went too far. There is nonetheless a powerful strand that views the self-governing, voluntary association as more accessible and contestable than the male-dominated, rule-bound state.

Civil society matters, finally, because programs for radical change have to capture people's hearts and minds and cannot depend just on directives issuing from the state. When Antonio Gramsci tried to explain to his fellow communists why revolution in Italy would take so much longer than revolution in Russia, he argued that it had been easier to seize state power in Russia because the state there was not supported by anything else. "In Russia the State was everything, civil society was primordial and gelatinous; in the West, there was a proper relation between State and civil society, and when the State trembled a sturdy structure of civil society was at once revealed."[13] A coup d'etat was out of the question in Italy, where communists would have to wage a long "war of position," fought mainly on the cultural front, to capture the active support of the Italian people. Translated into the language of contemporary feminism, this is like saying that the battle for sexual equality has to be won in civil society, and that there is a limit to what can be achieved through the "right" legislation alone.

The point suggested by Fraser and Habermas is that the state can be more conservative (more stuck in the old grooves) than the free flow of opinion and argument in civil society. But we know that the opposite also happens: that state policies can get too far ahead of opinion formation in civil society, and that when this gap becomes too great, some kind of backlash often occurs. (Recent examples might include the attack on affirmative action in the United States and the revival of white-Australia nationalism in a country where a pluralistic multiculturalism seemed to have become the accepted view. In both cases, one might say that Gramsci's "war of position" had been inadequately waged, and that politicians had become overly confident about what could be achieved by fiat alone.) Feminists have, of course, been happy to seize any opportunities offered via equality legislation or affirmative action for promoting sexual equality. But being more attuned than some other traditions to the power of culture in regulating social relations, they have also been acutely aware that strategies for change have to intervene on a number of levels. This is not necessarily (indeed rarely) discussed under the rubric of civil society, but it does have the effect of directing feminism away from an exclusively state-centric politics and highlighting the role of nongovernmental associations and groups.

None of this adds up to a thesis about civil society as the source of social cohesion or the guarantor of freedom or the place where morality resides. When feminists indicate a preference for a thriving network of "counterpublics" or say they want to see child care organized by a local self-governing collective rather than some arm of the state, the value attached to civil society is still largely instrumental. It is not that civil society is being presented as a good in itself, but that there is more scope for identifying and exploring nonsexist, egalitarian ways of doing things when operating outside the heavy hand of state power; and that practices of sexual inequality are so insidious and pervasive that they cannot be tackled merely by initiatives from the top. This makes civil society important to feminist politics, but does not necessarily say anything about civil society as a value in itself.

The Counterattractions

Against this is the crucial problem with civil society: that it so often operates to keep women out. Think of the coffeehouse society of eighteenth-century Europe, where men had their clubs and meeting places and discussion groups and women their parallel life in salons. Think, more recently, of those London clubs that still close their doors to women and pride themselves on providing a safe haven for the exclusive use of men. Overt exclusion has become relatively rare by the opening years of the twenty-first century, but there can easily be a flourishing network of men's associations paralleled by a less flourishing network for women. In the absence of overlapping membership, this looks more like segregation than "society."

The associations of civil society are brought into existence by the actions and choices of their members. This being so, they will inevitably reflect whatever is the existing distribution of resources (money, information, contacts, time) and probably reflect whatever is the existing balance of power. With the requisite energy and determination, people can of course do extraordinary things. But when so much of what generates an organization is gendered—time, self-confidence, range of contacts, and, to a lesser extent, range of skills—it is most likely that the number and membership of organizations will turn out to be gendered as well. There are certain features of modern democracy that can be said to counteract background inequalities. At its best, this is what the right to vote does: makes differences of sex, class, or race temporarily irrelevant, and gives men and women a moment of equal power. Civil society is not open to regulation in the same kind of way. There is no body to oversee its activities, to check that each citizen joins an equal number of groups or that each is equally active; and because of this, civil society is likely to reflect and confirm whatever is the current distribution of sexual power. Individual associations may be wonderfully vibrant—stretching boundaries, contesting orthodoxies, generating new forms of power—but those that speak for subordinate groups are still likely to be less numerous and weaker than the rest.

The related difficulty is that the relatively unregulated nature of civil society associations can make them more prone to discriminatory behavior than the publicly scrutinized institutions of the state. I do not want to exaggerate this point, for I am continually struck by the lapses one finds in government departments and the failure to live up to standards one would have thought obligatory in the modern state. It is also important to recognize that voluntary associations are not entirely unregulated, and that while some may be exempt from some legislation against sexual or racial discrimination (there is provision for this in British law), they mostly come under the remit of national legislation and are required to operate in a reasonably honest and fair-minded way. Yet there are still many and invidious ways in which voluntary associations can reproduce social hierarchies and social exclusions, and even their voluntariness can discourage measures designed to equalize members' power. The more intimate the group, for example, the less willing it may be to put decisions to a vote; people may feel this makes things too formal or sets people up as adversaries when they ought to be thinking of one another as colleagues and friends. Voluntary associations often operate on a borderline between friendship and politics, bringing together like-minded people who share similar views or enjoy the same intellectual and leisure pursuits. Feminists have been quick to spot the potential coerciveness in this, and the way it can work to disempower those who feel at odds with the dominant consensus but lack the confidence to expose themselves before people they regard as "sisters" or friends.[14] In such circumstances, the associations of civil society can prove themselves more coercive and less protective of individual equalities and freedoms than the much-despised institutions of the state.

A third risk has less to do with civil society and more with the way the concept is invoked to support critiques of the welfare state. In some recent analysis, civil society figures as part of an argument against excessive state spending and in favor of self-help. Civil society then becomes a code name for people assuming responsibility for their own lives, and welfare spending is blamed for diminishing the role of the voluntary associations through which people once assumed this responsibility. To illustrate with an example from Britain, David Green recently contrasted the friendly societies of the late-nineteenth- and early-twentieth centuries, which sprung up through traditions of self-help and insured workers against hard times, with the national insurance scheme later introduced by the government, which made insurance against sickness and unemployment compulsory and organized the payments via the state. In Green's view, this shifted the balance between civil society and state disastrously in favor of the latter, encouraging inefficiency (because there was then only one provider of insurance or health) and discouraging "the spirit of personal responsibility on which a vibrant civil society rests."[15] As is often the case, Green's argument turns out to be linked to the increase in one-parent families and the rise of illegitimacy, divorce, separation; the revival of civic traditions of self-help and responsibility is then connected in some obscure (to me) way with restoring marriage as a lifelong commitment and getting the family back on its traditional tracks.

At this point in the argument, feminists usually become rather restive about the delights of civil society. Celebrations of the active citizenry or a vibrant civic culture frequently signal policy shifts that aim to move responsibility from state to community. All too often, this "community" turns out to mean women, who are expected in their capacity as wives, mothers, and daughters to resume responsibility for more damaged members of their family, including those previously cared for in mental hospitals and not yet equipped for returning to noninstitutional life. This requisitioning of female labor may not be what most theorists have understood by civil society, but the term has undoubtedly come to carry this additional connotation. Where it does so, it rings all the alarm bells. Despite the points developed earlier, many feminists have continued to look to the state as one of the sources of gender justice, believing (a) that publicly sanctioned principles of sexual equality will help protect women exposed to wage exploitation, domestic violence, or the cultural pressures of their community or group; and (b) that public provision for child care, health care, and age care is an intrinsic part of the "feminization" of policy and the creation of a sexually egalitarian world. It is more often men than women who celebrate "a vibrant civil society" as the alternative to this.

VOLUNTARY ASSOCIATIONS AND PUBLIC PROVISION

One of the key ambiguities, then, is that feminism is simultaneously anti- and pro-state. It is critical of the state as an exclusive forum for political action; tends to see state institutions as hidebound, unresponsive, promoting a conservative political agenda; tends, for these reasons, to see the more amorphous, decentralized, and pluralistic activities of civil society as better suited to the development of feminist politics. But feminism is also supportive of the state as an agent of redistribution; regards the market as peculiarly unsuited to meeting the welfare needs that dominate so many women's lives; and considers the patchy network of voluntary associations a poor substitute for universal provision via the state. This last is particularly important for those who take sexual equality to be the overriding normative principle of the feminist tradition.

Feminism is about equality, understood here as no significant difference between the sexes in the distribution of jobs or responsibilities or roles. This implies equality in respect of employment; more far-reaching and demanding, it also implies equal responsibility for the sexes for caring for the young, sick, and old. Leaving aside as implausible the notion that this equality will arise spontaneously from the workings of the market, there are basically two different ways of imagining this development. The first concentrates on the public provision of services that were previously carried out by women in the home: setting up publicly funded and subsidised nurseries, providing a network of publicly employed careworkers to cook meals and do the shopping for the elderly or disabled, providing high-quality full-time care in residential homes. Responsibilities that used to fall on the shoulders of mothers, wives, and daughters (but hardly ever on fathers, husbands, and sons) would then be recognized as social responsibilities, to be funded out of general taxation.

Elements of this strategy have always featured in feminist campaigns, but when followed through to what might seem the logical conclusion, it usually generates disquiet. One problem is that this approach promises equality for the sexes without changing what the men have to do: this looks rather like the man who extricates himself from pressure to do an equal part of the housework by buying a dishwasher or employing a cleaner. The deeper problem is that handing children or aging parents over to full-time institutional care falls short of most people's vision of a humane and caring society—and certainly falls short of what most feminists have wanted to see. In opposition to this, an alternative approach has developed, premised on enabling a different division of labor between the sexes inside the home. This second strategy leaves the responsibility for carework primarily as a private responsibility, but sees it as being shared equally between women and men.

Those pursuing this second line of argument rarely think of "shared parenting"[16] as a matter of exhortation, for there are clearly structural features in contemporary societies that encourage us to carry on in the old unequal way. Most obviously, women still tend to earn less than men. In domestic units containing two parents, it then makes economic sense for the woman rather than the man to leave employment in order to care for the children or for the women to change to a job she can do part-time. Wage differentials thereby reinforce responsibility differentials, while the hours and timing of work are very unforgiving toward those trying to combine paid employment with parenthood. As a serious alternative, the equal shares model depends on major changes in the hours and conditions of work to enable both women *and* men to work what would currently be considered part-time: each doing a maximum of (say) thirty hours a week in paid employment, each then able to take an equal part in the unpaid labors of care.

The scenario premised on public provision has obvious limits, set by our perceptions of what counts as loving care. The second scenario is also limited, if only because many households contain only one adult and would not benefit from any strategy of equal shares. The best solution lies somewhere between the two, with a significant increase in public provision combined with a redistribution of responsibilities between women and men.

The state, that is, should assume more responsibility than it currently does for human well-being, should not treat looking after the vulnerable as a predominantly private (read, female) responsibility, and should shift its order of priorities so as to give greater prominence to questions of care. But simply handing over to the state what used to be carried out within the hierarchical family (moving women, as Nordic feminists have described it, from private to public dependence) can never be a complete answer. It is also at odds with what I have indicated as a long-standing feminist distrust of the overcentralized state.

Where private and/or voluntary associations fit in is probably the least developed part of this. There are feminists who see sexual equality as incompatible with the market economy, and these would argue for a much reduced role for market-based private associations engaged in production or marketing. There are feminists who favor greater decentralization, and these would argue for a much increased role for nongovernmental, voluntary associations in the organization of social life. There are still others who regard voluntary associations as the last resort of the reactionary traditionalist, and the least amenable to sexual equality: these would regard a redistribution of responsibilites from family to the voluntary sector as making things worse rather than better. This is perhaps a point at which the other side of the hyphen takes over: whether one is a liberal-feminist, socialist-feminist, postmodern-feminist, and so on. The feminism tells us to check out the consequences for sexual equality. It may be the other elements in the ethical system that determine the standpoint on private associations.

"Good" and "Bad" Associations

There is one question, however, that any version will have to address, which is what to do when the fluidity of civil society throws up groups that discourage equality between women and men. The associations of civil society are likely to include a number that operate on principles antithetical to feminist beliefs: churches that require segregation between women and men; cultural associations that promote sexist cultures; campaign groups working to overturn what have been seen as advances for sexual equality. How much policing should there be of associations that refuse basic principles of sexual equality? How much tolerance can feminists extend to groups they see as subordinating women to men?

These are questions endemic to liberal democracy, where the right to free association always generates "bad" as well as "good" associations—generates organizations dedicated to the expulsion of nonwhite immigrants as well as organizations dedicated to making opera available to all. There is a range of responses on offer, some stressing the overriding importance of individual and—by extension—group autonomy, others insisting that democracy requires all associations to abide by certain egalitarian norms. Given the historical as well contemporary connections with liberal democracy, it is not surprising that feminism tends to reproduce a similar range of more permissive to more interventionist positions. There are nonetheless three distinctive features. The first is that the number of associations one might object to is even higher for feminism because it promotes a version of sexual equality that is more demanding than currently accepted norms. The second—a counterweight to the first—is that feminism has developed a particular sensitivity about reading "basic principles" off one's own preferences, and is highly attuned to the dangers of cultural imperialism. The third is that feminism has recently moved into alliance with multiculturalism, and that this mutes some of its criticism of sexual subordination and inequality.

Most societies impose some constraint on the associations of civil society, perhaps banning those deemed to promote racial hatred, perhaps providing legal redress against those whose practices can be shown to discriminate against women, perhaps (to take an example from a different part of the spectrum) banning those that allow men and women to mingle freely together. But voluntary associations are normally allowed more leeway than those officially condoned by the state, and even when there is some requirement about abiding by "basic" principles of sexual or racial equality, these principles will usually be interpreted in the most basic of ways. Since feminists have, by definition, higher standards than currently prevail about what counts as sexual equality, they are going to find themselves at odds with a larger number of associations. This being so, one might expect a strongly interventionist approach to civil society, with the requirements of sexual equality repeatedly trumping the freedoms of association or speech.

This does not, on the whole, happen, for while the tradition draws on universalistic values of freedom and equality, it tempers these with a sharp sense of particularity and difference. The exploratory and pluralistic character of feminism has made it unusually sensitive to accusations of cultural imperialism, and highly attuned to the way groups can convince themselves that their own preoccupations and priorities are "the" overriding concerns. So when Islamic women, for example, have argued that wearing the veil frees them from sexual stereotyping and enables them to play a more active political role, many Western feminists have asked themselves whether their previous criticism of this practice was based on ignorance and self-conceit. Requiring women to veil themselves in men's presence looks self-evidently at odds with feminist views on equality and autonomy, but it is a rather strained notion of autonomy that requires women, against their stated wishes, to throw off this particular constraint. One might plausibly argue that the "wishes" are a product of male pressure. But there is always something a bit suspect about attributing people's choices to false consciousness or saying they did not "really" choose something they claim as their own decision. Feminists have become unusually self-conscious about this, and while speaking with reasonably unified voice on matters like female genital mutilation (mainly practiced on minors who cannot by any stretch of imagination be said to give their "consent"), they are far more divided on other issues.

Put positively, this means an openness to divergent voices and a vigilance against the arrogance of those who think they already know best. Put more negatively, it can lead to a loss of nerve in the face of inequality and an inability to act. This tension has become particularly evident in the alliance recently forged between feminism and multiculturalism. The problems women face in contemporary society bear a close family resemblance to the problems faced by members of minority cultural and ethnic groups: in both cases, an experience of being marginalized by dominant values and norms; in both cases, a perception that difference is being pretended away. When feminists defend affirmative action as a way of addressing deep structures of inequality that prevent women taking up their so-called equal opportunities, the argument points toward a parallel defense of affirmative action for members of racial and ethnic minorities. When feminists argue that legislation has been framed without reference to women's experience and that giving women an equal voice would alter the prevailing norms, this echoes similar charges that have been made by members of minority cultures. A feminism that focuses on the experience of marginalization and exclusion suggests numerous points of contact with other groups that have felt themselves defined out of the dominant norms.

But the alliance is also fraught with difficulties, and particularly so when one considers the centrality of conventions regulating sexual relationships to the definition of most cultures. What makes one culture different from another is very often the principles it adopts regarding the relative position of women and men: whether it regards marriage as a free contract between consenting individuals, as something that deprives women of their independent legal standing (this was the case in nineteenth-century Britain), or as something best arranged by parents acting on what they conceive to be the best interests of their children. Add on to this the fact that religion may be a central defining element, and one can see all kinds of difficulties arising. Most religions have experienced difficulty with sexual equality, and despite some notable exceptions (including the many early feminists who belonged to the Unitarian Church), many feminists experience difficulty with religion. That this should be so is hardly surprising, for religions tend to build into their moral prescriptions part of what have been the customs and conventions in the societies from which they arose. They then weight these customs with all the power of religious prescription. Religion is not in-trinsically mysogynistic—every religion contains a variety of traditions, and these have included a wide range of views on sexual equality. But religion is not, on the whole, associated with a strong defense of women's equal-ity. This promises some troubled moments in the alliance between femi-nism and multiculturalism.[17]

On an axis that runs from total toleration of all associations that spring up in civil society to state interventionism to enforce egalitarian norms, feminism has been closer to the first than might have been expected, and certainly closer than in popular mythology. There is a good side to this: the openness to revision, the recognition of cultural bias, the critique of "top-down" intervention. But where relations between the sexes are concerned, there has to be a limit to the idea that practices are acceptable so long as the practitioners "freely" agree to them. One of the characteristics of sub-ordination is that it makes people internalize their own submission; if points made earlier about the pervasiveness/invasiveness of sexual identity are correct, this is going to be particularly relevant to women. What is "freely" chosen is not by definition defensible. What is supported by a ma-jority of women is not thereby immune to critique.

Though this tells us little about what might be the criteria differentiating "acceptable" from "unacceptable" practices, "good" from "bad" associa-tions, it does clear the ground for more vigorous contestation. When so few agencies are prepared to speak out for sexual equality, the onus is on women to make their own needs and interests heard. And while feminists are rightly skeptical of the kind of interventionism that imposes the values of one group on the practices of another, they should also query the ab-stentionism that retreats from judgment and the justifications that depend on supposed consent. Celebrating civil society as the sphere of freedom and autonomy is not really an option for feminism, given the inequalities that so often mar the cozy associational world.

FURTHER READING

The diversity of feminism means that there in no agreed central work, but Mary Wollstonecraft's *Vindication of the Rights of Woman* (first published in 1792) is often cited as a founding text. Carole Pateman, *The Sexual Contract* (Cam-bridge: Polity Press, 1988), reinterprets the social contract tradition from a fem-inist perspective, while Susan Moller Okin, *Justice, Gender, and the Family* (New York: Basic Books, 1989), is particularly useful for understanding how feminism engages with other traditions in contemporary political theory. Carol Gilligan, *In a Different Voice* (Cambridge: Harvard University Press, 1988), developed influential arguments about the relationship between justice and care. Judith Butler, *Gender Trouble: Feminism and the Subversion of Identity* (London: Rout-ledge, 1989), has framed many of the debates in the 1990s. Jodi Dean, ed., *Fem-*

inism and the New Democracy: Re-Siting the Political (London: Sage, 1997), is particularly useful in thinking about civil society.

NOTES

An earlier version of this essay appeared in *Dissent* magazine.

1. Catharine MacKinnon, *Unmodified Feminism* (Cambridge: Harvard University Press, 1987).

2. Jodi Dean, "Including Women: The Consequences and Side Effects of Feminist Critiques of Civil Society," *Philosophy and Social Criticism* 18, nos. 3/4 (1992): 379.

3. Carole Pateman, *The Sexual Contract* (Cambridge: Polity Press, 1988), p. 102.

4. G. W. F. Hegel, *The Philosophy of Right* (Oxford: Oxford University Press, 1967), para. 166.

5. For example, Robert D. Putnam, "Bowling Alone: America's Declining Social Capital," *Journal of Democracy* 6, no. 1 (January 1995): 65–78.

6. John Keane, *Democracy and Civil Society* (London: Verso, 1988), p. 15.

7. This is what seems to happen in Carole Pateman's influential essay "Feminist Critiques of the Public/Private Dichotomy," where civil society is defined as the public world—in contrast, then, to the private—and expands to include the economic as well as the political, society as well as the state. Essay first published in 1983, reprinted in Pateman, *The Disorder of Women* (Cambridge: Polity Press, 1989).

8. For example, Carole Pateman: "The sphere of domestic life is at the heart of civil society rather than apart or separate from it" ("Feminist Critiques," 132–33; or Drude Dahlerup, who employs a tripartite division between state, market, and civil society, but always stresses that civil society includes the family as well. "Learning to Live with the State—State, Market, and Civil Society: Women's Need for State Interventions in East and West," *Women's Studies International Forum* 17, nos. 2/3 (March–June 1994).

9. For example, Susan Moller Okin, *Justice, Gender and The Family* (New York: Basic Books, 1989).

10. Nancy Fraser, "Rethinking the Public Sphere: A Contribution to the Critique of Actually Existing Democracy," in *Justice Interruptus* (New York: Routledge, 1997), p. 81. Fraser prefers the language of multiple publics to that of civil society (partly because she feels a sharp separation between civil society and state gives the impression that nongovernmental associations are only about opinion formation and do not have decision-making power), but her argument clearly covers the kind of ground that is indicated in discussions of civil society.

11. Jürgen Habermas, *Between Facts and Norms* (Cambridge: Polity Press, 1996), p. 309.

12. Dean, "Including Women," p. 400.

13. Antonio Gramsci, *Selections from the Prison Notebooks* (London: Lawrence and Wishart, 1970), p. 238.

14. Jane Manbridge, "Time, Emotion and Inequality: Three Problems of Participatory Groups," *Journal of Applied Behavioral Science* 9, nos. 2/3 (1973).

15. David Green, *Reinventing Civil Society: The Rediscovery of Welfare without Politics* (London: Institute for Economic Affairs, 1993), p. 147.

16. Not just parenting, of course, for the care of the sick or elderly takes up more of women's lives than the care of preschool children.

17. For an important recent debate on this see Susan Moller Okin, ed., *Is Multiculturalism Bad for Women?* (Princeton: Princeton University Press, 1999).

CHAPTER 5

A Critical Theory of Civil Society

Simone Chambers

THE INSTITUTIONS OF CULTURAL HEGEMONY

WITH SOME NOTABLE seventeenth-century exceptions, civil society is most often understood as one-half of the distinction civil society/state, rather than as a freestanding concept.[1] Critical theory is no exception;[2] it also sees civil society as an essentially relational concept. Civil society is defined in contrast to the state and is defended as a realm that ought to be insulated in certain ways from the state. From here, however, critical theory departs in significant ways from the mainstream or liberal conception of civil society. It is not only the state that is perceived to be a potential threat to the freedom of civil society; capitalist economic relations are also considered to be harmfully intrusive. Thus, civil society is distinguished from the state *and* the economy. In addition to the economy being out, critical theory differs from liberalism in that the family is usually considered to be in. These exclusions and inclusions might seem rather odd at first glance, as critical theory is one of the contemporary heirs to Marx, and Marx certainly considered the economy to be part of civil society; indeed, economic relations were the quintessential relations of civil society. A quick look at Gramsci's contribution to the Marxist debate about civil society will be helpful in explaining the shift in status of the family and economy.[3]

Gramsci, along with many other Marxists of the early-twentieth century, was consumed by the question Why are the masses not revolutionary? His answer was that the bourgeois/capitalist alliance was much more effective in hanging on to power than Marx had been able to anticipate. Rather than through brute domination in the form of state repression, economic blackmail, or payoffs, the stability of the system was ensured through the manufacture of consent. Hegemony, not force, was the weapon of the ruling class. Hegemonic power rested on the socialization of the masses into the ideology of the dominant class. Thus, Gramsci turned away from material relations and toward ideological/cultural relations. Power resides in the production of ideas, not so much the production of things, although the production of ideas is put into the service of the production of things.

For Gramsci, the family is included in civil society because it is an institution that can be and usually is central in shaping the general political dispositions of citizens. The family is a vehicle of culture and therefore of hegemony. Also central are the ingredients more commonly associated with civil society: churches, clubs, universities, associations, unions, cultural institutions, political parties, social movements, and so on. These are included not because of their voluntary character, however, but because of their role in reproducing the ideas necessary to maintain stability.

The turn toward the cultural sphere marks a break with the economic reductionism of Marx in two senses. First, civil society is no longer considered a system of needs understood primarily in economic terms. Now civil society is seen as a system of ideas, values, ideologies, and, yes, interests understood primarily in sociological and political terms. Second, the central role of hegemony leads to the semiautonomy of the world of ideas from the economy. The superstructure takes on a more complex relationship with the base, which eventually leads to the rejection of the causal connection between the two. Today, critical theory as one of the heirs to Gramsci and neo-Marxism sees civil society as a sphere of identity formation, social integration, and cultural reproduction, and although economic relations and the state play a part in these functions, their roles are, or ought to be, supporting, not leading.

Gramsci inaugurates a culture critique that takes the critical left in many directions. The direction that I pursue here leads eventually to the work of Jürgen Habermas and his influential theory of communication and democracy.[4] The road from Gramsci through the Frankfurt School to Habermas has two important turning points. The first is a linguistic turn, in which the culture critique of earlier critical theory is joined to a theory of communication and social evolution.[5] The second is what could be called a liberal Kantian turn, which sees Habermas defending some core liberal characteristics of civil society while at the same time maintaining a critical perspective.[6]

This second turn has been the more prominent one in recent years. Habermas is much more likely to engage the debates surrounding the work of Rawls and Dworkin than to engage Marxist theory. Can we still call him a critical theorist? The defining feature of critical theory has been and remains a unique melding of a Kantian critical method with a Marxist interest in the critique of ideology. Kantian critique involves investigation of the conditions of possibility for some given phenomenon. A Marxist critique of ideology involves investigating the ways in which ideas contribute to or hinder human emancipation. David Held describes the common thread that unites critical theory as an interest in "the conditions which make possible the reproduction and transformation of society, the meaning of culture, and the relation between the individual, society and nature. While there are differences in the way they formulate questions, the critical theorists believe that through an examination of contemporary social and political issues they could contribute to a critique of ideology and to the development of a non-authoritarian and non-bureaucratic politics."[7] Habermas is engaged in an enterprise that is very similar to his Frankfurt School predecessors. One major difference, however, is how Habermas assesses the role of liberal institutions in social development. While thinkers like Horkheimer and Adorno saw little hope for liberal institutions to break out of authoritarian and bureaucratic modes of domination, Habermas sees a potential to use liberal institutions (like the public sphere, equal citizen rights, and constitutions) to mitigate the worst effects of liberalism. He is in many senses more a liberal than a Marxist but, as I hope to show in this chapter, he is still a critical theorist. Perhaps he is best described as a critical liberal theorist.

Habermas's Marxist roots lead him to investigate and expose the forms of domination practiced in civil society, while his liberal Kantianism leads him to identify the sources of authentic autonomy that can be found within the institutions of civil society. The former is elaborated in a theory of the colonization of the lifeworld and the latter in a theory of discursive democracy. I discuss these two turns in the following two sections.

LIFEWORLD VERSUS SYSTEM

Habermas develops his theory of communicative action and social evolution as, among other things, a corrective to the Marxist tradition that saw labor as the driving force in social evolution. In the Marxist view, social reproduction is defined and given content through our interaction with nature; inquiry focuses on how we remake our external world generation after generation. Habermas argues that the overarching place of labor within this theoretical approach has produced a one-sided view of social dynamics that leaves out what he calls the lifeworld.[8] Not only do we remake the external/natural world through labor, but we also remake, generation after generation, our inner/sociocultural world through symbolic interaction or communication.

The lifeworld is the background against which all social interaction takes place. It is a repository and contains the accumulated interpretations of past generations: how the people who went before us understood their world, themselves and each other, their duties, commitments and allegiances, their art and literature, the place of science, religion, and law, and so on. As social actors, we draw upon these understandings when trying to make sense of the things that go on around us (or even inside of us).

The lifeworld is made up of meanings. We are connected to it via our interpretations and understandings. It is transmitted, altered, and reproduced via communication. The lifeworld stands in contrast to state and economic systems. These systems operate according to a different logic. The state is distinguished from the lifeworld in that power rather than communication is the medium through which it operates. Power is essentially hierarchical and coercive, while communication is egalitarian and persuasive. These are, of course, ideal types. Rarely is reality so neatly divided. Furthermore, one without the other is nonviable: power without communication would look something like Hobbes's state of nature; the state without the lifeworld might be seen in equally fictional accounts of *1984*-type antiutopias. A modern lifeworld without the state is also difficult to imagine, as the state offers legal guarantees that protect the integrity of the lifeworld. For its part, the lifeworld acts as a source of legitimacy for the state. Although interdependent, the lifeworld and state are analytically distinct in many of the same ways that the liberal conception of civil society is distinct from the state. Where liberals see individual voluntarism as the defining feature of civil society, however, critical theorists see communicative autonomy. Communicative autonomy refers to the freedom of actors in society to shape, criticize, and reproduce essential norms, meanings, values, and identities through communicative (as opposed to coercive) interaction. Communicative autonomy is linked to individual autonomy in that the former is a condition of the latter. Individuals do not develop life plans in isolation. They develop them in interaction with others in society. The freer that interaction is from the distorting effects of power and domination, the more opportunity actors have to explore and exercise individual autonomy.

While power is the medium through which the state operates, money drives the economy. Like power, money has a different modus operandi than communication. The ends of economic exchange are profit, efficiency, and instrumental success. The ends of communication are the production and transmission of meaning. When power coordinates action, it does so via sanctions—that is, coercion. When money coordinates action, it does so via the "laws" of supply and demand. When communication coordinates action, it does so via communicatively achieved norms.

Civil society is the lifeworld as it is expressed in institutions. As Cohen and Arato describe it, "[C]ivil society would include all the institutions and associational forms that require communicative interaction for their reproduction and that rely primarily on processes of social integration for coordinating action within their boundaries."[9] Thus, the unifying link within civil society is communication. Civil society is autonomous when its activities are governed by norms that are drawn from the lifeworld and reproduced or reformulated though communication. With the communicative rather than voluntarist nature of civil society as the defining feature, it becomes clear how the economy can be excluded along with the state.

The most important normative implication of the liberal civil society/ state distinction is the delineation of a sphere in which individuals are free from government control and interference and can develop and pursue self-chosen interests, pastimes, causes, careers, and so on. Critical theory defends a similar ideal; that is, it defends the protection from government control and interference of venues of communicative interaction through which individuals shape and choose interests, pastimes, causes, careers, and so on. The difference is subtle but significant. Critical theory sees potential threats to civil society as threats to the ways in which we interact, whereas liberals traditionally view threats as straightforward threats to individual choice. For critical theorists, a healthy civil society is one that is steered by its members through shared meanings. An unhealthy civil society is one that has been colonized by power or money or both.

A somewhat simplistic illustration of the ways in which economic factors can "colonize" civil society might help. A neighborhood association forms to create support and opportunity for "teens at risk." Citizens come together and discuss their goals and agree upon a general direction. To raise money, they market local teen art. They are very successful; Nike and Coca-Cola want to use their products as logos; there is a national demand for their art. Their financial success requires that they incorporate. Gradually their status changes from neighborhood association to company with the attendant constraints of profitability, and so forth. Profitable marketing is transformed from a means to an end. Rather than being guided by communicatively achieved ends, they are guided or constrained by market factors. From a liberal point of view we have a voluntary association that has simply shifted its priorities. Critical theory wants to say that there is something disturbing going on here. It might not be disturbing if it happened only sporadically. But if this sort of colonization is a persistent and widespread trend where economic ends come to overwhelm the character of civil society, then the autonomous nature of civil society is in jeopardy. For example, we usually think something has gone wrong when family members view their membership primarily as an economic partnership or, worse, a zero-sum economic game. When members of churches, universities, unions, associations, and political parties think of their mission in instrumental terms of efficiency, a source of new meanings is lost.[10] When business views the associations of civil society as pieces in marketing strategies and sets out to capture, infiltrate, or simply influence these organizations, then we have cause to worry. When counterculture is absorbed into the market, it loses its power to shape and transform the way we view the world. Finally, when the distribution of wealth is the most important factor in determining the richness of one's civil life, the value of civil society is compromised.

At an intuitive level, then, it is not difficult to understand how the economy can distort the communicative life of civil society. What is difficult is separating out the economy from civil society in any actual sense. Is a chamber of commerce or a community development corporation part of civil society or the economy? All economic enterprises involve some level of communication. Can we really say they are not part of the communicative network through which we form our identities and become integrated into social groups? The civil society/economy distinction (as well as the civil society/state distinction) is an analytic/normative distinction that does not correspond to categorical sets of institutions, associations, and groups that we can clearly identify as being one or the other. The analytic component identifies three different, if empirically intertwined, means of coordinating action. These means are communication, power, and money, any one of which may predominate in a social activity. The normative component identifies the circumstances under which it is appropriate for communication, power, or money to coordinate action.

Liberals sometimes argue that excluding the economy is suspect because civil society and the economy are not empirically separable, and even if they were, this distinction amounts to excluding certain things from civil society simply because one does not like them; that is, it is an overly normative as opposed to descriptive distinction. The liberal distinction between civil society and the state is open these same objections, however. The modern state has penetrated civil society in all sorts of ways that makes the liberal distinction empirically difficult to maintain. Is Legal Aid or Americorps part of civil society or the state? In participating in voter registration campaigns, am I acting on behalf of civil society or the state? Furthermore, the fact that law establishes the shape and latitude of civil society means that civil society and the state are intertwined at the same time as being distinct. The accusation that the critical theory distinction is overly normative also seems to apply to liberalism. The liberal "descriptive" distinction between civil society and the state is interesting only because it also contains a normative distinction: liberals do not like it when the state interferes too much in civil society. Excluding things you do not like makes sense if you do not like them for a good reason. Liberals do not like the state in civil society because it is coercive; critical theorists do not like the economy in civil society because it has a tendency to distort communication.

To conclude then, the civil society/economy distinction leads to a critical perspective that identifies the ways in which economic rationality has a tendency to overwhelm and crowd out other rationalities. The central and most important institutions for maintaining a healthy and vibrant civil society are not economic ones or ones that pursue economic ends. When more and more institutions of civil society are swallowed up by and become colonies of economic interests, then our freedom is in jeopardy. Our freedom is in jeopardy because the basis for a healthy democracy is undermined.

DEMOCRACY AND THE PUBLIC SPHERE

Critical theory is interested in a critique of civil society; it investigates the ways in which domination and alienation insinuate themselves into the social lives of citizens. While Marx believed that social emancipation was an essentially economic question, early critical theorists like Horkheimer and Adorno believed it was a question of ideas and culture. While Horkheimer and Adorno believed that liberal democratic institutions did more to reinforce domination than weaken it, Habermas believes that the institutions of liberal democracy can be used in the service of emancipation. The basic components of Habermas's critical liberalism are the following: civil society is the site of resistance and emancipation; the exemplary actors are social movements, although all citizens can share in this potential; the arena of action is the public sphere; the type of action is democratic deliberation.

The public sphere is an important extension of civil society. It is where the ideas, interests, values, and ideologies formed within the relations of civil society are voiced and made politically efficacious. As Habermas notes,

> Its [civil society] institutional core comprises those nongovernmental and noneconomic connections and voluntary associations that anchor the communication structures of the public sphere in the society component of the lifeworld. Civil society is composed of those more or less spontaneously emergent associations, organizations, and movements that, attuned to how societal problems resonate in the private life spheres, distill and transmit such reactions in amplified form to the public sphere.[11]

Habermas's interest in the public sphere begins in the 1960s with *The Structural Transformation of the Public Sphere*. He tells a Marxist-inspired story of how the rise of bourgeois civil society is paralleled by the rise of a corresponding pubic sphere. In this space, private citizens come together to form a public for the first time. Political clubs, journals, and pamphlet writing, as well as regular but informal political meetings in coffeehouses, salons, and the like, serve as venues for the formation of a public opinion that is not simply the aggregation of private opinions about public matters. Rather, it is an opinion that is formed publicly, that is, in critical public debate. Thus, opinion is public in three senses: it is about public matters; it is in the public domain; it is produced by a public, that is, private citizens interacting in the public sphere.

At first, the political function of public opinion is simply public criticism. But as state actors come to heed the voice of public opinion, a new and stronger role is envisioned. "Since the critical public debate of private people convincingly claimed to be in the nature of a noncoercive enquiry into what was at the same time correct and right, a legislation that had recourse to public opinion thus could not be explicitly considered as domination."[12]

Critical debate in the public becomes a test of rationality and right. By making public the grounds for state action and subjecting these grounds to the critical force of public debate, citizens can insure that the state has just reasons for its actions as well as that citizens believe that these reasons are just. Following Kant, this has come to be known as the principle of publicity.[13] The optimistic assumption at work here is that injustice and domination cannot survive the scrutiny of an enlightened and civic-minded public.

In Habermas's early discussions, although he was sympathetic to the ideal of publicity, he nevertheless argued that such a principle inevitably succumbed to the contradictions of the liberal/capitalist order.[14] Kant's public might have been critical but it was very bourgeois, both in the sense that it was restricted to property owners and that it primarily pursued economic interests in the public sphere. Inclusiveness, however, brought a degeneration of the quality of discourse. Critical debate gets replaced by the consumption of culture and an apolitical sociability. Participation is fatally altered, and the public sphere becomes an arena of advertising rather than a site of criticism. Capitalism colonizes and commodifies the public sphere primarily through a "profit-hungry" mass media, but also through the growing power and voice of economic interests like the "insurance industry," which can literally buy up public time and space. This pessimistic diagnosis is very much in keeping with his Frankfurt School roots. Habermas's later career, however, has seen the development of a theoretical approach that is much more optimistic about the possibility of rekindling the emancipatory potential of the public sphere first identified by Enlightenment thinkers of the eighteenth century. Much of contemporary critical theory has taken his lead in this matter, finding the possibility of emancipation in a revitalized and democratized principle of publicity.

How can we transform the public sphere into an arena of critical autonomous debate that is insulated from the distorting effects of power and money? The first components are legal and constitutional safeguards. Contemporary critical theorists have no quarrel with fundamental liberal rights, although they might offer a different justification for them, relying more on their role as essential preconditions for a healthy democratic sphere than on either notions of natural right or individual autonomy. Habermas argues, however, that freedom of speech and association are a necessary but not sufficient condition of a strong public sphere: "basic constitutional guarantees alone cannot preserve the public sphere and civil society from deformations. The communicative structures of the public sphere must rather be kept intact by an energetic civil society."[15] Not the state, but members of civil society bear the responsibility of sustaining an effective democratic public sphere. Only when actors consciously try to enhance, expand, and transform the public sphere as they participate in it do we have the critical buffers against deformation. The contrast is between mere "users" of the public sphere, who pursue their political goals within already existing forums and with little or no interest in the procedures themselves, and "creators" of the public sphere, who are interested in expanding democracy as they pursue their more particularist goals. Habermas observes that

> actors who support the public sphere are distinguished by the *dual orientation* of their political engagement: with their programs, they directly influence the political system, but at the same time they are also reflexively concerned with revitalizing and enlarging civil society and the public sphere as well as with confirming their own identities and capacities to act.[16]

Habermas, along with Cohen and Arato, identifies new social movements as the actors who have most characteristically taken on this dual role. Cohen and Arato identify this dualism as offensive and defensive strategies. Offensively, groups set out to influence the state and economy. So, for example, environmental movements are intent on influencing legislation, shaping public opinion, and containing economic growth. But at the same time, the environmental movement has consciously contributed to the expansion of associational life, to the encouragement of grass-roots participation, to the development of new and innovative forms of involvement, and to the extension of public forums of debate and deliberation. This sort of activity empowers citizens within civil society, helps maintain autonomy, and expands and strengthens democracy by giving citizens effective means of shaping their world.

The focus on social movements as important democratic actors is part of a larger trend in critical theory to develop a democratic theory that offers an alternative to liberal, pluralist, or economistic understandings of democracy. Voting-centric democratic theory is being replaced by talk-centric democratic theory.[17] The voting-centric view sees democracy as the arena in which fixed preferences and interests compete via fair mechanisms of aggregation. This model has proven unsatisfactory on both sociological as well as normative grounds. From a sociological point of view, the problem is that the economistic model is unable to say anything interesting about the formation of interests within civil society that are to be fed into the mechanisms of aggregation. From a normative perspective, the criticisms are that voting-centric democracy is attached to a politics of self-interest that produces social fragmentation; it cannot live up to ideals of legitimacy because outcomes are determined by numbers rather than by reasons; and finally, the marginalized, the powerless, and minorities are disadvantaged within the system.[18]

The remedy for these ills has been found in a democratic theory that focuses on the communicative processes of opinion and will-formation that precede voting. Theorists are interested in how deliberation can shape preferences, moderate self-interest, maintain conditions of equality, enable dialogic empowerment, and produce reasonable justification for majority decisions. In other words, interest has shifted from what goes on in the voting booth to what goes on in the discursive interactions of civil society. While nineteenth- and early-twentieth-century democratization focused on expanding the vote to include everybody, today democratization focuses on expanding the public sphere to give everyone a say. Voice, rather than votes, is the vehicle of empowerment. A democratized public sphere that offers everyone, especially marginalized groups, the opportunity to participate in shaping, influencing, and criticizing public opinion begins with a democratized civil society—that is, a civil society in which everyone can find a voice.

One implication of the argument I have just outlined is that we value civil society because it makes democracy possible and we value democracy because, if authentic, it transforms domination into self-rule. A liberal might worry that this is a weak defense of civil society. Do we mean, for example, that only associations that make clear contributions to democracy are given strong protection within civil society, while other, say, private or apolitical groups are less important and therefore given less protection?

Habermas answers this objection in *Between Facts and Norms* by appealing to the interdependence of individual and public autonomy.[19] Individual autonomy corresponds to the liberal notion of individual freedom safeguarded, for the most part, through a system of rights. Public autonomy refers to notions of popular sovereignty. These notions can be very abstract, as in liberal contract theory, or more concrete, as in theories of strong democracy. Habermas argues that authentic public autonomy is impossible without private autonomy and private autonomy can be justified only through public autonomy. If we did not have strong guarantees of individual autonomy in the private sphere, our democratic outcomes would be suspect. For example, no one was under the illusion that the votes taken in the Supreme Soviet of the USSR represented authentic democracy. These votes were suspect because there was no corresponding system of rights and protections that could give us confidence that individuals had been able to develop and express their true interests or opinions. Similarly, contract theories make sense only given the assumption that the parties are free and equal. Thus, authentic and healthy democracy requires a system of wide guarantees in civil society that encompasses much more than groups who choose to use that freedom in democracy-enhancing ways.

Without those wider guarantees, we would have no confidence that the opinions brought to the public (or the choice to remain silent) are authentic and autonomous. Protecting people's rights to join political or apolitical groups is a necessary condition of democracy.

From the opposite angle, the interdependence between public and private autonomy yields a different conclusion: because we can no longer rely on God, or Nature, or self-evident truth as a shared justification for rights, some version of public autonomy (Rawls's original position or Habermas's discursive democracy are two such versions) must be introduced to justify and legitimize the institutions of private rights. In answer to the liberal objection that discursive democracy privileges the people's will over rights, and to the democrat's objection that it privileges rights over the people's will, Habermas defends the "co-originality" (*Gleichursprünglichkeit*) of rights and popular sovereignty; the chicken and the egg cannot be prioritized.[20] There is no people's will to speak of without rights, and there are no rights without some theory of consent.

There is a sociological and Millian version of this argument as well. Critical public debate goes below the surface and asks hard questions, unmasks interests and manipulation, highlights hidden prejudices and bias, publicizes invisible injustice, and so on. This kind of debate emerges only out of a diverse civil society. A world in which there are many options, many contrasts to one's chosen way of life, many moral differences, many conflicting identities to chose from, and many different associations to join is a world that has a built-in critical component. Indeed, the more diverse is civil society, the more critical will be the public sphere. Although it is true that critical theory has a special place for groups that engage in action that directly enhances democracy, a civil society that protects and guarantees a wide range of activities indirectly enhances democracy. Diversity is the watchdog of democracy, ensuring that outcomes are viewed and tested from many different perspectives.

Can civil society survive all types of diversity or an infinitely expanding diversity? Is there a point at which difference is so wide that we can no longer call civil society a society? Or are there some types of difference that do not enhance democracy or that enhance democracy only if they stay on the fringes and attract very small numbers of people? These are some of the issues I address in the next section.

BAD CIVIL SOCIETY

Critical theory is generally very well disposed toward civil society and the progressive and critical movements to emerge from self-organized citizens' groups. In this assessment, critical theory has been influenced by certain analyses of the demise of Soviet and East European communism. Along with liberals and communitarians, critical theorists tend to see an active civil society as almost always a good thing and almost always a force on the side of democracy and freedom. There is, of course, something to this assessment. One need think only of Konrad's antipolitics, Havel's living in truth, and Poland's Solidarity to appreciate the democratic potential of civil society. A great deal of contemporary theory, however, fails to see the dangers that civil society can pose for democracy. As two critics of civil society literature put it, "[I]f civil society is a beachhead secure enough to be of use in thwarting tyrannical regimes, what prevents it from being used to undermine democratic governments?"[21]

The Weimar Republic had a vibrant and well-organized civil society that gave birth to and nurtured the Nazi movement. High levels of associational participation in pre-war Italy correlated very nicely with votes for Mussolini.[22] The new civil societies of Russia and Eastern Europe are home to groups like the Russian National Union and the Romanian National Union, which organize large numbers of citizens around fascist ideologies. The former Yugoslavia arguably had one of the most developed civil societies of any Eastern European country, and yet this did little to prevent the war and the "worst massacre in Europe since WW II."[23] Conversely, some have argued that one of the factors protecting Russia from an antiliberal takeover is the relative weakness of its civil society, which makes it difficult to organize a large-scale social movement.[24] Closer to home we see grassroots fascist and extreme-right movements in all Western civil societies. The militia and "patriot" movements in the United States appear to be gaining converts and support even in the face of the Oklahoma City bombing. Less extreme but perhaps more worrisome is the fact that civil society is home to many citizens' initiatives that are motivated by thinly veiled intolerance, mistrust, and xenophobia.

Civil society can be a place where citizens retreat into insular and defensive groups. It can be a place where particularism and difference define participation and where the self-organization of citizens contributes to a general atmosphere of distrust and misunderstanding. It is not the case, as is sometimes implied by communitarians, that active associational life is a good in and of itself.[25] Associations, clubs, churches, and, of course, families can and do promote antidemocratic illiberal ideas and when they do, bad civil society emerges. Bad civil society is one that promotes or is hospitable to particularist civility—that is, a civility that does not cross group boundaries. How do we protect ourselves from this risk?

For some, the risk posed by illiberal groups is greatly outweighed by the risk involved in limiting such groups. When freedom of association is the primary focus, the response to the dilemma of bad civil society has often been a combination laissez-faire/rights strategy. If people want to join mean-spirited, antidemocratic, even racist organizations, that's their business. As long as they stay within the law and refrain from violating other people's rights, they can do what they want. In this tradition, activism tends to be legal activism aimed at the recognition and enforcement of neglected or abused rights. Although civil society presupposes a system of rights, I want to suggest that civil society cannot depend exclusively on those rights to keep it intact. The courts cannot, by themselves, sustain a stable system of justice over time. If citizens are not in some way attached to that system, if they do not respect it, revere it, or believe in it, then no number of court orders will sustain its viability. One need think only of the highly juridified system of the Weimar Republic to see the limits of a system of justice that is not mirrored in the hearts and minds of citizens. Both feminists and civil rights activists are learning this lesson the hard way. The rights strategy of the pro-choice movement has proven only partially effective in the face of pro-life political activism. The pro-life movement has been very successful in mobilizing forces within civil society (I might add, despite the violence committed in its name) and is chipping away at *Roe v. Wade* at a grass-roots level.[26] Clinton's presidential initiatives on race were an admission that civil rights legislation and the legal activism of the 1960s were less than successful in capturing the hearts and minds of citizens. The new strategy was discursive and aimed at doing away with a *culture* of racism and distrust.

Certain civic republican approaches to civil society, although open to the problem of the cultural erosion of values, sometimes fail to acknowledge that that erosion can take the form of membership in associations. Robert Putnam's embrace of Tocqueville, for example, has until now been uncritical of the ways group solidarity and participation can cut both ways in democracy—reinforcing it in such groups like the Boy Scouts but undermining it in racist hate groups like the World Church of the Creator.[27] In this tradition, associational involvement is thought almost always to weigh in on the side of good citizenship. This claim, however, is sometimes circular or empirically questionable. It is circular if what defenders of civil society are really saying is that civil society promotes democracy because only democracy-promoting groups are considered part of civil society.[28] As an empirical claim, the idea that strong civil society is a friend of democracy is only sometimes true, as my counterexamples have suggested. The interesting question, then, is when is it true? Under what conditions or in what circumstances does strong and vigorous associational life promote civility and democracy, and when can we expect it to undermine democratic values? I cannot give a full answer to this question here, but I do think that critical theory has an important contribution to make to this debate, although critical theorists, for the most part, have not pursued this line of inquiry in any detail.

Critical theory, like defenders of freedom of association, is committed to individual rights. If people want to join mean-spirited, antidemocratic, even racist groups, the state is not going to stop them. What critical theory asks, which a rights-based approach often does not ask, is why people want to join mean-spirited, antidemocratic, even racist groups in the first place. While the rights strategy is to contain antidemocratic movements within the bounds of the law, the critical theory strategy is to consider the forces at work shaping antidemocratic interests. If we knew for certain that movements that are bound together by hate or that advocate antidemocratic principles would always remain marginal and few in number, then the rights strategy might make sense. But we do not know that. It is important to know why people join such groups in order to address the problem before it is too late.

Like many civic republicans, then, critical theorists are interested in what Sandel has called the "formative project," that is, the ways in which institutions, social structures, and economic forces shape identity, affect interest-formation, and influence value orientation. Critical theory differs from communitarianism, however, in that it takes a procedural, rather than perfectionist, approach to interest formation. For example, in distinguishing critical theory from civic republican approaches to modernity, Seyla Benhabib acknowledges that both approaches identify a pervasive discontent on the part of social actors.[29] Civic republicans attribute that discontent to a loss of a sense of belonging, which results in a loss of civic virtue. The cure they prescribe is active associational life. In contrast, Benhabib attributes discontent to a lack of political efficacy. The "malaise" of modernity can be traced to a loss of control over one's life and the conditions that determine one's chances. The cure is an accessible and efficacious public sphere. Benhabib does not explicitly use this argument to address what I have called the problem of bad civil society. Instead, her concern is for marginalized and disempowered groups like women and the poor. So, for example, she argues that a lack of political efficacy might be the result of the structural impediments placed in the path of women, who, in taking on the duties of motherhood, find it difficult to also pursue public agendas. In this case, public funds used to support better and more affordable child care might be one small step in addressing the problem.

Where do people turn when their frustration is not addressed? Benhabib is primarily concerned with the retreat into apathy and passivity. There are other options, however. They may turn to groups that appear to offer answers to their frustrations but in fact only offer scapegoats to blame. In these situations the political efficacy argument does speak to the problem of bad civil society. Indeed, there is some empirical research that connects a lack of efficacy in the public sphere with gravitation toward antidemocratic groups. This is Sheri Berman's conclusion, for example, about the Weimar Republic: "[I]nstead of responding to the demands of an increasingly mobilized population, the country's political structures obstructed meaningful participation in public life. As a result, citizens' energies and interests were deflected into private associational activities, which were generally organized within rather than across group boundaries."[30]

I am not saying that a vibrant and effective public sphere will magically transform racists into liberal democrats. Nor am I saying that we should encourage the expression of antidemocratic sentiment in the public sphere so that it does not infect private associations. The argument goes more like this: there will always be a certain number of people who reject the core principles of liberal democracy. There is nothing much we can do about this hard core. It is the "swing vote," if you will, that should interest us. These are the people *who come to be persuaded* that Jews, immigrants, African Americans, Croats, or liberal democracy as a whole is to blame for their predicament. I do not think that an effective and democratic public sphere will make any difference to people like the Communist Deputy Albert Makashov, who stood up in the Russian Parliament and lamented that "life in our country is getting worse and worse. Never before has it been this bad in Russia. . . . Who is to blame? The executive branch, the bankers, and the mass media are to blame. Usury, deceit, corruption, and thievery are flourishing in the country. That is why I call the reformers yids. Who are these Jews?"[31] What is worth investigating is how many of the people looking for answers will find his explanation convincing and why.

Although the causes of the frustration and discontent that Makashov hopes to tap into are economic, his "explanation" targets a group as the villainous force behind all the bad things that are happening. This type of explanation is only likely persuade the "swing vote" if they have no other reasonable alternative—that is, if all efforts to understand and get a hold of the circumstances of their life fail. Powerlessness makes people susceptible to solutions that, at the very least, offer the satisfaction of venting one's anger and frustration onto a clearly identified villain. This conclusion is supported by some research on social movements. For example, Foley and Edwards argue that "where the state is unresponsive, its institutions are undemocratic, or its democracy is ill designed to recognize and respond to citizens' demands, the character of collective action will be decidedly different than under a strong and democratic system. Citizens will find their efforts to organize for civil ends frustrated by state policy—at some times actively repressed, at others simply ignored. Increasingly aggressive forms of civil association will spring up, and more and more ordinary citizens will be driven into active militancy against the state or self-protective apathy."[32]

Critical theory has an important contribution to make to this debate because it focuses on empowerment and the forces that block empowerment. While scholars like Sheri Berman and Theda Skocpol talk in general terms about the need for strong national institutions to counter the particularism of a civil society gone insular, critical theory talks about a democratized public sphere that would include much more than responsive national parties and parliaments that listen to citizens.[33] Bad civil society develops when groups fail to live up to the ideals of democratic citizenship: when groups advocate hate, organize around xenophobia, and generally contribute to an atmosphere of distrust and suspicion between social actors. In extreme cases, where, for example, violence is suspected, the state can step in and censure the group. In most established liberal democracies, however, the more serious problem is with groups that spread a culture of hate rather than engage in violence. Here the defense must be alternative venues of cultural creation. These venues must both empower and engage citizens across group boundaries. The work that many critical theorists are doing in developing alternative institutions of deliberative democracy will be important in this respect.

The question of bad civil society deals with levels of intergroup democracy. What about levels of intragroup democracy? Is there a connection between whether a group is a good democratic citizen in the public sphere and what level of democracy and equality is maintained within the group? This is the question I address in the next section.

DEMOCRACY IN THE PRIVATE SPHERE

At first sight there appears to be no necessary connection between levels of internal democracy and equality and how groups perform as democratic citizens. There are militia groups, for example, that are internally highly egalitarian and consensually governed. They are not, however, very good democratic citizens in that they advocate an ideology that essentially undermines the possibility of cooperative democracy. Conversely, there are religious organizations that are hierarchical, patriarchal, and nondemocratic that are good democratic citizens in the sense that they are willing to engage others in egalitarian and respectful debate. Nevertheless, it is difficult to imagine a healthy democratized civil society that is home to nothing but undemocratically organized groups. How much internal democracy is enough democracy?

Democratized civil society, according to Cohen and Arato, is "compatible with spheres of life that are not discursively or democratically organized, as long as the need for non-discursive organizational principles and the boundaries between them and democratic organizations are established and confirmed in discursive procedures."[34] What does this mean? Cohen and Arato elide two overlapping yet distinct issues here. The first concerns the establishment of nondiscursive organizational principles and the second concerns the establishment of boundaries between non-discursive organizations and the state. The essence of a discursive principle of organization is that all those affected by the organizational rule ought to agree to that rule. Organizations that are hierarchical or even patriarchal are acceptable if the *members* can be said to have agreed to the hierarchy or patriarchy. The rest of society or the state does not have to agree with the way in which the organization is structured, although the rest of society and the state must be convinced that the members have agreed with the way in which the organization is structured. Agreement among members need not be reached in an explicit discursive procedure. Take, for example, the Catholic Church. The argument here is that Catholics, if asked, would agree that the pope ought to rule because he is Christ's envoy here on earth. This is not to say that members believe that the pope's legitimacy rests on consent; they clearly do not. Nor is it to say that the pope's right to rule has been established or confirmed in an actual, as opposed to hypothetical, discourse. Nevertheless, there is a sense that members of the church *would agree* if a discourse were to take place. Conversely, members can and do leave the church when they no longer *agree* with the basis of hierarchical organization.

In the case of the organizing principles for groups, the group members must agree; in the case of organizing principles for society as a whole, the ideal is general and public agreement. As an issue that affects all in society, the boundary between public and private should be established and confirmed in discursive procedures that include all. Because citizens cannot exit society in the same way that members can exit churches, there is a higher standard for establishing agreement. Simply remaining in the organization as opposed to exiting is not evidence of agreement in the case of society. Here we need to establish democratic procedures to measure agreement.[35] At first sight this argument might appear to weaken the protection of private sphere against public interference. This is not necessarily the case. The United States and Canada draw the line between public and private in slightly different ways and in slightly different places. In Canada, for example, individuals can be prosecuted for publishing and distributing hate literature, while it would be difficult to imagine such legislation surviving judicial review in the United State. While it can be said that the public has more latitude in Canada, the decisions about whether hate speech is protected or not is just as much a public decision in the United States as in Canada. The power to draw the line (regardless of where that line is drawn) is a public power. Advocates of more stringent regulation on hate speech in the United States (or victims of such speech) feel that the lack of such regulation represents an unjust *public* imposition that turns a blind eye to many serious civil injuries. Thus, Cohen and Arato are not necessarily saying that the burden of proof regarding which organizations we tolerate and which we do not lies either with the state or with the groups themselves. They are saying that the decision about where the burden of proof lies is itself a public decision and requires a discursive justification.

CONCLUSION

In "On the Jewish Question," Marx complained that liberal rights were a sham because they made everyone equal in the eyes of the state, and this was as real as making everyone equal in the eyes of God. In both cases, attention is diverted away from the site of real inequality: civil society. People live out their lives in civil society. If we are interested in bringing justice to their lives, then we must bring it to civil society. Marx got a lot of things wrong, including the worthlessness of rights and God in fighting injustice. What he got right, though, was that civil society is where it happens or does not happen.

Marx was interested in the contrast between the economic inequality of individuals in civil society and the political equality of citizens of the liberal state. Critical theory is also interested in this contrast. But it is now seen as connected to a deeper contrast that must also be overcome. That is the contrast between a culture of inequality in civil society and an ideology of equality in the state that appears more and more ineffectual in shaping the daily lives of citizens. The struggle is no longer over the means of production or the reins of power, but over the hearts and minds of individuals. Marxist economic reductionism says, transform economic relations and hearts and minds will follow. Marxist totalitarianism says, capture the state and if hearts and minds do not follow, we can make them follow. Because critical theory rejects both these roads to equality, it is left with a direct appeal to the hearts and minds of individuals. This is why democratic theory, and in particular participatory public opinion formation, has become so central in critical theory overshadowing, for example, theories of social justice. Democratic deliberation is seen as a noncoercive means of creating the social solidarity necessary to overcome a culture of inequality.

FURTHER READING

Andrew Arato and Eike Gebhardt. *The Essential Frankfurt School Reader.* New York: Continuum, 1982.

Norberto Bobbio. "Gramsci and the Concept of Civil Society." In *Civil Society and the State: New European Perspectives,* edited by John Keane, pp. 73–100. New York: Verso, 1988.

Jean L. Cohen and Andrew Arato. *Civil Society and Political Theory.* Cambridge: MIT Press, 1992.

Jürgen Habermas. *The Structural Transformation of the Public Sphere.* Translated by Thomas Berger with the assistance of Frederick Lawrence. Cambridge: MIT Press, 1989.

————. *Between Facts and Norms: Contributions to a Discourse Theory of Law and Democracy.* Translated by William Rehg. Cambridge: MIT Press, 1996.

David Held. *Introduction to Critical Theory: Horkheimer to Habermas.* Berkeley and Los Angeles: University of California Press, 1980.

Martin Jay. *The Dialectical Imagination: A History of the Frankfurt School and the Institute of Social Research, 1923–1950.* Boston: Little, Brown, 1973.

NOTES

1. For Hobbes, Bodin, and Spinoza the crucial distinction is not civil society/ state but rather a state of nature and a civil society created by the state. See John Keane, *Democracy and Civil Society* (New York: Verso, 1988), p. 35.

2. The first generation of critical theory is also known as the Frankfurt School, as it comprised a group of left intellectuals from disparate disciplines who came together in the Frankfurt Institute for Social Research. Some of the more famous names associated with early critical theory are Max Horkheimer, Theodor Adorno, Otto Kirhheimer, Herbert Marcuse, Walter Benjamin, and Erich Fromm. The Frankfurt School called their approach critical theory not simply because it criticized (i.e., found fault with) existing conditions. *Critical* was used in a more technical sense to refer to Kant's idea of critique (as in *The Critique of Pure Reason*). This is sometimes also called immanent critique because it is an analysis of a phenomenon from inside that phenomenon: we set out to understand human reason, fully aware that we cannot step outside of human reason to do so.

Today, second- and even third-generation critical theorists include Jürgen Habermas, Claus Offe, Günter Frankenberg, Helmut Dubiel, Axel Honneth, Hauke Brunkhorst, Seyla Benhabib, Jean Cohen, Andrew Arato, Nancy Fraser, Stephen White, Ken Baynes, Bill Scheurmann, and Thomas McCarthy, among others. See Andrew Arato and Eike Gebhardt, *The Essential Frankfurt School Reader* (New York: Continuum, 1982); Martin Jay, *The Dialectical Imagination: A History of the Frankfurt School and the Institute of Social Research, 1923–1950* (Boston: Little, Brown, 1973); David Held, *Introduction to Critical Theory: Horkheimer to Habermas* (Berkeley and Los Angeles: University of California Press, 1980).

3. See Norberto Bobbio, "Gramsci and the Concept of Civil Society," in *Civil Society and the State: New European Perspectives,* ed. John Keane (New York: Verso, 1988), pp. 73–100. See also Jean L. Cohen and Andrew Arato, *Civil Society and Political Theory* (Cambridge: MIT Press, 1992), pp. 142–59.

4. Habermas's interest in civil society spans his whole career beginning with *Strukturwandel der Öffentlichkeit* (Darmstadt: Hermann Luchterhand Verlag, 1962), now in translation as *The Structural Transformation of the Public Sphere,* translated by Thomas Berger with the assistance of Frederick Lawrence (Cambridge: MIT Press, 1989), and continuing into his latest major publication, *Between Facts and Norms: Contributions to a Discourse Theory of Law and Democracy,* translated by William Rehg (Cambridge: MIT Press, 1996). Jean Cohen and Andrew Arato in their book *Civil Society and Political Theory* go the furthest in developing a comprehensive theory of civil society inspired by Habermas and critical theory.

5. For more on this subject see Albrecht Wellmer, "Communications and Emancipation: Reflections on the Linguistic Turn in Critical Theory," in *On Critical Theory,* ed. John O'Neill (New York: Continuum, 1976), pp. 231–63.

6. On Habermas's liberal Kantianism see Kenneth Baynes, *The Normative Grounds of Social Criticism: Kant, Rawls, and Habermas* (Albany: State University of New York Press, 1992).

7. Held, *Introduction to Critical Theory,* p. 16.

8. Habermas borrows the concept of the lifeworld from phenomenology and most particularly Husserl. See Jürgen Habermas, *The Theory of Communicative Action,* translated by Thomas McCarthy (Boston: Beacon Press, 1987), 2:119.

9. Cohen and Arato, *Civil Society and Political Theory,* p. 429.

10. This intuition is reflected in our tax laws concerning nonprofit organizations and NGOs.

11. Habermas, *Between Facts and Norms,* p. 367.

12. Habermas, *Structural Transformation of the Public Sphere,* p. 82.

13. Immanuel Kant, "Perpetual Peace," in *Kant's Political Writings,* ed. Hans Reiss (Cambridge: Cambridge University Press, 1970), p. 130; Immanuel Kant, "On the Common Saying: 'This May Be True in Theory, But It Does Not Apply in Practice,'" in *Kant's Political Writings,* p. 85.

14. Habermas, *The Structural Transformation of the Public Sphere,* pp. 141–235.

15. Habermas, *Between Facts and Norms,* p. 369.

16. Habermas, *Between Facts and Norms,* p. 370.

17. Some of the main contributors to talk-centric critical theory of democracy are Seyla Benhabib, "Toward a Deliberative Model of Democratic Legitimacy," in *Democracy and Difference: Contesting the Boundaries of the Political,* ed. Seyla Benhabib (Princeton: Princeton University Press, 1996); James Bohman *Public Deliberation: Pluralism, Complexity, and Democracy* (Cambridge: MIT Press, 1996); Simone Chambers, *Reasonable Democracy: Jürgen Habermas and the Politics of Discourse* (Ithaca: Cornell University press, 1996).

18. Bohman, *Public Deliberation,* pp. 1–2; Benhabib, "Toward a Deliberative Model of Democratic Legitimacy," pp. 67–80; Jon Elster, "The Market and the Forum: Three Varieties of Political Theory," in *Foundations of Social Choice Theory,* ed. Jon Elster and Aanund Hylland (Cambridge: Cambridge University Press, 1986); Iris Marion Young, "Communication and the Other: Beyond Deliberative Democracy," in Benhabib, *Democracy and Difference,* pp. 120–36.

19. Habermas, *Between Facts and Norms,* pp. 84–118.

20. Habermas, *Between Facts and Norms,* p. 104.

21. Michael W. Foley and Bob Edwards, "The Paradox of Civil Society," *Journal of Democracy* 7, no. 3 (July 1996): 46.

22. Sheri Berman, "Civil Society and the Collapse of the Weimar Republic," *World Politics* 49, no. 3 (1997): 401–29; Stephen Hanson and Jeffrey Kopstein, "The Weimar/Russia Comparison," *Post-Soviet Affairs* 13, no. 3 (1997): 252–83; Filippo Sabetti, "Path Dependency and Civic Culture: Some Lessons from Italy about Interpreting Social Experiments," *Politics and Society* 24, no. 1 (1996).

23. David Rohde, *Endgame: The Betrayal and Fall of Srebrenica: Europe's Worst Massacre since World War II* (New York: Farrar, Straus, and Giroux, 1997).

24. Jeffrey Kopstein and Stephen Hanson, "Paths to Uncivil Societies and Anti-Liberal States," *Post-Soviet Affairs* 14, no. 4 (1998): 369–76.

25. See, for example, Robert D. Putnam, *Making Democracy Work: Civic Traditions in Modern Italy* (Princeton: Princeton University Press, 1993), p. 182.

26. Theda Skocpol argues that many of the recently founded large voluntary associations in the United States are staff-led (as opposed to volunteer-led) mailing list associations. The exceptions to this are mostly found on the right and include the National Right to Life Committee, the Christian Coalition, the National Riffle Association, and the Promise Keepers, all of which have mobilized on the ground and at the local, state, and national level. See Theda Skocpol, "Civic Engagement in American Democracy," *Social Science History* 21, no. 4 (Winter 1997): 473.

27. Putnam, *Making Democracy Work,* p. 182.

28. This is a common criticism of Putnam's definition of civil society. A similar example of circularity appears in the following definition: "to the extent that a group seeks to conquer the state or other competitors, or rejects the rule of law and the authority of the democratic state, it is not a component of civil society at all." Larry Diamond, "Toward Democratic Consolidation," *Journal of Democracy* 5, no. 3 (July 1994): 11.

29. Seyla Benhabib, *Situating the Self: Gender, Community, and Postmodernism in Contemporary Ethics* (New York: Routledge, 1992), pp. 77–78.

30. Berman, "Civil Society and the Collapse of the Weimar Republic," pp. 424–25.

31. Albert Makashov, "Usurers of Russia" quoted in *Johnson's Russia List* 7, no. 2461, November 6, 1998.

32. Foley and Edwards, "The Paradox of Civil Society," p. 48.

33. Compare, for example, Theda Skocpol, "The Tocqueville Problem: Civic Engagement in American Democracy," Presidential Address for the Annual Meeting of the Social Science History Association, Oct. 12, 1996, and Nancy Fraser, "Rethinking the Public Sphere," in *Habermas and the Public Sphere,* ed. Craig Calhoun (Cambridge: MIT Press, 1993), pp. 109–42.

34. Cohen and Arato, *Civil Society and Political Theory,* p. 412.

35. That the state is not a voluntary association is only one reason among many why constitutional essentials ought to be endorsed by a general agreement.

PART III

CHAPTER 6

Christianity and Civil Society

Michael Banner

IN ITS CONTEMPORARY USAGE the term *civil society* typically refers to the totality of structured associations, relationships, and forms of cooperation between persons that exist in the realm between the family and the state. Where such patterns of association, cooperation, and structured relationships are thought to be weak or inconsequential, as in the corporatist East of yesteryear (where individuals are said to have related chiefly to the State) or as in the capitalist and individualistic West (where personal relationships may arguably occur only within the family and perhaps not even there), it has become commonplace to lament the nonexistence of civil society. Christianity, it is usually supposed, will be prominent among the mourners on whichever side of the globe the wake is observed.

I shall suggest in this chapter, however, that the relationship of Christian thought to the question of civil society is a matter of some complexity. This complexity is not a matter of the simple muddle that occurs where the ambiguities of the term *civil society* are not recognized and addressed, but has to do with the history and variety of Christian social thought. Obviously enough, the tradition of Christian thought about society and community predates questions concerning the existence, character, and qualities of civil society, without thereby having nothing to say in answer to them. Thus, though one might, in delineating a Christian conception of civil society, chart only the reaction of Christian thought to the rise of civil society under the patronage of modern liberalism, the intellectual roots of any such reactions would not necessarily emerge clearly into view, and thus the reactions might seem somewhat thinner than they really are. Such an approach might also conceal the stimulus that Christianity itself gave to the emergence of civil society in its modern form. The tradition of Christian social thought is, however, not just lengthy but also varied. Even if its different strands possess, naturally, a certain family resemblance, it is not monolithic. There is, then, nothing that can be identified as the Christian answer to the question of civil society. Rather, there is a tradition of social thought that, in its different versions, is relevant to the questions posed by the modern debate about the existence, character, and qualities of civil society.

In the light of these considerations, this chapter approaches the task of answering some of these questions by attempting to outline particular and important moments in this tradition, taking as a point of departure Augustine's understanding of the two cities, which, as I shall point out, is questioned in different ways by Thomas and Calvin, and reconceived by Luther. In turn, the Lutheran reconception of the Augustinian approach is, it will be noted, criticized in the work of such figures as Bonhoeffer and Barth, while the Thomist tradition is developed in the social teaching of the Roman Magisterium. Attention will be drawn to the implications of these different approaches for contemporary questions regarding civil society, though the survey can, at best, be illustrative and not exhaustive.

INGREDIENTS

The question "Who or what does civil society include?" has been posed from within the Christian tradition as a question, in effect, about where and in what form society is instantiated. And one influential answer from within the Christian tradition to that question is, in brief, "the church," since outside that community social relations, public or private in modern terms, lack characteristics or qualities essential to them. Though this Augustinian answer was highly influential, it was in turn, however, as we must presently indicate, contested or reconceived, giving rise to different answers, or at least different emphases, in Christian thinking about the nature of human community.

Crucial to the thought of the New Testament in general, and the thought of Paul in particular, is the contrast underlying Paul's exhortation to the Romans: "Do not be conformed to this world, but be transformed by the renewal of your mind."[1] The character and significance of this contrast must, however, be properly understood. Wolin gets it right when, having cited this verse, he comments:

> This attitude must not be understood as mere alienation or the expression of an unfulfilled need to belong. Nor is it to be accounted for in terms of the stark contrasts that Christians drew between eternal and temporal goods, between the life of the spirit held out by the Gospel and the life of the flesh symbolized by political and social relationships. What is fundamental to an understanding of the entire range of [early] Christian political attitudes was that they issued from a group that regarded itself as already in a society, one of far greater purity and higher purpose: "a chosen generation, a royal priesthood, an holy nation, a peculiar people."[2]

Wolin is also right to observe of a much used and misused text that "the critical significance of the Pauline teaching [in Rom. 13] was that it brought the political order within the divine economy and thereby compelled its confrontation by Christians."[3]

Given such roots, it is hardly surprising that a dominant strand in the

Christian tradition has thought about society by means of a contrast between two kingdoms, realms or—as in the locus classicus of Christian social thought, Augustine's *City of God*—between two cities. According to Augustine,

> although there are many great peoples throughout the world, living under different customs in religion and morality and distinguished by a complex variety of languages, arms and dress, it is still true that there have come into being only two main divisions, as we may call them, in human society: and we are justified in following the lead of our Scriptures and calling them two cities.[4]

What is here characterized as a division *within* society is for Augustine in another sense, however, a division *between* societies, only one of which properly deserves the name. That this is a division between societies is the force of the use of the word *city* to mark the two divisions, since, employed where in Greek one might read *polis,* the word serves to indicate all-encompassing communities. The two cities, that is to say—the city of God (sometimes the heavenly city) and the earthly city—are to be understood as two polities, "two political entities coexistent in one space and time," "distinct social entities, each with its principle . . . and each with its political expression, Roman empire and church."[5] But these distinct "social entities," in virtue of their different origins, histories, and ends, are to be contrasted more starkly still; for if we quibbled with the notion that the division between the two cities was one within society, and noted that it is actually a division between societies, we must also reckon with the fact that one of these is for Augustine the form, here on earth, of the one true society, whereas the other is a society only in a superficial sense. How so?

"The two cities," says Augustine, "were created by two kinds of love: the earthly city was created by self-love reaching the point of contempt for God, the Heavenly City by the love of God carried as far as contempt of self."[6] Now the difference in ends or objects of love creates two quite different cities: "the citizens of each of these [two cities] desire their own kind of peace, and when they achieve their aim, this is the peace in which they live."[7] The heavenly city, united in love of God, enjoys a peace that "is a perfectly ordered and perfectly harmonious fellowship in the enjoyment of God and mutual fellowship in God."[8] The earthly city also desires peace, but its peace is of a different kind. The citizens of the earthly city, in a prideful love of self over love of God, have each rejected the rule of God and chosen in preference a self-rule as intolerant of any other rule as it is of God's; for "pride is a perverted imitation of God . . . [that] hates a fellowship of equality under God, and seeks to impose its own dominion on fellow men, in place of God's rule. This means that it hates the just peace of God, and loves its own peace of injustice."[9] The love of self becomes, then, that *libido dominandi,* or lust for domination, that has driven the Roman

Empire. Peace is achieved through the imposition of one's own will by the exercise of force, and is at once costly in its creation,[10] unjust in its character,[11] and unstable in its existence.[12] This is not to say that there is no difference between the Roman Empire and a band of brigands, to refer to Augustine's infamous jibe,[13] but it is to say that the peace of all other societies is different in kind from the just and certain peace of the true society found in the city of God, represented here on earth in the church, which is the city of God "on pilgrimage."[14]

The implications of Augustine's thought for the question where, and in what form, society is instantiated, are brought out in Joan Lockwood O'Donovan's summary of his argument:

> Augustine's polarising of the two cities . . . radically questioned the sense in which the social relations belonging to the *saeculum*, the passing order of the world, could be thought to comprise a society, a unity in plurality or harmonised totality. For on his view the secular *res publica* is not a true community knit together by charity and consensus in right—that is present only where faith in Christ and obedience to His law of love bind persons together—but a fragile and shifting convergence of human wills with respect to limited categories of earthly goods in a sea of moral disorder, of personal and group hostilities.[15]

Society, properly so called, exists in the city of God, and not in the earthly city. And so too civil society—for if the grounds for a stable structure of association and cooperation are certainly lacking for the whole, they are finally lacking for simple human associations as such.

The claim that society, properly understood, exists in the church is lost, however, if the theme of the "two cities" as Augustine develops it is transposed by an interpretation of the two cities as two spheres, a move associated with Lutheranism (if not quite so certainly with Luther).[16] Such a move dissolves the tension between the differently characterized cities by construing their relationship in terms of a functional division concerning, say, the worldly and the spiritual, or outer and inner. With the imagery thus construed, it becomes possible for the church to understand itself as an instance of civil society, rather than as its locus. But this is just what is prohibited in Augustine's thought, in which the two cities are not related spatially, to use Bonhoeffer's term,[17] but temporally or eschatologically; that is to say, the cities do not rule *over* different *spheres*, but rather, ruling over the same spheres, rule *in* different, albeit overlapping, *times*.[18] Just because of this overlap, the city of God must seek its distinctive peace amid the earthly peace and will make use of it as it makes use of earthly things in general (and thus has grounds for distinguishing between the different forms of the earthly city insofar as they do or do not prove useful to its purpose). But this overlap does not license the granting of autonomy, if one may put it so, to the earthly city. Coming at the point from the other side, one can agree with Markus when he observes that according to the Augustinian picture, "there was no need for Christians to be set apart sociologically, as a community separated from the 'world,' . . . uncontaminated by it and visibly 'over against the world.' On the contrary: the Christian community was, quite simply, the world redeemed and reconciled."[19] Monasticism (at least in its distinctly Augustinian theory in the *Rule of St. Benedict*, if not in its later, less-Augustinian practice) maintains this insight, presupposing not an autonomy of spheres (and thus, in our terms, that there are versions of society), but rather that the monastery, which was first of all a lay movement, displays the secular (i.e., temporal) form of society, of which the earthly city is but a sorry caricature.

If Luther subtly reconceives the Augustinian picture, Thomas and Calvin offer more straightforward challenges to it, while Orthodoxy developed independently of it, though struggling with essentially the same issues and problems. Although Augustine was writing at a time when Christianity had become the official and favored religion of the Empire, it was chiefly in Byzantium that the "conversion of the state" led to a radical questioning of the contrast between civil church and uncivil society, to put it in modern terms, that belongs to early Christian thought. This conversion did not unsettle Augustine's picture: the earthly city had not become the city of God "merely because the kings serve it [i.e., the church], wherein lies greater and more perilous temptations."[20] In the East this sense of danger or tension was not always maintained, even if the charge of "caesaropapism" (i.e., the subordination of the church to political rule) risks ignoring some of the subtleties involved, or at least the predominantly pragmatic character of the handling of these issues. It does, however, indicate the danger to which Orthodoxy has seemed especially prone, at least to Western eyes; that is, of having a "charismatic understanding of the state" that "lacked political realism,"[21] and that thus too readily assumed the possibility of Christian society outside the immediate life of the church. Arguably Eastern monasticism, like its Western counterpart, preserved a rather different perspective.[22]

In the West, "the alternative theological answers . . . to the Augustinian problematic of secular society are," to cite Joan Lockwood O'Donovan again, "the Thomistic-Aristotelian rejection of it and the Calvinist-Puritan conversion of it."[23] She continues:

> Under Aristotelian influence St. Thomas exchanged the Augustinian conception of a conflictual and disjunctive social order for a more organically harmonious one. His minimising of the spiritual distance between the traditionally "pre-lapsarian" institutions such as marriage and family and the post-lapsarian institutions such as private property and political rule enabled him to weave social life into a unified moral texture. He viewed sinful society as retaining the inherent harmony of a hierarchy of natural ends and functions, each part having its ap-

pointed place within the teleological whole. With no disjunctive division between different communities, especially between political and non-political communities, all together constituted a real social totality, a common will directed toward a common good.

For Calvin the handling of Augustine was different:

Unlike St. Thomas, Calvin's response to the Augustinian problematic of secular society was a reorientation rather than a displacement of it. For Calvin the disorder of sinful social relations could not be mitigated by an appeal to a natural social teleology, but required a different conception of order: a more exclusively political/juridical one based immediately on God's providential rule over sinful humanity and elaborated in the (largely Old Testament) ideas of divine-human covenant, divine commandment and divinely established offices. The unity of civil as well as of ecclesiastical society depended on their institutional structuring by God's commandments that defined the rights and duties of every social "office" as a vehicle of His revealed law in the creation and redemption of the world.

SOCIETY

According to the tradition that flows from Augustine, then, civil society as genuine society—that is, even minimally, as a stable structure of association and cooperation between persons—exists in the city of God, or in the church that is, here and now, its imperfect token. In contrast with this society, all other associations are radically defective. But what makes the church, or the city of God, itself a society and not a simple aggregate?

It might be supposed that this is not a problem, or not a very severe problem, within the Augustinian framework, simply because in identifying the church as society we avoid the issue that must arise for those who think of society as variously realized and manifested and thus as having parts. This supposition would, however, be mistaken for two reasons. In the first place, even of the church it can be asked what unites its members. Furthermore, and in the second place, in stressing that talk of "two cities" does not presuppose a division of spheres—that is, to repeat Markus's formulation of Augustine's viewpoint, that "the Christian community was, quite simply, the world redeemed and reconciled"—attention is drawn to the fact that the life of the church might be expected itself to be differentiated, since it will comprise more than those functions that might be attributed to a church by a contemporary sociologist. Thus Bonhoeffer, for example, to be regarded as a modern exponent of this tradition, thinks of the Christian life as structured according to "divine mandates," including labor (or culture), marriage, and government, and the first of these may involve patterns and instances of association and cooperation which will raise a question as to the coordination or unity of what is in another sense a single society.

In his dispute with the Donatists, Augustine came to stress order, sacraments, and doctrine, and most importantly baptism, as what renders real within the church the rule of Christ, and thus unites the church as one body. This rule of Christ within the life of the church in, or rather as, the world brings unity to this differentiated society as each of its members uses everything for the sake of a higher end, namely, God.

For the Thomist tradition, which thinks of society as existing outside the church in virtue of the claims made upon human life by its natural ends, it is the common good that serves to unite its parts. The classical organic image of society thus maintains its naturalistic quality, with a special emphasis, however, on the need for the head to identify the common good and coordinate its pursuit.[24] The sense in which the unity of society is an achievement is heightened in Calvin's conception. Order for Calvin, as Wolin points out, "required a constant exercise of power,"[25] though here the instrument of its realization is not a single head, but a wider structure of institutions and offices. This structuring of Christian society, giving participation a more crucial role than any direct and individual rule, whether in matters civil or more narrowly ecclesiastical, was to have significant consequences for the growth and development of civil society in the particular sense in which that term is now most often used. It was in the Calvinist congregations of New England that there developed a practice of association, cooperation, and self-government that was determined to protect the social space thus revealed, occupied, and mapped out against encroachment by the state. This space is, of course, the space of civil society as it is classically conceived, and its imagining has roots, as we shall have cause to note again, in Reformation thought and perhaps even further back in the Christian tradition.

VALUES

Though Thomas and Augustine may have looked for society in different places, and expected it to be sustained in different ways, there was no difference between them in believing that the good or value of such society (within the church in Augustine's account, or outside it in Thomas's) lies precisely in its sociality, since it is in sociality that the human good is realized.

Augustine had been tempted to represent the good life as a neo-Platonic quest with contemplation at its core. As he distanced himself from these philosophic roots, however, he came to stress the thoroughly social character of human life. Thus, though the earthly city is contrasted with the

city of God, the contrast is not between the sociality of one and the aso-
ciality of the other, but rather between the doubtful sociality of one and
the true sociality of the other, a sociality with a horizontal as well as a ver-
tical dimension. The heavenly city, we will recall, united in love of God, enjoys a peace that "is a perfectly ordered and perfectly harmonious fellowship in the enjoyment of God and *mutual fellowship in God.*"

Thomas's grounding in Aristotle required a move in the other direction,
so to speak: not in explicit recognition of the value of society, but rather a
modest qualification of the assumption in its favor. (Thus in his commentary on *The Politics,* in glossing Aristotle's reflection on the "monstrous,"
we might say "inhuman," condition of those deprived of society and isolated from political life, Thomas, as D'Entrèves puts it, "finds it necessary
to make an express reservation with regard to asceticism, in favour of the
idea of a higher degree of perfection to be attained by retiring from the
world rather than by participating in it. But he is at pains to emphasize
the exceptional character of a life of this kind, and the necessity, for the at-
tainment of such an ideal, of more than human capacities.")[26] But however that may be, the essential agreement between Thomas and Augustine
is evidenced in the former employing the latter's argument in justifying or
explaining the prohibition of incest. According to Thomas, an end of marriage is "the binding together of mankind and the extension of friendship:
for a husband regards his wife's kindred as his own. Hence it would be prej-
udicial to this extension of friendship if a man could take a woman of his
kindred to wife since no new friendship would accrue to anyone from such
a marriage. Wherefore, according to human law and the ordinances of the
Church, several degrees of consanguinity are debarred from marriage."[27]
Here he simply repeats the reasoning of Augustine when he explains why,
apart from in the first generations, men were forbidden to take their sisters
as wives: "the aim was that one man should not combine many relationships in his one self, but that those connections should be separated and
spread among individuals, and that in this way they should help to bind social life more effectively by involving in their plurality a plurality of persons."[28] (What is striking here is that the freedom of marriage, which the
church vigorously maintained in other ways, gives way before the good of
the extension of sociality.)

The good of sociality is, then, a presupposition of both these streams of
thought within the Christian tradition. And, according to Leo XIII in
Rerum Novarum, it is the fact that this is a good that explains the existence
of civil society in the modern sense, as well as in its older sense: "Just as
man is led by [a] natural propensity to associate with others in a political
society, so also he finds it advantageous to join with his fellows in other
kinds of societies, which though small and not independent are nonetheless true societies."[29] Thus "the natural sociability of men" is held to be

the principle from which both the state and private associations are born and the good that they serve, and this prior grounding of both determines the relationship between them: "It is by virtue of the law of nature that men may enter into private societies and it is for the defence of that law, not its destruction, that the state comes into being."[30]

In the Thomist tradition, however, this "natural propensity" to association in society and societies has been understood as more than a tendency to mere association. Rather, it is a tendency to association in societies that presuppose and foster that community of purpose, interest, and sympathy that is expressed by the notion of solidarity. It is on the basis of such anthropological presuppositions that modern Roman Catholic social thought from *Rerum Novarum* on (through, for example, Pius XI's *Quadragesimo Anno* and down to John Paul II's *Laborem Exercens*) has offered a critique of liberalism and socialism that both, though in different ways, deny the naturalness of human solidarity. Free-market liberalism is thought to conceive of humanity as made up of competitive individuals lacking a common good distinct from the aggregate of individual preferences. Socialism seems no less to doubt the naturalness of social solidarity, albeit that the conflictual character of society is a matter of class, rather than individual, interests and is, furthermore, not intrinsic, but is historically conditioned and contingent.

The recent *Catechism* of the Roman Catholic church extends this analysis somewhat by finding what we might think of as a hierarchy of values in society, each serving the human good. In the first place the *Catechism* offers what seems like a pragmatic reason for "socialization" (meaning here "the creation of voluntary associations and institutions . . . 'on both national and international levels, which relate to economic and social goals, to cultural and recreational activities, to sport, to various professions, and to political affairs'"),[31] namely, that it "expresses the natural tendency for human beings to associate with one another for the sake of attaining objectives that exceed individual capacities."[32] In the second place, however, in mentioning again humankind's natural sociability and thus entertaining the thought that human society is an end in itself, it goes on to connect "socialization" with a further good:

> The human person needs to live in society. Society is not for him an extraneous addition but a requirement of his nature. Through the exchange with others, mutual service and dialogue with his brethren, man develops his potential; he thus responds to his vocation.[33]

Elsewhere it is said that the "the vocation of man" is "made up of divine charity and human solidarity,"[34] just because "the human person is . . . ordered to God" as well as to others.[35] The *Catechism* notes in addition, however, that "[a]ll men are called to the same end: God himself" and that "there is a certain resemblance between the union of the divine persons and the fraternity that men are to establish among themselves in truth and love."[36]

The further good that might be found in human society in virtue of this "resemblance" has been more central to Protestant thought that, if it affirms the "natural sociability" of human kind, does so not on the basis of supposed knowledge of the natural law, but more definitely on the basis of a theological anthropology. For Karl Barth, for example, that "the humanity of man consists in the determination of his being as a being with the other" is a counterpart of the prior fact of humankind's calling to be the covenant-partner of God.[37] Thus here the value that might be attributed to civil society is found not only in its satisfying human sociability or solidarity as such, but in the fact of this human sociability and solidarity being a likeness of, and a preparation for, the sociability and solidarity of the life of God, into which humans are called. The value of civil society is for this tradition, then, firmly eschatological, so we might say.

RISKS

In recent Roman Catholic teaching the risks associated with civil society are the risks associated with society itself, namely, that higher levels of association will tend to deprive lower levels of association and individuals of their proper responsibilities. According to Pius XI in *Quadragesimo Anno:*

> Just as it is gravely wrong to take from individuals what they can accomplish by their own initiative and industry and give it to the community, so also it is an injustice and at the same time a grave evil and disturbance of right order to assign to a greater and higher association what lesser and subordinate organizations can do. For every social activity ought of its very nature to furnish help to the members of the body social, and never destroy and absorb them.[38]

This wrong is to be prevented by respect for the principle of subsidiarity (a term first employed in Pius's encyclical, though plainly the idea is much older). This principle, which functions as a balance to the emphasis on the common good that had been central to *Rerum Novarum*, states that

> a community of a higher order should not interfere in the internal life of a community of a lower order, depriving the latter of its functions, but rather should support it in case of need and help to co-ordinate its activity with the activities of the rest of society, always with a view to the common good.[39]

The *Catechism* offers a theological rationale for this principle, which protects civil society against the state, but also individuals against civil society:

> God has not willed to reserve to himself all exercise of power. He entrusts to every creature the functions it is capable of performing, according to the capac-

ities of its own nature. This mode of governance ought to be followed in social life. The way God acts in governing the world, which bears witness to such great regard for human freedom, should inspire the wisdom of those who govern human communities. They should behave as ministers of divine providence.[40]

Thus behaving, those with authority will acknowledge the existence of lower authorities and the rights of the individual, a theme that has been increasingly important in Roman Catholic social thought of the last fifty years and that features prominently in the *Catechism*, even though there is some evidence (in *Evangelium Vitae*, for example) of a growing sense of the need to bring some order and discipline to a mode of discourse that has given us rights to abortion, to die, and so on.

The Augustinian tradition, as we have seen, was suspicious of the exercise of power because of the fundamental corruption of the human will. Societies and associations, at whatever level, may provide occasions for domination and oppression. (Liberation Theology is, in a sense, an heir to this tradition and has sought to supplement and strengthen it by learning from the Marxist critique of society and civil society. The complaint against it from some of its critics, however, has been that it has not related what it has learned from Marx to the major themes of Christian doctrine, but rather has allowed the latter to be replaced by, or wholly subordinated to, other categories and concepts.) The Augustinian tradition has addressed and characterized the risks that societies pose, however, not by the formulation of an abstract principle, such as the principle of subsidiarity, nor necessarily by an elaboration of an account of human rights. Apart from anything else, to have taken this route might appear to treat the two brackets, so to speak, of the modern discussion of civil society (namely, the state and the individual in his or her privacy) as themselves autonomous and beyond criticism, when against the command of God they can possess no such autonomy. The command of God is in principle, in a manner of speaking, totalitarian, as the monastic rules we have already referred to presuppose in opening the whole of the life of ruled (monks) and ruler (abbot) to the Rule.

If, however, there is a suspicion of the principle of subsidiarity and rights, it is plain enough that the totalitarian character of the rule of God itself provides a basis for a critique of all social institutions and associations, a point that was formulated with a certain clarity and force in the *Barmen Declaration* of 1934. This document can be seen as a protest at the tendency of Lutheranism, having converted Augustine's two cities into two spheres, to accord a certain independence to the state and civil society as concerned with the outer and not the inner life, which is the concern of the church. In Luther's most important treatment of this matter, the distinction is used to "safeguard religion against the unwelcome attentions of ungodly princes,"[41] and thus (by the way and to mention another occasion when Christian thought is found at the origins of civil society) provides arguments that would later be taken over almost *tout court* by advocates of religious toleration.[42] But the distinction of spheres seemed also to deny to the church in principle, the right to offer a critique of action in the public realm, even when that action involved, as here, the determination of the limits and character of society by myths of *Volk*, blood, and soil. Against such a distinction the *Barmen Declaration* asserts that "Jesus Christ is . . . God's vigorous announcement of his claim upon our whole life" and that "through him there comes to us joyful liberation from the godless ties of this world," and rejects "the false doctrine that there could be areas of our life in which we would belong not to Jesus Christ but to other lords, areas in which we would not need justification and sanctification through him."[43] As Torrance comments: "[T]o confess the Lordship of Christ over all areas of life (intellectual and cultural, ecclesial and civil) means that, in the light of the Gospel, we are unconditionally obliged to be true to and obedient to the One who is in his person God's Word to humankind. Culture, therefore, may neither determine the sphere of the Gospel nor relativise its imperatives but, conversely, culture and society require to be perceived, interpreted and evaluated critically in the light of the Gospel."[44] (This point will be important in relation to the issue of freedom, treated below.)

If the Protestant tradition has had cause to recapture a sense of its critical responsibility toward society, civil or otherwise, the Roman tradition, which has perhaps never lost this sense, has had cause to consider whether its own hierarchies, structures, and government are themselves in need of critical examination in the light of the principles of subsidiarity and a proper respect for the individual that have been used to examine secular society. Since Vatican II, at least, there has been a wide recognition that if society and civil society pose certain risks to the individual, so too may certain understandings of the church and of its "Magisterium" (i.e., teaching office and authority).[45] The disputes within Roman Catholicism concerning the bearers of this authority and its scope point to the fact that the principle of subsidiarity is not so much a rule by which precise boundaries can be determined, as a general caution against interventions from above except as a last resort.

RESPONSIBILITY

We have already seen how the principle of subsidiarity focuses the question as to who is to do what in civil society. According to this norm, responsibility is to remain at the lowest level from state to individual, provided that its remaining there is compatible with the common good. This serves, subject to interpretation and judgment, to attribute responsibilities to individuals, families, local communities and associations, and so on, to vindicate them in their different roles and, against certain understandings of its duties, to restrain the state. Of course the interpretation of this principle is a matter of contention, as we have noted, and no more so, perhaps, than in relation to the discussion of the market that stimulated the Encyclicals that first brought the theme of subsidiarity to attention. While a libertarian approach is likely to think that responsibility for human well-being lies with the individual pursuing his or her interests in the marketplace, on certain interpretations of the principle of subsidiarity and on certain understandings of the common good, this responsibility does not lie at this level alone but is shared with others, including the state.

Within Protestant thought the question of responsibilities is handled in effect by means of a theme already mentioned, namely, that of the so-called mandates or orders of creation. Reflection on this theme is an attempt to elaborate an ethic that takes seriously the fact, as Brunner puts it, that

> [t]he world, that which is not "I," is not something material, needing to be shaped and moulded by us. To think it is betrays an impertinent, arrogant habit of mind springing from the delusion that man is a god. The world is not a shapeless mass of matter, it is not a chaos which we have to reduce to form and order. It was formed long ago: it is given to us in a rich variety of form. In its *form* the will of God is stamped upon that which exists. We ought to understand this existing shape or order as the expression of the Divine Will. . . . We are to range ourselves within this order.[46]

According to Brunner the order we are called to respect does not consist only in "our natural existence, but also . . . [in] our historical existence." Thus, when he claims that "Reverence for the Creator, whose work, in spite of all human perversion, is the one existing reality, demands as our first reaction obedience to the existing order, and grateful acceptance of the goodness of the Creator in the orders, through which alone He makes it possible for us to serve our neighbour, and, indeed, to live at all,"[47] he means by the "orders," something more than the mere biological givens of human existence. He means, in fact, "those existing facts of human corporate life which lie at the root of all historical life as unalterable presuppositions, which, although their historical forms may vary, are unalterable in their fundamental structure, and, at the same time, relate and unite men to one another in a definite way."[48] Brunner names five such orders: the family, the state, culture, the church, and the economic order, and concludes that "the Command of God comes to us related to these orders of reality . . . [and] can be perceived in and through them."[49]

Brunner's handling of this theme was the cause of considerable controversy; Barth (sharply and with some imprecision) and Bonhoeffer (sympathetically and with more care) took exception to it.[50] The details of this controversy need not trouble us, since what is important to note here is that in seeking to handle the theme better, Brunner's critics share the underlying conviction that provides the basis of his concern, namely, that the created order possesses a good that makes a moral demand on us and on our ordering of social life. This has the implication for Bonhoeffer that even if government is itself, or has, a mandate, "[i]t is not creative. It preserves what has already been created, maintaining it in the order which is assigned to it through the task which is imposed by God. It protects it by making law to consist in the acknowledgement of the divine mandates and by securing respect for this law by the force of the sword. Thus [for example] the governing authority is not the performer but the witness and guarantor of marriage."[51]

The seeming specificity of the principle of subsidiarity may be lacking, and the need to develop a fuller account of the parts of society and their relationship may be obvious, but what is also evident is that the Protestant treatment of the ethics of creation leads to a belief in a differentiated society, with various responsibilities lying with different forms of social life that extend from the individual to the state.

FREEDOM

Again, the principle of subsidiarity, which has already been stated, provides a way of approaching the question of the appropriate balance between individual autonomy and the organizations and associations of society. It is plain here, however, that the interpretation of its precise requirements is a matter of some difficulty, as is evident when the *Catechism* asserts that the "right to the exercise of freedom . . . must be recognised and protected by civil authority within the limits of the common good and public order."[52] What is equally plain is that the freedom which is here in question is a freedom within or under the moral law, and not the absolute freedom of those versions of liberalism that the affirmation of solidarity was meant to preclude. According to *Evangelium Vitae:*

> When freedom, out of a desire to emancipate itself from all forms of tradition and authority, shuts out even the most obvious evidence of an objective and universal truth, which is the foundation of personal and social life, then the person ends up by no longer taking as the sole and indisputable point of reference for his own choices the truth about good and evil, but only his subjective and changeable opinion or, indeed, his selfish interest and whim. This view of freedom leads to a distortion of life in society. If the promotion of the self is understood in terms of absolute autonomy, people inevitably reach the point of rejecting one another. Everyone else is considered an enemy from whom one has to defend oneself. Thus society becomes a mass of individuals placed side by side, but without any mutual bonds.[53]

It is this notion of freedom, according to the Encyclical, that "exalts the isolated individual in an absolute way, and gives no place to solidarity," which lies at the root of "the contradiction between the solemn affirmation of human rights and their tragic denial in practice" in abortion and euthanasia.

For O'Donovan, the modern liberalism with which Christianity may need to contend has its beginning in the church's assertion of what he terms "evangelical liberty," "which is to say, the freedom freely to obey Christ."[54] The assertion of this freedom could not but have consequences for society: "the voice of a prophetic church in its midst, which speaks with divine authority, loosens the hold of existing authorities and evokes the prospect of liberty"[55]—for here the freedom of the individual against certain authorities is a presupposition of the assertion of the existence of yet higher authorities to which these others must themselves submit. Thus,

> [f]reedom . . . is not conceived primarily as an assertion of *individuality,* whether positively, in terms of individual creativity and impulse, or negatively, in terms of "rights," which is to say immunities from harm. It is a social reality, a new disposition of society around its supreme Lord which sets it loose from its traditional lords. Yet individual liberty is not far away. For the implication of this new social reality is that the individual can no longer simply be carried within the social setting to which she or he was born; for that setting is under challenge from the new social centre. This requires she give herself to the service of the Lord within the new society, in defiance, if need be, of the old lords and societies that claim her. She emerges in differentiation from her family, tribe and nation, making decisions of discipleship which were not given her from within them.[56]

In the early period it was perhaps the practice of avowed virginity that was the most marked sign of this freedom of decision and differentiation against authorities for the sake of a yet higher authority. But in relation to all earthly societies, the exercise of freedom thus conceived remains vital to Christian self-understanding, just because the ordered and differentiated society of the city that God intends is not to be identified with the imperfect societies of other cities that recognize other authorities or none.

Further Reading

Aquinas: Selected Political Writings. Edited by A. P. D'Entrèves (Oxford: Blackwell, 1959).

Augustine. *City of God.* Translated by H. Bettenson (Harmondsworth: Penguin, 1972), esp. bk. 19.

Barmen Declaration. Translated by D. S. Bax. *Journal of Theology for Southern Africa* 47 (1984).

D. Bonhoeffer. *Ethics.* Edited by E. Bethge, translated by N. H. Smith (London: SCM, 1955).

Catechism of the Catholic Church (London: Chapman, 1994).

Martin Luther and John Calvin. *On Secular Authority.* Edited and Translated by H. Höpfl (Cambridge: Cambridge University Press, 1991).

The Rule of St. Benedict. Translated by J. McCann (London: Sheed and Ward, 1976).

NOTES

1. Rom. 12:2 (in the Revised Standard Version).

2. S. S. Wolin, *Politics and Vision: Continuity and Innovation in Western Political Thought* (Boston: Little, Brown, 1960), p. 99, citing 1 Pet.: 2, 9.

3. Wolin, *Politics and Vision,* p. 98.

4. Augustine, *City of God,* trans. H. Bettenson (Harmondsworth: Penguin, 1972), 14.1.

5. O. M. T. O'Donovan, *The Desire of the Nations* (Cambridge: Cambridge University Press, 1996), pp. 83 and 203.

6. Augustine *City of God* 14.28.

7. Augustine *City of God* 14.1.

8. Augustine *City of God* 19.13.

9. Augustine *City of God* 19.12.

10. Of the imperial peace, Augustine exclaims (*City of God* 19.7): "think of the cost of this achievement! Consider the scale of those wars with all that slaughter of human beings, all the human blood that was shed!"

11. The prime mark of this injustice is the existence of slavery. According to Augustine (*City of God* 19.15), the proper relationship between human beings is "prescribed by the order of nature, and it is in this situation that God created man. For he says, 'Let him have lordship over the fish of the sea, the birds of the sky . . . and all the reptiles that crawl on the earth.' He did not wish the rational being, made in his own image, to have dominion over any but irrational creatures, not man over man, but man over beasts. Hence the first just men were set up as shepherds of flocks, rather than as kings of men."

12. In the midst of a melancholy review of the woes of life produced by division and conflict within house, city, world, and even within that "angelic fellowship" posited by "those philosophers" who insist that "the gods are our friends," Augustine notes (*City of God* 19.5) that the peace of the earthly city is "a doubtful good, since we do not know the hearts of those with whom we wish to maintain peace, and even if we could know them today, we should not know what they might be like tomorrow."

13. "Remove justice," writes Augustine (*City of God* 4.4), "and what are kingdoms but gangs of criminals on a large scale? . . . For it was a witty and a truthful rejoinder which was given by a captured pirate to Alexander the Great. The king asked the fellow, 'What is your idea, in infesting this sea?' And the pirate answered, with uninhibited insolence, 'The same as yours, in infesting the earth! But because I do it with a tiny craft, I'm called a pirate: because you have a mighty navy, you're called an emperor.'"

14. Augustine *City of God* 15.21.

15. J. L. O'Donovan, "Société," in *Dictionnaire Critique de Théologie*, ed. J-Y. Lacoste (Paris: Presse Universitaires de France, 1998). For a fuller account and discussion of Augustine's argument, see O. M. T. O'Donovan, "Augustine's *City of God* XIX and Western Political Thought," *Dionysius* 40 (1987): 89–110.

16. For Luther's most important grappling with the issues, see *On Secular Authority*, ed. and trans. H. Höpfl (Cambridge: Cambridge University Press, 1991).

17. D. Bonhoeffer, *Ethics*, ed. E. Bethge, trans. N. H. Smith (London: SCM, 1955), p. 178: "God and the world are thus at one in Christ in a way which means that although the Church and the world are different from each other, yet there cannot be a static spatial borderline between them."

18. The city of God is a "city whose kingdom will be eternal" (*City of God* 15.8), whereas the earthly city persists only until the day "when all human lordship and power is annihilated and God is all in all" (*City of God* 19.15).

19. R. A. Markus, *Saeculum: History and Society in the Theology of St. Augustine* (Cambridge: Cambridge University Press, 1970), p. 167.

20. Cited in O'Donovan, *The Desire of the Nations*, p. 197.

21. J. Meyendorff, *Byzantine Theology: Historical Trends and Doctrinal Themes* (Oxford: Mowbray's, 1975), p. 216.

22. See G. Florovsky, "Antinomies of Christian History: Empire and Desert," in his *Christianity and Culture* (Belmont, Mass.: Nordland, 1974), pp. 67–100.

23. O'Donovan, "Société."

24. In, for example, "On Princely Government" (*De Regimine Principum*), having rehearsed arguments that demonstrate that "the fellowship of society" is "natural and necessary to man," Thomas continues: "It follows with equal necessity that there must be some principle of government within the society. For if a great number of people were to live, each intent upon his own interests, such a community would surely disintegrate unless there were one of its number to have a care for the common good: just as the body of a man or of any other animal would disintegrate were there not in the body itself a single and controlling force, sustaining the general vitality of all the members. As Solomon tells us (Prov xi, 14): 'Where there is no ruler the people shall be scattered.' This conclusion is quite reasonable; for the particular interest and the common good are not identical." See *Aquinas: Selected Political Writings*, ed. A. P. D'Entrèves (Oxford: Blackwell, 1959), p. 3.

25. Wolin, *Politics and Vision*, p. 171.

26. D'Entrèves, *Aquinas: Selected Political Writings*, xvii; citing *Commentary on the Politics* 1.1: "If any man should be such that he is not a political being by nature, he is either wicked—as when this happens through the corruption of human nature—or he is better than man—in that he has a nature more perfect than that of other men in general, so that he is able to be sufficient to himself without the society of men, as were John the Baptist and St Anthony the hermit."

27. Aquinas, *Supplement to the Summa Theologiae*, trans. Fathers of the English Dominican Province (London: Burns Oates, 1920), 54.3.

28. Augustine *City of God* 15.16.

29. Leo XIII, *Rerum Novarum*, trans. Catholic Truth Society (London: CTS, 1983), par. 37.

30. Leo XIII, *Rerum Novarum,* par. 38.

31. *Catechism of the Catholic Church* (London: Chapman, 1994), par. 1882, citing *Mater et Magistra* 60.

32. *Catechism,* par. 1882.

33. *Catechism,* par. 1879.

34. *Catechism,* par. 1699.

35. *Catechism,* par. 1711.

36. *Catechism,* par. 1878.

37. K. Barth, *Church Dogmatics,* III/2, ed. G. Bromiley and T. F. Torrance, trans. H. Knight et al. (Edinburgh: T and T Clark, 1960), p. 243.

38. Cited in "Subsidiarity, Principle of," in *The New Dictionary of Catholic Social Thought,* ed. J. A. Dwyer and E. L. Montgomery (Collegeville, Minn.: Liturgical Press, 1994).

39. *Catechism,* par. 1183, citing *Centesimus Annus.*

40. *Catechism,* par. 1184.

41. H. Höpfl, editor's introduction to Luther, *On Secular Authority,* xiii.

42. Höpfl, introduction to Luther, *On Secular Authority,* xi.

43. *Barmen Declaration,* trans. D. S. Bax, *Journal of Theology for Southern Africa* 47 (1984): 1.1.

44. A. J. Torrance, introductory essay to *Christ, Justice, and Peace,* by E. Jüngel (Edinburgh: T and T Clark, 1992), p. xii.

45. For a treatment of subsidiarity in relation to the teaching authority of the church and for further references, see J. Mahoney, *The Making of Moral Theology* (Oxford: Oxford University Press, 1987), pp. 169–74.

46. E. Brunner, *The Divine Imperative,* trans. O. Wyon (London: Lutterworth Press, 1937), pp. 124–25.

47. Brunner, *The Divine Imperative,* p. 214.

48. Brunner, *The Divine Imperative,* p. 210.

49. Brunner, *The Divine Imperative,* p. 93.

50. For Barth see especially "Nein" in E. Brunner and K. Barth, *Natural Theology,* trans. P. Fraenkel (London: Centenary Press, 1946), pp. 65–128; and for Bonhoeffer, see *Ethics,* especially the section entitled "The Last Things and the Things before the Last."

51. Bonhoeffer, *Ethics,* p. 182.

52. *Catechism,* par. 1738.

53. John Paul II, *Evangelium Vitae,* English trans. (London: Catholic Truth Society, 1995), pars. 19 and 20.

54. O'Donovan, *The Desire of the Nations,* p. 255.

55. O'Donovan, *The Desire of the Nations,* p. 252.

56. O'Donovan, *The Desire of the Nations,* p. 254.

CHAPTER 7

Natural Law and Civil Society

Michael Pakaluk

NO DOUBT THERE IS *some* sort of connection between adherence to natural law theory and advocacy of civil society.[1] The Catholic Church, for example, which styles itself an interpreter of natural law, has long upheld the notion of *subsidiarity,* which seems to imply a rich notion of civil society. Aquinas[2] and Aristotle,[3] both natural law theorists in some sense, favored a conception of political society in which authority is shared among families, clans, guilds, fraternities, and religious associations. Yet it is unclear whether this connection is principled or merely accidental: How exactly is a certain conception of civil society implied by principles of natural law?

INGREDIENTS

The difficulty is compounded by the variety of conceptions of natural law. It is necessary to begin by fixing ideas. Let us stipulate that no theory may be properly called a "natural law theory" unless it holds all of the following three principles. First, there are objective moral principles, duties, claims, or rights that exist prior to, and are not dependent upon, human convention, choice, or positive law. Second, positive law is appropriately understood as consisting of precepts that bind in conscience and not merely on prudential grounds. Finally, positive law binds in conscience only to the extent that it incorporates, or mirrors, objective moral principles, requires or prohibits some matter not falling within the scope of objective moral principles, or does not *contravene* objective moral principles.[4]

Here is a simple example to illustrate the three basic building blocks of natural law theory. Every innocent human being has a right to life, that is, a right not to have his life deliberately taken by another; thus, laws against murder bind in conscience by mirroring the duties implied by this prior, objective right. Furthermore, if a public official commands that an innocent person be put to death, then his command has no binding force, that it has no force should be recognizable to all, and the command should be disregarded.

Thus far, natural law theory is a thesis about law, not about nature or naturalness: it could be endorsed by anyone who believed in objective moral principles of any sort. Moreover, natural law theory in this sense evidently implies no particular viewpoint on civil society. We get no clearer view of civil society if we give natural law theory more content by adopting the traditional way of stipulating the chief objective moral principles that are held to be prior to law. According to Aquinas, for example, the objective principles of morality form a hierarchy. Most basic are the twin precepts "love God above all" and "love your neighbor as yourself." The Ten Commandments are then said to follow from these two first principles. Various more refined and qualified precepts follow from the Ten Commandments, and so on. The precept that honor should be showed to all elderly persons by those who are younger, for example, follows from the commandment to honor one's mother and father.[5] Yet, clearly, even if we adopt this fuller theory, we are not bound to adopt any particular view on civil society.

If natural law theory is to have something interesting to say about civil society, we need a richer theory, one that takes a position on 'nature' as well as law. And indeed we do find a richer theory of this sort in the work of important natural law theorists, such as Aquinas, the Stoics,[6] Aristotle,[7] and the Scottish moralists.[8] We arrive at this richer theory by adding two more principles to the three we specified above. First, there are 'natures' in the world. A nature is what a thing is, its essential properties. These properties are typically dynamic potentials to act or be acted upon in various ways, given various conditions. Second, the natural world as a whole is, at least for the most part, an ordered system, marked by intelligibility, similarity of action across diverse domains, and goal-directedness.

If these assumptions are granted, then morality does not simply involve the identification of universal and abstract principles governing human actions alone; rather, it involves particular claims and duties that attach to particular things in virtue of what they are (the question of what is 'due' to a thing of that kind), or what they have effected (what is 'due' to an action of that sort). These entities may be considered either in themselves (e.g., what is 'due' to a human being, as such) or in relationship to others (e.g., whether food in short supply is 'due' more to a human being than to a dog). For instance, if we suppose that the sort of thing a human being is, is an animal with the capacity to know and to love (when these are suitably specified), then we might hold that what is 'due' to a human being, as such, is simply whatever helps it in its activities of knowing and loving. Again, if we suppose that, in human work, the worker's product is some sort of *actualization* of the worker and that this is an objective, metaphysical truth (as Aristotle[9] and Locke[10] held), then what is 'due' to the worker, in virtue of his having produced something, is that he have some degree of control over his product—that is, what is to be done with the work is something 'proper' to him to determine; the work is his 'property'. On the natural law viewpoint, this would be a claim he could rightfully press, prior to any convention, choice, or positive law, simply because of what productive work is. Again, and for similar reasons, when a man and woman conceive a child, the consequence is that what is 'due' the child is that he be cared for by the persons responsible for his existence, and what is 'due' the parents is that they be honored and obeyed by the child—claims that, again, would be prior to human convention, choice, or positive law.

It is easy to see that, on this view, associations or communities will typically have a certain internal coherence, autonomy, and independence because of various claims and duties, binding upon their members, that arise out of the relationships and activities constitutive of those associations or communities. We can therefore speak of any association as having its own 'law', formulated and administered by whichever person or persons has authority for that association, and the law of that association is appropriately based upon these claims and duties, and gets its force from them.

Furthermore, when one association is lower than, or a part of, another association, its autonomy and independence will not disappear, but only be modified—since those prior claims and duties do not disappear. Let us say that an association is lower than, or a part of, another if its purpose contributes to the ends of that other association. For instance, a philosophy department in a college is a constitutive part of the college, because the purpose of the department—namely, imparting a philosophical education and contributing to philosophical understanding—is a constitutive part of what is aimed at by the college, namely, imparting a liberal education and contributing to knowledge and understanding generally. The higher association would have authority to regulate the activity of the lower, by modifying and adapting it so that it fits into the whole, and to prevent abuses; also the higher should presumably assist the lower in its activities; yet the lower would have its own distinctive activity and function, which, again, would imply various claims and duties that would have force prior to any administrative decisions by, or laws of, the higher.

When a large number and variety of associations come together to form a higher association, we would expect various, overlapping hierarchical arrangements of associations to emerge. To stay with our academic example, the philosophy department in a modern research university is part of the college and part of the graduate school; it contributes to teaching and to research; its funds are derived from a common endowment and its own endowments, and so on. In this situation authority would properly be diffused among the various associations with ample scope allowed for discretion and prudential judgment by the authorities of those associations, in matters proper to those associations. The law of the whole would properly be conceived of as simply coordinating and regulating the quasi-autonomous activities of those associations. If political society is simply such a large association—as is typically held by natural law theorists—then it similarly should be marked by a wide dispersion of authority and a limited scope of law.

If we define 'civil society' to be simply political society, then, according to natural law theory in its richer version, civil society should have the sort of structure just described. If, however, by 'civil society' we mean those associations that *make up* political society, then natural law theory argues for the modified autonomy and independence of such associations. It holds that such autonomy and discretion are a matter of right. The force of the law of political society depends upon its recognition of the claims and duties constitutive of these associations, and the law of political society may, in some instances, lose its force if it contravenes these claims and duties.

Some further remarks about natural law reasoning are in order in this introductory section, since the natural law viewpoint concerning particular associations in civil society, especially the family, is not readily intelligible unless it is seen as arrived at through distinctive types of reasoning. Someone who operates with the idea that nature is what a thing essentially is and, further, that nature is an intelligible, teleological system, will reason about the world in certain way. It is this way of reasoning that sets natural law theorists apart as much as anything. We can distinguish seven characteristics of this mode of reasoning.

(i) *The complementarity of art and nature.* Human artifact and technology are to be regarded as properly complementary to nature, but incapable of supplanting it. This means that conventions or techniques that appear to subvert, undermine, or wholly replace nature will turn out to bring along with them bad consequences.

(ii) *Ideal type analysis.* Inherent in each sort of thing is an ideal of how that thing ought to be. Analysis of an object, therefore, involves the articulation of the ideal, and the arrangement of phenomena in relation to it.

(iii) *Analogy.* Nature follows principles that exhibit uniformity and constancy. In particular, nature will often act similarly across different domains; hence it can be useful to regard some structures in nature as 'standing for' or 'representing' others, insofar as the former display, perhaps more clearly, principles similar to those at work in the latter.

(iv) *Reciprocal systems:* it is characteristic of natural structures to contain elements that are mutually adapted to attain, by working together, some end that neither could attain through its own function.

(v) *Proximate versus remote motivation.* The motive cause at work in an element in such a system, then, will typically not be itself directed at the end attained by both, but rather at the particular function to be exercised by just that element; nonetheless, the system admits of the interpretation that it aims at that end.

(vi) *Unintended consequences.* In particular, living beings that act with some degree of volition or deliberateness, by acting according to natural motives, may work so as to bring about some good, perhaps for others as well as themselves, without intending it.

(vii) *Empathetic reasoning*. Human beings, because they are intelligent parts of nature, are capable of arriving at an understanding of what is good or bad for particular sorts of things, but especially for human beings, by a kind of intuition of what is ideally good for a being of that sort.

It would be easy enough to illustrate all of these topoi with examples from the writings of Adam Ferguson, or various Stoic moralists. It should be noted that such patterns of reasoning are not confined to natural law philosophy. They would seem, for instance, to be indispensable to poetry: it is difficult to say how poetry can arrive at truth, unless nature admits of being reasoned about in such ways. They seem inherent, too, in moralistic reasoning (e.g., Johnson's *Rambler* essays or the *Meditations* of Marcus Aurelius), and also, of course, in religious thought, which typically views nature as a kind of elaborate parable.

It is necessary to distinguish, then, between natural law reasoning, so characterized, and a *theory* of natural law. As I understand the matter, any time a father enjoins obedience on his child, on the grounds that "I'm your father," or a person employs a proverb that instructs on account of an implied analogy between human endeavor and the larger realm of nature, we are engaging in natural law reasoning. *Theories* of natural law are presumably to be judged according to how they account for the force of such reasoning.[11] It should be said that, historically, there have been various types of natural law theory, so understood. I have been sketching one that makes crucial use of ideas derived from Aristotle and is similar in spirit to Stoic and Thomistic conceptions. But the Scottish moralists devised another kind of theory, which appealed not to 'natures' as essences, but rather to the de facto 'natural constitution' of human emotional life.

All theories of natural law, however, maintain that at least the more fundamental claims of morality are discernible by the ordinary operation of human intelligence, without any support from a putative revelation or a specifically religious doctrine. If morality is something natural, and a human being is by nature equipped with intelligence, one would expect that this natural equipment would, in typical circumstances, be sufficient for the successful identification and completion of that activity which is, so to speak, required by nature for a thing of that kind. Yet this is not to say, of course, that a particular religion could not incorporate into its teachings this very affirmation. And in fact the Catholic Church has held that human reason is sufficient on its own for discerning, say, the bindingness of the basic content of the Ten Commandments upon all human beings. To be sure, it has held, furthermore, that the revelation it claims to have received makes it an authoritative judge and interpreter of the claims of reason in connection with morality, particularly in difficult cases. This claim, however, clearly requires a theological justification, which we cannot evaluate here.

Note that the distinction between natural law reasoning and theory, furnishes a response to the objection to natural law theory, namely, that few persons are professed adherents of it, for, it may be replied, everyone uses, and *must*, practically speaking, continue to use reasons that are best accounted for by natural law theory, and are not easily accounted for, if at all, by rival versions of moral theory.

Note too that a natural law theorist need not hold that agreement must be reached on the theoretical account of a pattern of reasoning for that reasoning to have force, any more than we all need to accept some schematization of logic in order to argue logically. A 'natural law framework' might very well constitute some shared frame of reference, then, even among persons who do not regard themselves as believers in 'natural law theory'. And that 'framework' might very well be promoted more by the earnest study of, say, Demosthenes or Shakespeare than by an examination of the philosophical soundness of Thomas Reid's system. But presumably there would be an advantage in studying such a good theory of natural law, insofar as this would make persons more disposed to look for bases of agreement that the theory predicts would exist, or insofar as the theory, as is to be expected, provided guidance as to the construction of arguments capable of winning consent from reasonable persons generally.

SOCIETY

We shall understand a 'society' to mean simply an association, as a music society is an association for the promotion of some aspect of music. Let us define an association as the coordinated activity of more than one person, by which each aims to achieve what he could not achieve at all, or could not easily achieve, if he were acting on his own. For instance, a chess association makes it easy for its members to play games regularly with others of roughly the same ability, even as they improve in skill, which is difficult to arrange apart from something like a chess association.

The members of an association may all be aiming to achieve the same thing numerically, or the same *kind* of thing, or different sorts of things altogether. All the members of the Library Building Committee aim at numerically the same thing, that is, the construction of the new library. All the members of a chess club aim at the same kind of thing, that is, mastery of chess. The parties to a trade partnership, however, typically aim at different sorts of things, that is, each wants to obtain from their association what the other can provide. But even when the members of an association aim to achieve different sorts of things, still there is some sense in which all are aiming at the same thing: in the business partnership, the contract that is adopted articulates an exchange that both parties regard as fair and equal, and all parties have the aim that the exchange take place as specified in the contract.

Given this definition of 'society', 'civil society' should be taken to indicate political society itself, together with all of those associations that are parts of, contained within, or under political society and its institutions of government. Subordinate associations include groups that are small enough in scale that members can come to know one another's character and aim to associate with a view to helping one another show good character, especially families, religious congregations, and neighborhoods.

It is typical of natural law theory in the richer sense to hold that civil society is something natural. If it is also assumed that nature inherently aims at good ends, it seems plausible to suppose that a kind of complete or polished human character is one of the things that is 'supposed' to result from civil society. On this view, civil society would be a failure if its members did not hold in common a sound conception of human excellence and aim to foster it in their various dealings with one another.[12]

We might ask what would make civil society more or less of a society, or more or less unified? There are a number of criteria supplied by natural law theorists. Does government work for the good of the governed, or for its own good? If it acts for its own good, then it is impossible for the government and governed to share the same end, and thus there is disunity of purpose. Do the types of action and types of association allowed by law foster some aspect of the human good, or are they at odds with it? If at odds, then citizens become incapable of appropriating or enjoying, by a kind of analogical reasoning, the actions of others. For example, it is impossible for a person of good character, buying a good book at a bookstore, to look upon a person of bad character, who buys pornography in an "adult" bookstore, as engaged in something analogous. Do families and small-scale associations succeed in knitting together the citizens of a nation through many and diverse bonds of affection, which are in turn capable of becoming generalized and widely applied, amounting to 'solidarity'? Without such bonds citizens lack a concern for the true good of others, and their association with one another takes on an instrumental character. Is there a rough parity of material well-being and education, so that citizens find it easy to regard one another as equal, and so that their material interests roughly coincide? Without this condition class conflict becomes inevitable.

It is conformable with the natural law view articulated here to hold that there is no general 'problem of unity and diversity' in society, and therefore no general solution; rather, the question of what are allowable, desirable, or necessary types of diversity will arise for each *sort* of association.

Thus, for example, the diversity needed for an orchestra is: strings, brass, woodwinds, percussion. A type of diversity perhaps desirable, but not necessary, would be: that different musicians in the orchestra received their training from different schools. A type of unity is necessary: competence and musicianship (bad notes cannot be tolerated). A type of unity that would be desirable but not necessary: say, that which comes from their having worked together over a large period with a single conductor of great skill.

It will be objected that such "solutions" are obvious and trivial. Quite so. The natural law theorist, I maintain, will wish to hold, somewhat in the manner of Wittgenstein, that 'the problem of unity and diversity' is to be dissolved, not solved, by the consideration of particular cases where it admits of a clear formulation and then mundane resolution. We might expect that if the force of mundane unity and diversity is rightly appreciated across various domains, no *additional* difficulty about them will remain, or, if it does, say, in some matter concerning citizenship and political participation, this would be more easily decided if seen as an extension, by analogy, of the mundane sort of case. The claim is that just as democracy (it is admitted) requires training and an established culture of democratic participation if it is to work well, so the common resolution of political disagreements as regards unity and diversity is a matter of the extension to the political of a faculty for discernment that needs to be developed by practice in and appreciation of more mundane cases.

VALUES

Let us recall the picture of a well-ordered society presented above. In such a society, people will spontaneously enter into a variety of associations with one another to achieve things that they could not achieve easily or at all working on their own. Each association will have its own autonomy, authority, power of discretion, and 'law'. When one association falls under another, the higher will play the role largely of regulating and coordinating. We can therefore ask the question, what would be lost if in a larger association those associations that were its parts were to disappear or be destroyed, and we were left simply with the large-scale association? What would be lost, for instance, if a university abolished its departments and attempted to carry out all the same activities, but from the highest level of administration? What would be lost if a baseball league abolished management of individual clubs and attempted to manage and develop clubs from a central administration? The question about civil society is of exactly the same sort: What would be lost if associations other than the government and its creatures were abolished and the activities that might otherwise be carried out by other groups were managed from a central administration? The list is long, but it should include:

(a) *Motives for action*. People do more eagerly, with greater pleasure and more persistently, what they themselves recognize needs to be done, and what they have taken the initiative to accomplish. The correct model of society, I have argued, is one in which people constantly exercise initiative in forming associations to respond to felt need, with 'government' entering in simply to regulate and assist these. In such an arrangement, each person will be, as it were, well stocked with powerful motives for action. Since happiness, the natural law viewpoint assumes, comes of fruitful activity on behalf others, such an arrangement is one in which people have the motivations required actually to be happy.

(b) *Self government*. It is better for persons—for their development and happiness—that they govern their own actions, rather than being governed by others. The quasi autonomy that associations in civil society should enjoy maximizes the government that people exercise over their own activities, since, again, each association has its own authority and is allowed scope for discretion.

(c) *Sense of a bond across time*. Typically, the felt needs that give rise to associations will recur in different generations. For example, the need for easily accessible books, in response to which citizens have formed libraries, will be felt anew by each generation of parents. Thus, those who form associations naturally come to see themselves as carrying out for the next generation what they received from the previous generation and perhaps took for granted. Insofar as they look backward with gratitude, they are bound to the previous generation by the virtue traditionally called 'piety'; and insofar as they look forward with responsibility, taking up the torch in turn, they acquire a kind of paternal solicitude for those who follow. To take on such a role gives significance to a person that transcends the merely local in place and time.

(d) *Love and friendship*. Let us assume that, as Aristotle remarks, "no one can be happy without friends."[13] Let us assume that a friendship consists of two or more persons, of their own accord, wishing for the other some good that is theirs to give because of a recognition of the goodness of the other. Friendship, then, requires that you have goods at your disposal, that you can give them to another of your own accord, that you are able to recognize the goodness of others, and that this in turn is capable of becoming a motive for action. Clearly, friendships can develop only in associations that are small scale (which allow familiarity with another's character). That is to say that friendship is more likely to develop in associations that are not minutely controlled by law, but rather depend upon discretion and the exercise of good traits of character (otherwise members cannot allot goods 'on their own accord').The relationships between persons in a small-scale, quasi-autonomous association are capable, then, of being friendships; those in larger-scale associations, or in an association insofar as it is a creature of a higher association, are not. Thus, civil society provides its members with ample opportunities for forming friendships and acting out of friendship.

(*e*) *Education and development of character.* This point can be developed in two ways: first, as a corollary of the preceding point: it seems correct to say that good character in human beings is fostered only through love and friendship. Typically we are moved to emulate someone's good characteristics only to the extent that we have affection for him; and we are moved to encourage someone to develop good character only to the extent that we love him and care whether he has good character. If this is so, then civil society is important because its various small-scale associations are so many incubators of good character. A second argument depends upon a perhaps controversial distinction between following rules and having good character. Let us assume that even if morality can in some sense be expressed as a set of prescriptions and proscriptions, still, good character consists in acting in such a way that these rules are, as it were, irrelevant or beside the point. For instance, someone who loved every other human being dearly would hardly have to regulate his actions by the principle "Do not murder." Again, it seems correct that the skills involved in the interpretation and following of legal codes do not amount to good character. We might say, rather, that good character consists in recognizing the goods that are at stake in a certain domain and pursuing them appropriately, while avoiding or repelling the contrary evils. It would follow, then, that people would develop good character only to the extent that they developed habits of recognizing and pursuing goods relevant to their domains of action. For instance, a teacher would acquire good character in teaching precisely by coming to recognize and to pursue with persistence the good involved in his students' acquiring a sound education—rather than, say, through attempting to observe meticulously some set of regulations devised by a controlling authority. If this is correct, then civil society would be important as amply providing the right circumstances in which good character is consistently elicited, tested, and therefore acquired.

What has been said so far applies to civil society as a whole. Yet, as I said, it is usual for proponents of the natural law viewpoint to pick out some elements of civil society—the family, neighborhood, and churches—as being especially important. On what grounds is this done?

Natural law theory looks upon the family—father, mother, their offspring, and perhaps other close blood relatives sharing a household—as a naturally motivated reciprocal system, with numerous unintended good consequences. It would be impossible here to follow out even the most obvious of these good consequences, or to begin to list the various societal evils that can be accounted for by reference to the widespread falling away, in our society, from the ideal of family association. Very generally, we may observe that, as regards the ideal type, the family secures in a particularly compelling way all the goods listed above that come through associations. The family provides forceful motives for action, and indeed most people will work hard only in order to please or provide for some family member. The family constitutes the realm in which a person is most free to order as he sees best matters that are of greatest importance for his happiness. Procreation is the activity par excellence by which a person transcends his particular place and time. Family bonds are among the best and most enduring friendships, especially that between husband and wife. The extreme love of parent for child is perhaps the best way to teach a child his worth, whereas the love of child for parent naturally results in imitation.

It is plausible that family bonds are the basis of all social affection and concern, an idea first articulated by Aristotle in his criticism of Plato's communism (in book 2 of Aristotle's *Politics*) and that in recent times has been developed by sociologists under the notion of 'stem families.'[14] The reason for this is perhaps the following. True social concern plausibly involves regarding the good of another as essentially bound up with one's own, so that you look upon your own good as at least in part *defined* by what is good for another. It is easy to see how social concern, once acquired, could be extended: for example, if I regard X's good as in part defining of my own, and X regards Y's good as in part defining of his good, then I should presumably regard Y's good too as in part defining of my own (think of the maxim "Friends of friends are friends"). But such extension requires a foothold: it is difficult to see how a person who in no way regarded his own good as defined by what is good for another could come to acquire such a concern. But what is particularly interesting about family relations, and in fact is distinctive of them, is that within a family, each person rightly regards his very existence as something relative to that of others: a child is *of these parents;* two brothers are *of the same parents;* and so on. This is arguably enough to provide the foothold. Any child is in a position to look upon any fellow citizen, 'raised and sheltered' by the same country or laws, as like a brother; a father is in a position to view any citizen as someone whose welfare is to be looked out for, as his own child; and so on. The claim is that an association involving dependence or reciprocation, but based on human convention or contract, is capable of being viewed by its members as defining in part the good of each, only if each has come habitually to regard in that way those who are so related to him by nature, and *that* regard is extended.

Finally, natural law theory will regard certain sorts of religious association (not all) as especially significant, on the grounds that such associations support the basic ideas underlying the correct conception of civil society. The religious associations that play such a role are those that foster belief in claims of conscience that are prior to human convention or positive law, the view that nature is expressive of God's purposes, and the notion that a person's life has worth depending upon how it is judged from God's point of view, not a human viewpoint. For instance, a Christian who holds that "we must obey God rather than man" will look for and acknowledge objective principles, claims, and duties not dependent on human conventions, while regarding all human authority and positive law as necessarily restricted. Someone who holds that nature is created by God will interpret nature in the teleological manner recommended by natural law theory. Finally, someone who judges the worth of his action from what he takes to be God's point of view, an "inner-directed" personality,[15] will likely show the initiative and responsibility that are necessary to found and participate in the self-regulated associations constitutive of well-ordered civil society.

Associations will understandably differ in the degree to which they encourage their members to recognize and endorse the more fundamental principles involved in a correct conception of civil society. The claim of natural law theory is that certain sorts of religious association, for example, Orthodox Jewish, Islamic, and Christian, are especially important to civil society because they involve the clear articulation of such principles, and help to provide justifications for these. In contrast, a bowling league, for instance, will provide little support of that kind.

RISKS

We should distinguish two sorts of risk. First, assuming that civil society is more or less well ordered, what are the bad things to which individuals, associations, or society as a whole are exposed, precisely in virtue of civil society's being arranged as described? Second, in what ways would a civil society of the sort described be itself at risk, that is, which forces either internal or external to civil society tend to weaken or undermine it, or otherwise work for its destruction?[16] We may identify four risks of the first sort.

(1) *Unjustified civil disobedience.* Clearly, natural law theory assigns great scope to the judgment and discretion of individuals, who, it claims, should regard themselves as not bound to observe the law or command of a superior that contravenes principles, claims, or duties that are in some sense based upon nature. It can do this without concern that it promotes anarchy, since it holds that there are objective goods and evils, and that the more significant of these are accessible to the human mind. Nonetheless, mistakes in this matter would surely be possible. Natural law theory would also hold that a person's ability correctly to discern objective principles, claims, and duties will typically depend upon his having some minimal degree of virtue—which provides another reason why virtue has to be fostered in a well-ordered society.

(2) *Failure.* It is impossible for someone to be allotted real responsibility for something without there being the risk of failure. A subsistence farmer can starve; a business venture can go bust; a parent can neglect to educate his children well. And, of course, failures of this sort tend to carry along with them suffering inflicted on others not themselves responsible for the failure. If the subsistence farmer, through miscalculation or laziness, starves, then so does his family. If an entrepreneur goes bankrupt, his employees lose their jobs. Risks of this sort can often be reduced by the action of a higher association, but by the nature of the case the risk cannot be eliminated; at best it can be hidden or transferred.

(3) *Poor judgment.* Clearly, people can make bad use of discretion in the exercise of their authority; for example, a dean given broad discretion in the dispersal of research grants can choose to favor his friends or professors with suitable political views. Employers may refuse to hire someone for eccentric reasons. The risk can be lessened by a general recognition of the importance of due process; however, as with failure, it cannot be eliminated.

(4) *Inefficiency.* A society in which authority is not highly centralized will in many circumstances be less efficient, especially in responding to external threats, as in time of war. Yet there seems to be no reason why the difficulty could not be anticipated in advance and largely corrected for by putting in place procedures for a rapid but transient mobilization, for example.

Risks of the second sort to civil society may be identified as follows.

(1) *Forces that promote the centralization and homogenization of authority.* Alexis de Tocqueville argues that democracies favor simple principles of government.[17] The subtleties of federalism, for instance, are hard to understand, institute, and follow over time. Furthermore, citizens in a democracy tend to be envious of subsidiary authorities, since these seem to be like aristocracies. Robert Nisbet has argued that an emphasis on individual rights in fact threatens freedom, since typically the rights of individuals are enforced by higher levels of authority against lower.[18] Federal courts vindicate rights of individuals by taking authority away from school boards and states. Rights of individual spouses are vindicated at a cost to the family as a whole and its children. Michael Oakeshott has written about a misguided 'rationalism' that cannot countenance any authority not expressive of some single, overarching principle.[19] Such rationalism is inherently at odds with the deference to custom and tradition that seem necessary for quasi-autonomous associations in civil society. Robert Bork has spoken of the "ratcheting" effect inherent in government: since it is rare for someone who acquires power voluntarily to divest himself of that power, changes that bring about centralization are not reversible.[20] The

question becomes only how long it will take for power to become central-ized, not whether it will. This "ratcheting" is often accelerated by histori-cal accidents such as the Great Depression and World War II, which brought about much more centralization of governmental authority in the United States.

(2) *Legalism,* or the mistaken supposition that rights are created or en-dowed through acts of law. It is commonly thought today in the United States that human rights are somehow bestowed by the Bill of Rights. But what is bestowed by statute may be revoked by statute.

(3) *Misguided benevolence.* Utilitarian conceptions of morality, which are based upon some abstract principle of general benevolence, seem most congruent with government by a centralized administration in the service of social welfare. Again, it is common to argue, fallaciously, that if each per-son has a 'right' to some good or service, in the sense that this is 'due' to him as a human being (e.g., health care), this good or service should be supplied to everyone through the direct efforts of government at the high-est level (thus, a single-payer federal health plan). Again, in a system of gov-ernment that attempts, as much as possible, to be morally neutral, it will in practice be impossible for its efforts of relief not to work as an *incentive,* encouraging precisely the evil they were intended to relieve.

(4) *Passivity.* The receipt of assistance by a lower level association from a higher creates the expectation of further assistance, which leads to de-pendence and loss of autonomy. It is typical for those who receive assis-tance to view this receipt as in some way "shameful." As if to compensate or rationalize, it is imagined that the assistance comes merely in response to some 'right' to receive assistance (an 'entitlement'). Once the assistance is regarded as something to which one has a right, however, it appears an injustice not to receive the assistance. The result is that the idea that a per-son receiving an 'entitlement' should instead work to advance his own in-terests appears to be a counsel of injustice.

(5) *Individualism.* Tocqueville refers to the perversion of family life and life among intimate friends, whereby these relations are regarded simply as sources of private gratification, with the result that a person removes him-self from public life or regards himself as in no way bound to advance the public good.[21] Tocqueville explains this individualism as a consequence of egalitarianism, but clearly there can be other causes.

(6) *Loss of virtue.* If citizens lack virtue, it becomes difficult to preserve public peace without the use of severe constraints, penalties, and threats by government (e.g., metal detectors in the entrances of public schools). Law inevitably becomes constructed on the grounds that the typical subject is a lawbreaker or potential lawbreaker. The average citizen, then, becomes no longer worthy of trust. Citizens can have little confidence in the un-monitored behavior of their fellow citizens. Thus, the leeway and discre-tion required for civil society become difficult to maintain.

RESPONSIBILITY

Responsibility is a vast topic; it has to a great extent been touched upon already, but the general principles involved in the natural law viewpoint may be set forth as follows.

Responsibility for aiming at *happiness* belongs to two associations in particular, the family and the political association, because only these coordinate all goods relevant to happiness. The family does this by furnishing such goods directly to individuals, whereas the political association should do so only indirectly. Thus, those principally responsible for the welfare of a particular person are his relatives. Political association should care for individuals by supporting families of which the individuals are members, and by creating the conditions under which strong families can flourish.

In general, responsibility should be shared in accordance with the principle of subsidiarity, which is that those matters that *can* be overseen and taken care of by a smaller association *should* be. Subsidiarity implies that a higher association should not intervene in the activity of a lower without serious cause, that interventions, when necessary, should not undermine the functioning of the lower, or cause it to become dependent on the higher, that such intervention or assistance should therefore be temporary and calculated to restore the autonomy of the lower, and that finally, a lower association should not seek assistance from a higher in matters that it can accomplish on its own.

We may regard violations of this principle as types of injustice, on the grounds that the best goods available to human beings are in fact good actions, and that good actions belong to a person most fully when initiated by him and sought through the exercise of his own good judgment. Thus, the unnecessary intervention of a higher association in the affairs of a lower is akin to the *theft* of these goods, by the higher from the lower. Again, a lower association's becoming dependent upon a higher indicates a kind of *greediness* or graspingness on the part of the higher.

It is not unusual, of course, for power to be used to accomplish injustice; but the injustice involved in violations of subsidiarity is particularly insidious, because typically it takes place through intentions that have morally impeccable credentials, for example, relief of the poor, help of the distressed, and so on.

FREEDOM

The principle of subsidiarity can be applied to individuals as well as to groups. We should hold that any association of which an individual is a member should not, as an association, intervene in the individual's carrying out of functions that have reasonably been assumed by him, without good cause. If intervention is necessary, then it should be transient, not undermining the authority an individual has in his domain, and it should be calculated to help him continue carrying out his tasks on his own. The individual, correspondingly, should act from personal initiative and not expect that others, or the association, carry out what he can well enough carry out on his own.

Note that this way of stating the relationship between individual autonomy and group authority assumes that an individual is already inserted in a group, and his 'autonomy' consists in his carrying out appropriately his role or task in the group. On the natural law viewpoint, this is the correct way of conceiving of the matter: the autonomous individual, setting a law for himself in isolation from particular communities to which he belongs, is a philosopher's fiction. That "a human being is by nature social" implies that autonomy is to be understood simply as the freedom to operate with discretion and authority in matters falling within one's own domain, and cooperatively with others. On the natural law viewpoint, this is the only thing that 'individual autonomy' could mean; no other coherent notion is available.

On this point of view, there can be no question of settling in advance, by some general criterion, the 'appropriate balance' between individual autonomy and group constraints. The thing must be decided on a case-by-case basis, by those most involved, with reference to the limitations and abilities of particular persons. For instance, how much discretion should a professor be allowed in a philosophy program to determine the content and textbooks for his courses? There is of course no a priori appropriate answer: everything depends upon the abilities of the professor, the nature of his training, the purposes of the program of which he is a member, and so on. Sometimes of course the expectations of the individual diverge from those of the association; sometimes the expectations of the association are not clearly articulated, and disputes arise because of misunderstandings; sometimes rules or procedures appear onerous to someone but in fact are not so, and the person feels burdened by them because he lacks good character or has a bad outlook. But these are practical difficulties, involving no matter of philosophical principle.

Similarly, on this viewpoint, freedom is not incompatible with submission or obedience to the law of an association, but rather requires it. Let us define freedom as doing of one's own accord what one wishes. But, on the natural law viewpoint, we wish for what we regard as good for us. Thus, freedom would amount to doing of one's own accord what one regards as one's good. Yet it is possible to be mistaken as to what is good for oneself. Thus, freedom requires being correct about what things are good for oneself. If associations exist to procure what cannot be procured easily or at all by its members working on their own, and what they procure is in fact good for the members, then if this is recognized and pursued on those grounds, the activity that results will be freedom in the sense defined—that is, assuming it is done by each 'of his own accord'. But that is precisely what subsidiarity is meant to maximize, with its standard that what can be done by a lower level of association (i.e., 'of its own accord') should be.

Further Reading

Aristotle's *Politics*, books 1 and 2, is the classic statement of civil society as built up from the family and "voluntary associations." His discussion of how a society thus constituted results in bonds of friendship among citizens is found in *Nicomachean Ethics* 8.9–12. For a detailed examination of this text, see Michael Pakaluk, *Nicomachean Ethics Books VIII and IX: Translation with Commentary* (Oxford: Clarendon Press, 1998). The important modern discussion of these themes is to be found in Peter L. Berger and Richard John Neuhaus, *To Empower People*, 2d ed. (Washington, D.C.: AEI Press, 1996), which contains several useful essays by other authors reflecting on the Berger-Neuhaus thesis on the twentieth anniversary of the publication of the title essay. A brief but sufficient discussion of the notion of subsidiarity may be found in the new *Catechism of the Catholic Church*, paragraphs 1878–85.

Notes

1. Richard John Neuhaus, for example, a proponent of the natural law, is famously the author, with Peter Berger, of an influential recent essay on civil society, "To Empower People." Peter L. Berger and Richard John Neuhaus, *To Empower People*, 2d ed. (Washington, D.C.: AEI Press, 1996).

2. John Finnis, *Aquinas* (Oxford: Oxford University Press, 1998).

3. *Politics* 1.1–7.

4. As regards this last requirement, presumably some qualifications are necessary: it seems plausible to say that law ceases to bind in conscience only if it contravenes an 'important' principle, duty, etc.; also, it can be disputed whether 'contravention' *must* take the form of the law's commanding something prohibited by some principle, duty, etc., or whether in some cases the law's simply failing to prohibit something that *should* be prohibited counts as contravention.

5. Thomas Aquinas, *Summa Theologiae* 2a2ae, qq. 94–100.

6. Cf. Cicero, *De Respublica*.

7. Cf. *Nicomachean Ethics* 5.

8. Cf. Louis Schneider, ed., *The Scottish Moralists* (Chicago: University of Chicago Press, 1967).

9. *Nicomachean Ethics* 9.7, 1167b34–1168a9.

10. John Locke, *Second Treatise on Government*, chap. 5.

11. This is admittedly a bit oversimplified, since it is not correct to suggest that there is any antecedently agreed upon body of evidence, which it is thought such theories should account for. Indeed, it is a fault of some theories of natural law—namely, modern versions that are intent principally on accounting for claims based on 'human rights'—that they are too narrow in their explanatory aims.

12. This conception, perhaps, could itself admit of variation, at least through differences in emphasis; e.g., it might be held that the ideal of refinement characteristic of Confucian culture and that characteristic of households of the sort portrayed by Jane Austen were substantially the same, but different in *emphasis* and *arrangement*.

13. *Nicomachean Ethics* 9.9.

14. *La famille souche* of Frederick LePlay, cited in Robert Nisbet, *The Twilight of Authority* (New York: Oxford University Press, 1975), pp. 252–60.

15. David Riesman, *The Lonely Crowd* (New Haven: Yale University Press, 1950).

16. It should be noted that we hardly need to rely on natural law theory to answer these questions, since the risks of both sorts will for the most part be obvious; however, our results will nonetheless express a 'natural law viewpoint', in the sense that the risks we identify will be those that affect civil society in the form that it should ideally take according to natural law theory.

17. Alexis de Tocqueville, *Democracy in America*, 2.26.

18. Robert Nisbet, *Conservatism: Dream and Reality* (Minneapolis: University of Minnesota Press, 1986).

19. Michael Oakeshott, *Rationalism in Politics* (New York: Basic Books, 1962).

20. Robert Bork, *The Tempting of America* (New York: Free Press, 1989).

21. Alexis de Tocqueville, *Democracy in America*, 2.27.

PART IV

CHAPTER 8

The Jewish Tradition and Civil Society

Suzanne Last Stone

THERE IS NO term for, much less a theory of, civil society in classical Jewish texts.[1] Rabbinic writers do not produce theories; they produce commentaries on a biblical or talmudic text, codes of law, and legal responsa. These sources, moreover, are extremely diverse, covering over two millenniums of history, and were for the most part generated in premodern exile, when Jews lacked a state of their own; lived in compact, internally autonomous, and religiously homogenous communities scattered across continents; and were segregated from general society legally, politically, and socially. Without a state of their own, and with little sense of belonging to the host states in which they live, rabbinic writers do not discuss the role of society in relation to the state. So, the Jewish tradition has little to contribute to the civil society/state debate. If one understands civil society, instead, as "an ethical vision of social life,"[2] concerned with the conditions for establishing bonds of social solidarity between diverse members of society and shaping rights of association to promote such bonds, then Judaism has much to contribute to the discussion.

The topic of forging and maintaining overlapping bonds of social solidarity not only among the community of Jews but also in a pluralistic social world appears throughout Jewish literature, beginning with the biblical portrayal of the terms and conditions of Israelite associational life with other groups living in the biblical polity. This discussion is continued in rabbinic sources that reconstruct Israel's biblical past and messianic future, although without reference to any actually existing Jewish polity. The rabbinic tradition developed a theory of what constitutes not a "civil society" but, rather, a "civilized society." The Jewish tradition thus offers its own ethical perspective on the criteria necessary to establish trust, bonds of social solidarity, and duties of association in a pluralistic world, which I shall describe in the first part of this chapter.

Whether this particular ethical vision of social life can be applied meaningfully today is a difficult and pertinent question. Although the traditional rabbinic division of time views all history between the destruction of the Temple in the first century and its hoped-for rebuilding in the messianic age as an undifferentiated time of exile, modernity fundamentally altered the background conditions to which the classical sources respond. The extension of civil society itself to include Jews raises new questions about the terms of such inclusion. What rights of association do Jews require in order to thrive in a manner continuous with the Jewish tradition, and what does the rabbinic tradition say about the participation of Jews in the pluralistic, associational life of the nation? Moreover, the changes wrought by the "Jewish emancipation and self-emancipation"[3]—the breakup of homogeneous religious communities, the rise of secularism, and the consequent fragmentation of Jewish society—raise new questions for the rabbinic tradition about intragroup associational life itself. The most dramatic change is the creation of the state of Israel. Several Jewish intellectuals view the construction of a "Jewish" theory of civil society, one capable of encompassing the diverse groups, both Jewish and non-Jewish, that constitute Israeli society, as an urgent need—even though they are not at all sure how to connect such a theory to the rabbinic sources.

There are no developed answers to these questions. The rabbinic process is one of gradual adaptation, the search for legal responses to new problems through the slow accretion of consensus, and the use of the traditional talmudic categories developed in the earliest centuries. With respect to Israel, in particular, historical events have far preceded rabbinic legal development. So, in addressing these questions in the second part of this chapter, I shall speculate as much as report.

THE IDEAL JEWISH SOCIAL ORDER

Ingredients, Society

The Bible begins with the story of the creation of humans in God's image, endowing humanity with special worth and dignity. This idea embodies an ethical ideal of social harmony among humans, one that the prophets envision as the goal of the end of days. Humanity is not intended to be a universal human order, however, nor "one fellowship and societie," as Locke wrote.[4] Nor are humans made a community by any common enjoyment of natural rights. The lesson of the biblical story of the Tower of Babel is that a universal human order is potentially dangerous. Instead, humanity is divided into unique collectivities, each with its own language and laws, and each capable of attaining independent moral significance.

The biblical election of Israel at Sinai creates an immediate division within humanity between Israel and the other nations of the world. The community or nation of Israel comes into being through the covenant, a historical social contract between God and Israel at Sinai (described in most rabbinic sources as grounded in consent), which establishes the Torah as the law of the Israelites. What gives Israelite society its identity, without which it would cease to be a society or would become a different one, is the law. The Torah, the written and oral law given at Sinai, is the particu-

lar inheritance of Israel, and only Israel is bound by the 613 commandments contained in it. The law is permanent and binding on all future generations of Jews, because God included in the covenant all who stood at
Sinai and those who are "not here with us this day" (Deut. 29:14). As an
original member of the covenant, each Jew continues to be obligated to
perform the law even if he or she disassociates from the community. Although the concept of chosenness is sometimes linked, especially among
mystical thinkers, to the idea of a distinctive Jewish soul, for most chosenness is a societal concept, referring to the national community's obligation
to become a religious community by observing the law.

The unity of Jewish society derives from a common subjection of all its
constituent parts—political organs, the family, and the individual—to the
exclusive authority of the law. All aspects of life are governed by the law,
including private individual conduct, private family relations, social relations, and market activity. The organs that wield coercive power are similarly parts of the community that the law addresses. The monarch does not
exemplify divine law. He is essentially a magistrate who applies the law in
concrete circumstances such as in conditions of war, just as the judges apply
the law to concrete cases.

Nor is the individual a distinct unit possessed of individual rights that
separate him from other individuals and society itself. Covenantal obligations are imposed on the individual not as a singular human being but,
rather, as a member of the community. One cannot ignore one's obligations without endangering others. This is the meaning of the talmudic legal
principle that "all Jews are responsible [literally, sureties] for one another."[5]
Each Jew is held accountable for the preventable transgressions of another
and is responsible for the other's fulfillment of the commandments. Ritva
glosses this further: "All Jews are responsible for one another. They are like
[parts of] one body and like a guarantor who repays the debt of a friend."[6]
Such a system may, and does, respect individual rights of personhood and
property, but it cannot confer on its members the kind of freedom or autonomy presupposed by civil society. In the Jewish conception, the individual is neither sovereign over his or her own life and experience nor a
fully independent source of moral values. Freedom is not defined in terms
of subjective rights or the choice of one's aims and desires. Freedom means
individual accountability, the free will to obey or disobey the law.

Judaism thus lacks the building blocks, drawn largely from Christian
conceptions of society and the individual and the experience of European
Christendom, that gave rise to the idea of civil society in the West.[7] Given
the comprehensiveness of the law, Judaism could not develop a picture of
society as independent of its political organization, as did the Church; nor
a concept of independent realms of experience, separate domains such as
the household, the state, the economy, and society itself, each arranged ac-

cording to its own logic or laws; nor even a sharp distinction between public and private spheres. Nor could it develop a notion of the individual as an equal moral agent possessed of rights that separate him from society as a whole.

Civil society, it is worth underscoring, is a historical and culturally specific model, an outgrowth of and corrective to the Western tradition of individualism. The problem that the idea of civil society first sought to solve, how to synthesize individualism with community, cannot arise in a tradition that views the individual as heteronomous, not autonomous, and as located firmly in a particularist community. Nor does the ancillary problem that the idea of civil society seeks to solve, the development of a society strong enough to resist state hegemony and the concentration of power in the state, arise. Because power belongs properly to God, in the Jewish tradition power is dispersed throughout society. The law places limits on the accumulation of property and land, equalizing material resources, and on the accumulation of power by the monarchy or other coercive institutions. The Jewish tradition offers, then, precisely the kind of historical model that should be contrasted to civil society: what Ernest Gellner has called the "segmentary community which avoids central tyranny by firmly turning the individual into an integral part of the social sub-unit."[8] The individual is protected from central dictatorship but is subject instead to the dictatorship of friends and neighbors, for "the collective responsibility of members of the covenant invites mutual surveillance and pressure to conform to divine norms, as oppressive to the individual as any tyranny."[9]

The Jewish tradition provides not only an alternative historical option to civil society, but also an alternative ethical model of how associational life should be structured and concretized in a pluralistic society. The rabbinic vision reaches beyond the Jewish social structure. It contemplates a world populated by morally corrupt societies, on the one hand, and civilized societies, on the other—societies that adhere to the moral order given by God to humanity, according to the biblical account, prior to the Sinaitic election. The rabbinic tradition codifies this order as consisting of seven basic human obligations: to refrain from idolatry, blasphemy, homicide, incest and adultery, robbery, and eating the flesh of a live creature, and to establish a system of justice.[10] The nations of the world thus also potentially constitute societies of moral significance whose basic purpose is to establish justice in the social sphere; they are not merely aggregates of individuals. Only those who do not adhere to the (Jewish) universal moral code are not members of a true society. They live, instead, in a state of moral chaos.

So, there are other societies that overlap the covenantal one. The rabbinic tradition stipulates criteria, quite different from those proposed by other political traditions represented in this volume, for adjudicating which associations in a pluralistic society should be supported and which should not, which associations are mandatory and which impermissible. Communal bonds, social proximity, political and material dependence, and moral character determine the level of social solidarity owed to society's diverse members.[11]

I begin with the covenantal community, in which the strongest bonds of social solidarity are owed. Covenantal fellowship, unlike the friendship of citizens in the liberal state, is not voluntary. The law imposes a duty to associate with other covenantal members. It is not only that many legal obligations, from the cultic to the mundane, can only be performed within a group setting. Rather, as Maimonides summarizes, "one who diverges from communal paths, even if he commits no transgression but merely separates himself from the congregation of Israel, and does not participate in their sorrows, loses his share in the world to come."[12] The social solidarity that the law stipulates for covenantal fellows is regulated by two interrelated principles: to "love one's neighbor as oneself" (Lev. 19:18) and to "hate" evildoers (Psalms 139:21). The tradition is less concerned with the problem of commanding the emotions of love and hate and more concerned with concretizing these obligations in specific acts, such as visiting the sick, comforting mourners, and assisting in burials,[13] and with "interpreting and restricting the object of love" and hate.[14] Some acts of benevolence are so extraordinary that they are obligatory only among covenantal fellows: extending interest-free loans, redeeming captives, sabbatical cancellation of debts, just-pricing, rebuking fellows to prevent transgression, and special forms of charity. Certain objects of love cannot be subsumed under the general category of reciprocal love. It is not sufficient to love the unfortunate reciprocally, as one loves oneself; they require special protection.[15] Similarly, specific provisions are made for those one may view with hostility. The biblical ideal of a social bond among all Israelites assumes that social relations are a site not only of natural amity and affection but also of personal jealousy and conflict. The concrete obligations of fellowship extend to personal enemies.[16]

It is forbidden to extend social solidarity and assistance to the undeserving, however, for to do so implies a failure to employ critical judgment. In a society defined by common allegiance to the law, the undeserving are rebellious sinners, heretics, and apostates, who show through their actions that they reject the authority of the law.[17] Such rebellious sinners are no longer "fellows" to whom mutual social obligations are owed, and they no longer enjoy rights of association with covenantal members. Social contact with them is forbidden, they are neither mourned nor eulogized, and intermarriage with them is forbidden. The wish to preserve the historic community, which overlapped with the religious community, no doubt accounted for increasingly narrow definitions of what

constitutes deliberate defiance of the law and thus abdication of community membership.[18] But the core concept remained and was enforced.
Thus, one may be a Jew for purposes of incurring an obligation to God
to observe the law, yet not a Jew for purposes of asserting rights of fellowship.[19] The status of covenantal fellow turns on conduct, and not as-
cription, a concept that plays a critical role in defining who is included in
Jewish society, one that has assumed critical significance in modern conditions of Jewish social fragmentation.

An additional model of social solidarity overlapping the covenantal is
provided by the biblical portrayal of the associational life that Israelites
share with non-Israelites residing in the polity. The biblical concept of social solidarity among diverse ethnic members of the polity bears a resemblance to the fellowship of citizens in the modern nation. The Bible speaks
of three types potentially within the polity: the heathen, the stranger, and
the resident stranger. The heathen is an idolater who is not to associate with
Israelites. Idolatry is not only an absolute falsehood; it is linked in biblical
thought with moral corruption. The Bible repeatedly commands the community to rid the territory of idolatry and idolaters—pagan and Israel alike.

In contrast, Israelites are enjoined in the Bible to love the stranger as
oneself (Lev. 19:33–34), to provide one law for the stranger and the Israelite alike (Exod. 12–49), and to provide the stranger with food, cloth-
ing, and agricultural charity (Lev. 23:22; Deut. 24:19). The Hebrew word
stranger, *ger*, connotes both foreignness and residence. In its original biblical setting, the stranger is an individual of non-Jewish birth living in the
land in close proximity with Jews, who accepts Jewish political authority,
and obeys some, though not all, of the covenantal law. The social solidarity that Israelites owe to the stranger is ascribed specifically to the stranger's
material and political dependence. The stranger does not have an allotted
portion of the land and is therefore associated with the Levite, the widow,
and the orphan (Deut. 10:17–18), to whom special consideration must be
shown. The Bible also appeals to history to ground the obligations of social solidarity owed to those who are politically dependent on others. Israelites, too, were once strangers in Egypt (Deut. 10–19).

This sense of social obligation, rooted in political and material dependence and in social proximity, is muted in the rabbinic reworking of the
biblical model. The biblical stranger was gradually assimilated into the covenantal community and reconceived as a convert, who became a full member of the covenant upon assuming the obligations of the law. The rabbinic
tradition equates the biblical stranger with the resident stranger, which it
identifies as a non-Jew who formally accepts the Noahide laws as a condition of living in the land.[20] Social solidarity owed to those who are dependent and proximate is replaced by a more abstract ethical commitment
to those who accept the Jewish teaching of justice and morality.

The category of resident stranger had no practical application in exile. The early talmudic discussion of the obligations owed by Jews to non-Jews with whom they lived assumes that non-Jews are pagan idolaters and erects encumbrances against any association with them. The Talmud also discriminates against non-Jews with respect to juridical rights and obligations. Whether the legal inequality of non-Jews posited in the Talmud is based on their status as idolaters or, rather, reflects the mutual alienation between Jews and non-Jews or even a perception of an ontological division between the two groups is unclear.[21] Even in the talmudic period, however, the differential rules were sometimes held inapplicable, not because non-Jews were analogized to "strangers" but, rather, because other halakhic principles intervened. The principle of *darkhei shalom,* pursuing paths of peace in social life, was often invoked as a legal basis for supporting the pagan poor, visiting the sick of both groups, and burying their dead with Jews.[22] This principle reasserts the importance of extending social solidarity to those with whom one lives in close proximity.

In the medieval period, rabbinic jurists began to apply the concept of Noahides to Moslems and Christians. Menahem Ha-Me'iri, a thirteenth-century French decisor, presented an original synthesis of the entire talmudic system of discriminatory rules and exceptions, essentially rendering most obsolete. He held that juridical discrimination against non-Jews refers to non-Jewish idolaters who lived in the culture of the ancient world, who "were not bound by proper customs," and not to the people of the medieval era, who are disciplined by enlightened religion.[23] The latter are owed full charitable, legal, and ethical reciprocity.[24] Ha-Me'iri's formulation is of particular importance for two reasons. Although other jurists reached similar legal conclusions, they did so through the traditional talmudic, casuistic method and confined their rulings to the practical needs of the community. Ha-Me'iri, as Jacob Katz points out, formulated his distinction between the two periods as a "principle," and thus "transcended the conventional methods of halakhic thinking."[25] Moreover, although Ha-Me'iri compares religiously enlightened non-Jews to resident strangers who observe Noahide law, he does not equate them. Rather, Ha-Me'iri creates a new intermediate category between paganism and Judaism. This category consists of "nations that are restricted by the ways of religion." Societies that fear God are lawful, disciplined societies. As Moshe Halbertal points out, Ha-Me'iri emphasizes the functional aspect of all religions in creating a well-ordered society.[26] As Katz earlier suggested, Ha-Me'iri had in mind all societies that maintain legal institutions and enforce moral standards in society.[27]

The system of social solidarity that Judaism proposes is the product of its peculiar blend of particularism and universalism. Minimal obligations are owed to all humanity. Social solidarity is owed to civilized societies who adhere to universal criteria of morality. The deepest bonds of solidarity are reserved for covenantal fellows. "To renounce this distinction," as Gordon Lafer writes, "is not to extend the intimacy and commitment of communal relations to the world at large, but rather to reduce even familial and communal bonds to the level of our relations with strangers."[28]

Values, Responsibility

Maimonides identifies the command to love one's fellow and its corollary, to love the stranger, as the second cardinal principle of the Torah. For Maimonides, social solidarity is not a good in itself; it is linked to the first principle, love of God. It is through love of God that one comes to understand that social solidarity is based not on self-interest but, rather, on reciprocity, that those who obey the different sets of duties God has charged them with are "normatively interchangeable" in the eyes of God.[29]

In contrast to the Christian tradition, Judaism does not view sociality and solidarity as grounded in human nature. Human nature, in the traditional Jewish viewpoint, is too fragile a basis for ordering political, legal, and ethical obligations, for humanity is capable of moral corruption. Social bonds are a product of culture, of law. They are created and molded by the concrete obligations imposed by the law, mandating some associations and forbidding others. The legal principles regulating associational life are thus part and parcel of the larger purpose of the law: in biblical terminology, to mold a holy nation; in the philosophic language of Maimonides, to provide for the well-being of the community. In the Bible, holiness is defined as separation, both physical separation of Israelites from idolaters and social separation from general society. Such separation is designed to preserve cultural distinctiveness and prevent the infiltration of foreign norms. As Jacob Katz notes, even Ha-Me'iri refused to suspend various segregative laws that served to separate Jews from non-Jews.[30] The obligation to show social solidarity with all civilized societies cannot efface the biblical plan to create a unique national collectivity.

For Maimonides, the fellowship created by the social commandment assures general human well-being. The law does not take into account individual interests, however, as the individual is not a sufficient judge of his own well-being. Nor need individuals agree about the general justness of the law. A divine law addresses objective human well-being. Human well-being consists in the well-being of the body, that is, the human need for physical security and material sustenance. But human well-being consists, more importantly, of the creation of conditions that allow persons to perfect their moral character and their intellect. These laws are not only cultic. They include the obligation of fathers to educate their children, the obligation of children to care for parents, economic restrictions on maximizing profits designed to protect weaker parties and redistribute resources according to need, and the like. In short, the law is responsible for assuring human well-being, and it is the law that determines who is to do what.

Responsibility for performing the law and thus providing for the well-being of oneself and others rests on each individual community member in the first instance. The social organization of Judaism, which includes extensive education of children and adults as well as periodic public recitation of the law, is designed to promote self-governance, to enable persons to perform the law themselves. The pedagogic form in which the law is cast invites willing adherence to the law, although coercive institutions are also provided. But there is a marked tendency to devalue coercion. Many laws, particularly those that involve no public act, entail no public sanction. Even major criminal offenses are often unpunished by human authorities, as a result of the well-known biblical procedural rules that make conviction unlikely.

The principal function of judges (later, rabbinic authorities) is to determine the law that the individual community member is obliged to perform. In contrast to the natural law tradition, which posits that humans can discern their obligations through reason, or the Confucian tradition, which combines affective and cognitive modes of knowing one's obligations, in Judaism, the innate moral capacities of humans are developed within the context of revelation, the source of genuine moral knowledge. The law itself specifies the good, while human reason is employed to interpret the law so that its moral and ethical import is realized. The law is assumed to contain the principles for its own elaboration, serving as a broad mandate for judicial legislation and interpretation, including extending or adding to its provisions and restricting or annulling others.

Conspicuously absent from the biblical model is any assignment of responsibility for human well-being to private or communal associations. Communal associations first emerged in the talmudic period. According to the Talmud, the "townspeople," a legally recognized partnership, provided for local public needs, such as synagogues, schools, ritual baths, and police protection.[31] They also acted as labor unions, with the right to fix weights and measures, prices and wages.[32] The medieval *kehillot,* lay representative associations that legislated for the public good, were viewed as extensions of this talmudic model. The communal associations had the right to tax and to subject individuals within their geographic jurisdiction to their authority, subject to rabbinic review, a right medieval jurists justified as grounded in the consent of their membership.[33] They also became the vehicle for fulfilling various fellowship obligations, such as dispensing charity and redeeming captives. It is unclear whether the communal associations are properly classified as mediating institutions or political institutions. In a society without a state, the distinction is, needless to say, elusive. Genuinely private voluntary associations, organized for religious, charitable, educational, and occupational purposes, proliferated in the late-medieval period.[34] But these associations were not endowed with any legal or theoretical importance. From the tradition's perspective, these associations were the natural consequence of the law's social orientation.

POST-ENLIGHTENMENT JUDAISM AND CONTEMPORARY PLURALISM

Risks, Freedom

I have already suggested that the Jewish tradition has few resources from which to build a modern, liberal conception of civil society. Indeed, from the rabbinic perspective, liberal civil society, defined as a realm of voluntary association and free entry and exit, is the problem of modern Jewish existence because it liberates individuals from the group, enabling them to discard traditional forms of life, express their identity in nontraditional terms, or put aside the question of identity altogether. Liberal civil society encourages sectarian divisions to multiply and overlapping associations to proliferate, and interprets this fragmentation as benign because "plural memberships and divided loyalties make for toleration."[35]

The main risk that the rabbinic vision of associational life poses for its members in contemporary conditions of freedom is self-isolation and estrangement, both from general society and from nonconforming Jews. This isolation, although often seen by members as an intensification of the principle of holiness as separation embodied in the remnant of the faithful, is an abdication of rabbinic Judaism's historic role of assuring the survival of the religio-national community. In order for rabbinic Judaism to play a positive role in the drama of Jewish life, especially in Israel, it needs to develop a mode or theory of associational life in an ethically pluralistic society existing under modern conditions of freedom and equality—a new synthesis akin to that developed by Ha-Me'iri in the medieval period. No such theory has yet emerged. Instead, rabbinic authorities resort to casuistic reasoning, cast in a language that is, at best, strange to modern eyes, which has been only partially successful in accomplishing this goal.

The critical questions of associational life in Israel concern the place of secular Jews and non-Jews in a Jewish polity and the role of religious legislation. Rabbinic discussion of these issues sheds some light on what form of civil society the Jewish tradition could, at least, support or tolerate in a modern Jewish state.

Given the traditional definition of Jewish society as excluding deviants, including public desecrators of the Sabbath, the question arises whether secular Jews are, from the rabbinic perspective, within Jewish society. This question arose immediately on the heels of the Jewish Enlightenment, well before the creation of the state, when nontraditional denominations and secularist movements began to proliferate. As expulsion or banning was not an option, several traditional communities self-separated themselves from general Jewish society and formed segregated communities of the faithful.[36] The early settlement community in Israel raised the question in its most acute form but also spurred efforts at accommodation because the very fact of the individual's continued attachment to the idea of a Jewish nation softened the rabbinic category of rebellious sinners who reject the law.

Although one still can find contemporary rabbinic opinions holding that those who deny the divinity of Jewish law or publicly desecrate the Sabbath are no longer a part of the covenantal community,[37] most rabbinic authorities hold otherwise. These opinions, for the most part, continue earlier talmudic and medieval patterns of restricting the category of rebellious sinners by viewing sinners as not fully responsible for their actions. External factors, and not individual autonomous decision, cause the sin.[38] Rabbi Abraham Yeshayahu Karelitz, the Hazon Ish, argues more broadly, however, that the times have so changed that the traditional categories no longer even apply. Modernity is different because it is "a time of God's concealment."[39] Such rulings are motivated, however, by communitarian concerns, and not by respect for the value of diverse forms of Jewish life or of individual choice. As such, they create a virtual fellowship, in which the primordial obligation of social solidarity exists only on one side. An equally nettlesome issue for the rabbinic tradition is the place of the non-Jew within the state. Does the halakha provide an adequate "model of mutuality as a basis for stable group relations"?[40] Social reciprocity does not present a serious legal issue, given the norms of mutuality achieved even in the earlier talmudic model through invocation of the principle of pursuing paths of peace. (Political realia is a far greater impediment.) The more critical issue is the extension of full citizenship rights. According to Maimonides, non-Jews (and Jewish women) are forbidden to hold positions of political authority in the Jewish polity.[41] The exilic models of reciprocity do not resolve this issue because they address only sharing acts of benevolence.

The admission of non-Jews (and Jewish women) as equal partners in the polity would seem to require a bolder theory, one that affirms the equality of all persons under the law. The Jewish philosopher Hermann Cohen claimed that the biblical injunction to provide one law for the citizen and the stranger (who obeys Noahide law) was, in fact, the precursor of this emancipation ideal. "The Noahide," he writes, "is a citizen," a person whose equal moral worth is recognized, triggering full equality under the law.[42] Cohen seems to have no followers within the halakhic community, however, for the talmudic understanding of the laws of the resident stranger hedge the concept with restrictions that make it far less amenable to such uses. Rabbinic adoption of the approach of Ha-Me'iri, who equalizes the juridical rights of Jews and non-Jews "restricted by the ways of religion," would provide an alternative basis for a theory that affirms the equality of all persons under the law. But Ha-Me'iri's work, which was lost for centuries, has only now begun to penetrate mainstream rabbinic thought. Moreover, the application of Ha-Me'iri's view to members of secular societies, in which the empirical instantiation of a just and ethical society substitutes for adherence to religion that generates lawfulness, remains at issue.

The more common rabbinic strategy is to retain the differential rules in theory but to make them inapplicable to the issue at hand. Thus, Chief Rabbi Isaac Herzog argued that the ban on non-Jews holding political authority refers to the exercise of nonelective, life-tenure powers because it had in mind the office of the Jewish king.[43] Rabbi Shaul Yisraeli proposes to circumvent the ban by conceiving the state itself as no more than a partnership, modeled on the talmudic partnership of the "townspeople." He analogizes the holding of office in the state to holding office in a business, which a non-Jew may do.[44] The disturbing feature of these opinions is not their result but their rationales, which highlight the paucity of resources in the tradition for developing a comprehensive theory of equal citizenship.

The most controversial issue in Israel today is religious coercion. Must an authentic Jewish civil society incorporate religious law? Here rabbinic writers have been far bolder, drawing on a persistent tension in the halakha with respect to the validity of coercion in general and religious coercion in specific. Performance of the commandments is ideally undertaken freely. At the same time, the law was imposed both to preserve the character of the community as a whole and on the assumption that compelled observance produces "inner consent." More recent rabbinic writings seriously question whether coercion is valid in circumstances where it is unlikely to produce such inner consent.[45] Such inner recognition of the ultimate justice of coercion, possible in a religious age, does not exist in the modern era.

Although the roots of this view go back to talmudic debates about the validity of coercing religious behavior, the growing shift away from coercion suggests a genuine penetration of modern modes of thought into the halakha. Rather than lamenting the decline of a religious worldview, several rabbinic writers assign a positive value to the contraction of opportunities for religious coercion and attribute this contraction to the providential progression of Jewish and human history. Not only was the course of Jewish history providentially guided to limit the scope of coercive powers;[46] the progression of human history toward a maximizing of individual human freedom is a precursor of the messianic age, enabling the law to be performed under ideal conditions of free choice.[47] Thus, a political structure that protects autonomous decision making is superior to the political structure of the past, once a given society attains "intellectual and moral maturity."[48]

The far-reaching implication of this reconception of the value of religious coercion is that religious legislation in the secular state would have no halakhic justification if its purpose is to compel observance of Jewish law. Such legislation must be justified on other grounds, such as the will of the people—a return to the talmudic partnership model of the "towns-people" and its medieval successor, the *kehillah,* which legislated for the common good of the geographic community on the basis of consent. Thus, the critical question is what the communal will is at a given time. That religious legislation is still acceptable to various segments of Israeli society suggests that some form of consensus still exists about the form a Jewish civil society should take.

Debates about religious jurisdiction over marriage and divorce illuminate the differing reasons underlying such consensus. Pursuant to a political compromise between religious and secular parties entered into at the creation of the state, the state retains the Ottoman millet system, ceding matters of personal status to the jurisdiction of recognized religio-ethnic groups. Although it is fashionable to view the political arrangements as purely instrumental, the compromises are best understood as tentative agreements, subject to revision, about what a Jewish society that does not define its identity exclusively in terms of the halakha should entail. Religious parties advocate religious jurisdiction over marriage and divorce, not primarily in order to impose religious standards of behavior on individuals, but because they fear that civil marriage and divorce will produce two exogamous groups, which will lead to a rupture in the unity of the Jewish people living in close proximity in the state. For secular Zionists, religious jurisdiction over marriage and divorce is still largely viewed as in the interests of the collective to preserve a Jewish national identity as well as an expression of Jewish national and cultural norms. Zionism views the laws of society as reflections of the collective self, and not merely convergences of interest between individuals, and thus is also willing to subordinate individual rights (such as freedom from religion) for the welfare of the collective society.

A new "post-Zionist" group has entered this debate. This group wishes to establish a liberal democratic society in which rights are located in the individual and not in the collectivity that constitutes society and in which the "the individual is freed from the burden of a priori duty to a collectivity in which he was born 'by chance' and not of his own free choice."[49] They stress the heterogenous character of Israel, which includes other ethnicities and religious groups, and urge a liberal vision of civil society as one in which people freely enter and exit groups—a vision that requires civil marriage and divorce. So far, this perspective has not led to a call for complete reform of religious jurisdiction over marriage but rather for adjustments, the establishment of an alternative structure for those individuals who cannot be accommodated by the halakha.

These debates open a window onto what a distinctively "Jewish" form of civil society might look like. Both the rabbinic tradition and Zionism would be philosophically opposed to a model of society in which voluntarily chosen groups form and dissolve at the pleasure of their membership, as both stress the critical role of the community in defining individual identity and as both affirm nationhood, ethnicity, and peoplehood as ways to organize society. Both link the value of individual diversity to the uniqueness of human collectivities, which is valued over any abstract universal human order, and both see associational rights as lodged in the community or culture itself, not in individuals. Finally, both might claim that voluntarist groups are "parasitic" on cultural or religious communities, using their insights. If these communities disappeared, the intellectual resources of ad hoc groups would be diminished, nor could voluntary groups form around their traditions.[50] Thus, a distinctively "Jewish" form of civil society ideally should support a collectively held right of cultural and religious groups to cultural perpetuation.

On the question whether a liberal version of civil society could be tolerated, however, the rabbinic tradition and Zionism might part ways. The nationalist imagination is unconstrained by texts and traditions. In the rabbinic tradition, however, the issue is invariably a legal question, to be determined by the halakha. If there is no halakhic validity to religious legislation under modern conditions of freedom other than that rooted in consent, any model of civil society could be tolerated so long as it would not impinge on the halakhic practices and institutions of those desirous to observe the law. Whether a liberal version of civil society does indeed present such difficulties for the halakha is best analyzed by looking briefly at the problems traditional Judaism faces in the liberal West.

The transformation of Judaism from a corporate body enjoying group rights of religio-legal autonomy into a private, voluntary religious association within civil society, whose freedoms are protected through individual rights of free exercise and association, does not pose an insuperable obstacle for traditional Judaism. The particularity of Judaism means that the non-Jewish state is under no obligation to conduct itself in accordance with Jewish precepts or to impose such precepts on non-Jewish society. Nor does rabbinic Judaism contain any theories about state obligation to support or refrain from interfering with the activities of the smaller associations within its midst, akin to the Christian idea of subsidiarity. Rabbinic Judaism never entertained the possibility of dictating terms to its host states; it searched for legitimate halakhic ways to survive under conditions of foreign rule. The early talmudic principle that "the law of the state is the law," whether understood as a pragmatic concession to alien state power or as a principle of recognition of the legitimacy of all political governance, exemplifies the kinds of accommodation the halakha made.[51]

The relegation of religion to the private domain is not conflict free, however. The halakhic principle that "the law of the state is the law" cannot serve to legitimate state incursions on matters of religious prohibition or permission; its application is confined to fiscal matters.[52] Thus, it is axiomatic that halakhic Judaism cannot thrive in exile if the state prevents Jews from fulfilling their religious obligations, whether requiring Jews to perform acts that are forbidden or forbidding Jews from performing acts that are required.

Other effects of the reorganization of Judaism as a private religion within civil society present a different level of conflict because they bear on the question of cultural distinctiveness. One of the most intractable social problems within the Jewish community today is the dilemma of the Jewish woman unable to secure a Jewish divorce. Because marriage and divorce are matters of religious prohibition and permission, a Jewish divorce is required to dissolve a marriage valid under Jewish law. Such divorces must be initiated by the husband. Jewish law developed strategies that enabled the Jewish court to secure a bill of divorce from a recalcitrant husband in order to free a woman from the union. But the ability to do justice from within is difficult to achieve when the Jewish court lacks autonomy and when the husband can divorce and remarry under civil law, despite the failure of the husband to furnish a Jewish divorce. In the absence of comprehensive halakhic solutions, rabbinic authorities have sanctioned resort to the state for assistance, urging it either to recognize the authority of the Jewish court over parties who have evidenced a prior commitment to its jurisdiction or to enact special legislation to offset cultural disabilities unique to Jewish women, such as conditioning the grant of a civil divorce on removing barriers to the remarriage of a spouse.[53] But the argument for juridical recognition or for nonneutral legislation is not easily accommodated within the liberal individualist model of rights.

Education of children is another sensitive topic within the traditional Jewish community. May the state compel private associations to teach particular values that are seen as critical to the maintenance of a healthy civil society or that are based in comprehensive liberal principles, such as individual autonomy? Several participants in this symposium raise the question whether sexual inequality or illiberalism within the associations comprising civil society should be permitted in a democratic state. Michael Walzer, for example, proposes that "associational policies and practices that radically curtail the life chances of members" or that "limit the rights or deny the responsibilities of citizenship" should be resisted by the state, offering a hypothetical refusal by the Catholic Church to educate Catholic women as one example. These practices cannot be justified on grounds of free choice, for, as he points out, "voluntary associations are often in part involuntary: children are enrolled by parents and membership is tied up with fundamental aspects of identity that are powerful constraints on rights of exit."[54] If rights of association may be shaped by an ideal conception of civil society, liberal features of education could be imposed in the private sphere. Even in a liberal regime that regards civil society solely as a by-product of rights of association, associational rights, because of an a priori commitment to individual autonomy, may be limited in cases where it can be argued that group practices conflict with the production of an individual capable of selecting among alternative life choices.

The most traditional segments of halakhic Judaism are particularly vulnerable to this critique because they routinely curtail the life chances of their members for economic success or social integration by imposing restrictions on secular education. They believe that the development of integrated halakhic personalities, of individuals who internalize the Jewish system of obligation and who will embody its values both in their personal lives and in their role as transmitters of the tradition, requires near exclusive immersion in the intricate content and value system of the halakha, particularly at an early age. The Jewish tradition is thus more comfortable with the classically liberal position that views rights of association as independent of any ideal model of civil society and that seeks to avoid a comprehensive liberalism. It would also argue that it is a harm to prevent people from perpetuating a way of life of enormous significance to them and that toleration "based on the harm argument" is a more inclusive concept for those groups that do not themselves value autonomy.[55]

So far I have concentrated on what Jews require from civil society. But what do they owe to civil society? The existence of universals within Judaism, the Noahide commandments, raises the question whether Jews have a halakhic obligation to assure a civilized society by actively promoting observance of Noahide law. Although nominally seven, each Noahide principle is the subject of extensive rabbinic juridical elaboration so that Noahide law potentially covers a large variety of topics, including international human rights, euthanasia, abortion, and capital punishment. So far, the concept has been far less useful than one might suppose. Most rabbinic authorities hold that Jews are not legally obliged to promote observance of Noahide law.[56]

Noahide law aside, there is a constellation of halakhic principles that could be interpreted to impose an obligation on Jews to collaborate with other members of society in projects that better the ethical, moral, spiritual, and material condition of general society.[57] The intuition that such an obligation exists sustains those who interpret Judaism nontraditionally in terms of a Jewish mission to pursue justice in the social sphere and who define Jewish identity "associationally," as participation in "sub- or extra-communal voluntary social organizations."[58] The more traditional segments of religious Judaism have generally avoided this topic, in part out of reluctance to bolster nontraditional understandings of Judaism as a mission. But there is a growing, if tacit, acknowledgment that religious sources do obligate Jews to collaborate with others in projects designed to better the moral and material climate of society, even if the exact contours of this obligation are unclear. That observant Jews have failed to turn their energies in this direction, favoring projects that advance the interests of Jews to the exclusion of those involving humanity, is not surprising. This group was the most affected by the Holocaust, which led to despair over common projects of social solidarity and a pouring of energies into the reconstruction of Eastern European Jewry. Given time and stable political conditions, one may expect to see developments on this front.

CONCLUDING NOTE

The most glaring deficiency in the tradition that I have been reporting on is the lack of a model for the extension of equal citizenship rights in the Jewish polity. The biblical exhortation to provide one law for the citizen and stranger alike cannot bear this weight, given the restrictions that talmudic and medieval jurisprudence impose on the institution of the resident stranger. Although several rabbinic sources offer other pragmatic solutions to this issue, their rationales are unsatisfying. Resort to casuistic reasoning and other technical means of problem solving is, of course, a traditional rabbinic method. Such methods also often are accompanied by a genuine shift in consciousness about the justness of an institution. The abolition of slavery, for example, was accomplished through a series of technical restrictions, clearly motivated by a deep abhorrence to the institution. Whether such methods can do this work today is unclear.

It is time, Gerald Blidstein writes, to attempt a new position, based on the candid acknowledgment that Jews relate to the non-Jew, for example, as "fully human possessors" of the divine image.[59] Blidstein asks whether "the divine image of man" can "become a more powerful halakhic concept than it seems to be at present or than it has been historically."[60] To draw this question out: can the idea that man is created in the image of God provide a new universal category of membership in the Jewish polity and a new universal category for the creation of social bonds with all members of society, by virtue of their humanity alone? This is no easy task in a tradition that has as its centerpiece the idea of the distinctiveness of human collectivities, that eschews the creation of a universal human order, and that values the particular over the general. The tense coexistence of universalism and particularism within one tradition is both the problem of Judaism and its definition.

FURTHER READING

Gerald J. Blidstein. "Halakha and Democracy." *Tradition* 32, no. 1 (1997).

Jacob Katz. *Jewish Emancipation and Self-Emancipation* (Philadelphia: Jewish Publication Society, 1986).

Gordon Lafer. "Universalism and Particularism in Jewish Law: Making Sense of Political Loyalties." In *Jewish Identity,* ed. David Theo Goldberg and Michael Krausz (Philadelphia: Temple University Press, 1993).

David Shatz, Chaim I. Waxman, and Nathan Diament, eds. *Tikkum Olam: Social Responsibility in Jewish Thought and Law* (Mountvale, N.J.: Jason Aronson, 1997).

Eliezer Schweid, "'Beyond' All That—Modernization, Zionism, Judaism," *Israel Studies* 1, no. 1 (Spring 1996).

NOTES

1. Although the Jewish viewpoint on any given subject is no longer identical with the classical rabbinic viewpoint, until modernity the latter provided the intellectual framework within which all Jewish thought was set. Any understanding of how Judaism views a topic must begin with the rabbinic tradition, which still provides the primary intellectual constraint on the adoption of any political theory represented in this volume.

2. Adam B. Seligman, *The Idea of Civil Society* (Princeton: Princeton University Press, 1992), p. 10.

3. Jacob Katz, *Jewish Emancipation and Self-Emancipation* (Philadelphia: Jewish Publication Society, 1986).

4. John Locke, *The Second Treatise of Civil Government* in *Locke's Two Treatises of Government,* ed. Peter Laslett (Cambridge: Cambridge University Press, 1967), p. 401.

5. Sifra on Lev. 26:37; Babylonian Talmud, Shevuot 39a.

6. Ritva, Babylonian Talmud, Rosh Hashanah 29a.

7. See Charles Taylor, "Modes of Civil Society," *Public Culture* 3, no. 1 (Fall 1990): 95–118.

8. Ernest Gellner, *Conditions of Liberty: Civil Society and Its Rivals* (London: Penguin Books, 1996), p. 8.

9. Moshe Greenberg, *Studies in the Bible and Jewish Thought* (Philadelphia: Jewish Publication Society, 1995), p. 57.

10. On Noahide law, see David Novak, *The Image of the Non-Jew in Judaism: An Historical and Constructive Study of the Noahide Laws* (New York: Edwin Mellen Press, 1983); Suzanne Last Stone, "Sinaitic and Noahide Law: Legal Pluralism in Jewish Law," *Cardozo Law Review* 12 (1991): 1157–1214.

11. For a fuller discussion, see Greenberg, *Studies in the Bible and Jewish Thought,* pp. 369–94; Gordon Lafer, "Universalism and Particularism in Jewish Law: Making Sense of Political Loyalties," in *Jewish Identity,* ed. David Theo Gold-

berg and Michael Krausz (Philadelphia: Temple University Press, 1993), pp. 177–211.

12. Maimonides, Mishneh Torah, Hilkhot Teshuvah 3:11.

13. Maimonides, Mishneh Torah, Hilkhot Evel 14:1.

14. Steven Harvey, "Love," in *Contemporary Jewish Religious Thought,* ed. Arthur A. Cohen and Paul Mendes-Flohr (New York: Charles Scribner's Sons, 1987), p. 558.

15. This point is made by Lenn Evan Goodman, "Maimonides' Philosophy of Law," *Jewish Law Annual* 1 (1978): 88–89.

16. See Goodman, "Maimonides' Philosophy of Law," pp. 89–90.

17. For an analysis of these categories, see Samuel Morell, "The Halachic Status of Non-Halachic Jews," *Judaism* 18, no. 4 (Fall 1969): 448–57.

18. See Aviezer Ravitzky, "The Question of Tolerance in the Jewish Religious Tradition," in *Hazon Nahum: Studies in Jewish Law, Thought, and History,* ed. Yaakov Elman and Jeffrey S. Gurock (New York: Yeshiva University Press, 1997), 378–385.

19. For a fuller treatment of the topic, see Norman Lamm, "Loving and Hating Jews as Halakhic Categories" in *Jewish Tradition and the Nontraditional Jew,* ed. Jacob J. Schacter (Mountvale, N.J.: Jason Aronson, 1992), pp. 150–57.

20. Babylonian Talmud, Avodah Zarah 69b; Maimonides, Mishneh Torah, Hilkhot Melakhim 8:10.

21. See Moshe Halbertal, *Bein Hokhmah Le-Torah* [Between Torah and wisdom] (Jerusalem: Hebrew University Magnes Press, 2000), p. 84.

22. Babylonian Talmud, Gittin 61a.

23. Menahem Ha-Me'iri, Beit Ha-Behira, on Avodah Zara 22a.

24. Menahem Ha-Me'iri, Beit Ha-Behira, on Baba Qama 113b.

25. See Jacob Katz, *Exclusiveness and Tolerance* (New York: Schocken Books, 1961), p. 118.

26. See Halbertal, *Bein Hokhmah Le-Torah,* pp. 102–3.

27. See Katz, *Exclusiveness and Tolerance,* p. 121.

28. Lafer, "Universalism and Particularism," p. 195.

29. Goodman, "Maimonides' Philosophy of Law," p. 101.

30. See Katz, *Exclusiveness and Tolerance,* pp. 125–28.

31. See *Encyclopedia Talmudit,* vol. 3, s.v. "bene ha'ir."

32. Babylonian Talmud, Baba Bathra 8b.

33. See Martin P. Golding, "The Juridical Basis of Communal Associations in Mediaeval Rabbinic Legal Thought," *Jewish Social Studies* 18, no. 2 (1966): 67–78.

34. See Derek J. Penslar, "The Origins of Modern Jewish Philanthropy," in *Philanthropy in the World's Traditions,* ed. Warren F. Ilchman, Stanley N. Katz, and Edward L. Queen II (Bloomington: Indiana University Press, 1998), pp. 197–201.

35. Michael Walzer, "Rescuing Civil Society," *Dissent* (Winter 1999): 65.

36. See Judith Bleich, "Rabbinic Responses to Nonobservance in the Modern Era," in Schacter, *Jewish Tradition and the Nontraditional Jew,* pp. 37–115.

37. For examples, see Lamm, "Loving and Hating Jews as Halakhic Categories," p. 158 n. 22.

38. See Ravitzky, "The Question of Tolerance in the Jewish Religious Tradition," pp. 381–84.

39. Hazon Ish 13:16, cited in Lamm, "Loving and Hating Jews as Halakhic Categories," pp. 160–61.

40. Gerald J. Blidstein, "Halakha and Democracy," *Tradition* 32, no. 1 (1997): 28.

41. Maimonides, Mishneh Torah, Hilkhot Melakhim 1:4–5.

42. Quoted in David Novak, "Universal Moral Law in the Theology of Hermann Cohen," *Modern Judaism* 1 (1981): 105.

43. The opinion is discussed in Blidstein, "Halakha and Democracy," pp. 25–27.

44. Rabbi Shaul Yisraeli, Ha-Torah ve-ha-Medina, again discussed in Blidstein, "Halakha and Democracy," p. 27.

45. Rabbi Meir Simha of Dvinsk, Or Sameakh, Hilkhot Gerushin 2:20; Hilkhot Mamrim 4:3.

46. This is the view of Rabbi Yosef Eliyahu Henkin, Ha-Darom 10 (Elul 1959), pp. 5–9, cited in Blidstein, "Halakha and Democracy," p. 37 n. 22.

47. This is the view of Rabbi Abraham Isaac Kook, according to Tamar Ross, "Between Metaphysical and Liberal Pluralism: A Reappraisal of Rabbi A. I. Kook's Espousal of Toleration," *AJS Review: Journal of the Association of Jewish Studies* 21 (1996): 82, 101–2.

48. Ross, "Between Metaphysical and Liberal Pluralism," p. 82.

49. Eliezer Schweid, "'Beyond' All That—Modernism, Zionism, Judaism," *Israel Studies* 1, no. 1 (Spring 1996): 240.

50. Diana Tietjens Meyers, "Cultural Goals: Rights, Goals, and Competing Values," in Goldberg and Krausz, *Jewish Identity,* p. 21.

51. For a systematic treatment of the doctrine, see Shmuel Shilo, *Dina De-Malkhuta Dina* (Heb. 1974).

52. See Shmuel Shilo, "Dina de-Malkhuta Dina," *Encyclopaedia Judaica* (1972), 6:53–54.

53. For a full treatment of this issue, see Irving Breitowitz, *Between Civil and Religious Law: The Plight of the Agunah in American Society* (Westport, Conn.: Greenwood Press, 1993).

54. Walzer, chap. 2, this vol.

55. For a fuller articulation of this position, see Moshe Halbertal, "Autonomy, Toleration, and Group Rights: A Response to Will Kymlicka," in *Toleration: An Elusive Virtue,* ed. David Heyd (Princeton: Princeton University Press, 1996), 110–13.

56. See J. David Bleich, "Tikkun Olam: Jewish Obligations to Non-Jewish Society," in *Tikkun Olam: Social Responsibility in Jewish Thought and Law,* ed. David Shatz, Chaim I. Waxman, and Nathan Diament (Mountvale, N.J.: Jason Aronson, 1997), pp. 61–102.

57. This issue is discussed extensively in a collection of essays appearing in Shatz, Waxman, and Diament,170 *Tikkun Olam: Social Responsibility in Jewish Thought and Law.*

58. See Penslar, "The Origins of Modern Jewish Philanthropy," p. 205–8.

59. Blidstein, "Halakhah and Democracy," p. 29.

60. Blidstein, "Halakhah and Democracy," p. 33.

CHAPTER 9

Alternative Conceptions of Civil Society
A Reflective Islamic Approach

Hasan Hanafi

CONTEMPORARY MUSLIMS articulate a number of alternative conceptions of civil society. First, there are some who reject the very idea of civil society as alien to Islam, a concept coming from the West: secular, antireligious, and aiming at Westernizing Muslim societies. This is the radical fundamentalist position. Second, there are some who affirm the concept of civil society as a universal concept, a global ideal irrespective of its Western origins. They accept it as a model, a norm of practice, and an ideal in lifestyle for individuals and societies. In this view, Islamic tradition becomes an archaic expression of bygone values reflective of their own peculiar historical conditions. This is the other radical position—the secular, Westernized alternative. Third, there are some who argue for the possibility of developing the ingredients of classical Islam to reflect modern social needs. They argue that similarities can be maintained and differences can be bridged through creative reinterpretation—or *ijtihad*—of the basic ethical sources of Islam. This final position is the reformist or modernist alternative.

These three broadly defined alternative conceptions of civil society are not merely theoretical constructs. We can find each position reflected in the spectrum of Muslim political societies; in practice, civil society is not one uniform type in the Muslim world. It varies from Lebanon to Afghanistan. In Lebanon today, civil society is reemerging after having been ripped apart by a decade of civil war. It exists because of the relatively equal power between society and state. Lebanon is unified in the public space by the general allegiance to the civil law, in spite of some balancing of power between different religious groups required by its multiethnic and multireligious composition. Still present are some illiberal vestiges of the old Lebanon: a Christian head of state, a Sunni prime minister, a Shi'i house speaker. Nevertheless, the civil war minimized the weight of sectarianism and maximized the feeling of citizenship, which has been reinforced by the resistance to the Israeli occupation in the south.

On the other extreme, Afghanistan under the Taliban offers a strict application of Islamic law, especially in family law and the penal code, the two obsessions of religious conservatism. The same practice in a more sophisticated way exists in Saudi Arabia and Sudan under the banner of applying

Islamic law (*shari'a*), using religion as a camouflage for patriarchal society and for military dictatorship. Human rights in this type of state are routinely violated and human rights organizations are even banned.

The third practice is a middle course, which is more common in the rest of the Arab and Muslim world, in states such as Morocco, Tunisia, Libya, Egypt, Syria, Jordan, Kuwait, the United Arab Emirates, and Oman, where we find a balance between civil society and the dictates of medieval Islamic law. In the public sphere, the rules of civil society are maintained: citizenship, equality of all in front of the law, the constitution, freedom of expression, democracy, pluralism, and the like. In the private sphere, such as family law, the shari'a is maintained since it is one of the sources of civil law.

It is clear from the above list of states following the middle course that civil society in its fullest sense is still far from realized in most of the Muslim world.[1] But the fact that democracy and respect for human rights are still the exception rather than the norm in the Muslim world does not reflect in my view the validity of either of the two extreme conceptions of civil society that I outlined above. Indeed, I believe that while the concept of civil society may be of Western origin, most of its key features may be found in Islamic ethical theory, and these features are slowly being realized in cultural contexts as different as the Moroccan and the Malaysian. Indeed, as I will argue in this chapter, the development of the third approach to civil society—the reformist, modernist approach—is the only viable one for pluralistic Muslim societies, whether they are African, Asian, or European. An Islamic state is not one that advocates only the application of the penal code or the observance of external rituals, but the state that implements the spirit or intent of the law (*maqasid al-shari'a*). A state that pursues this spirit may not replicate all the institutions associated with Western civil society, but it will foster and protect many of the values that underlie it.[2]

INGREDIENTS

The concept of civil society is a Western concept, coined in the seventeenth century by the English political philosopher Thomas Hobbes as an alternative to Kingdom and Church. The human being is neither a subject of a king nor a believer in a church. He is a citizen of a state, where everybody is equal to everybody, where all citizens are governed by the same law embedded in the constitution. Hegel in his *Philosophy of Right* considered civil society as a step toward the state. The original concept held more political rather than economic connotations: equal citizenship, social contract, equality in front of the law, a constitution, and freedom and democracy.

That liberal concept of civil society was the foundation for liberal economics, and found expression in the rise of capitalism, free enterprise, and private property.

Civil society is not a panacea for the age-old problem of balancing the powers of the state, the society, and the individual. When it does exist, however, it provides a certain balance between the power of the ruler and the power of the people, between power from the top and power from the bottom, between the government and the opposition, which allows state and society to coexist without falling into the extremes of authoritarian rule or popular revolt.

Islamic culture historically has shared this concern for limiting the power of political authorities by diffusing it among a number of formal and informal institutions. If civil society means a system of checks and balances that prevent a preponderance of power residing in either the state or societal institutions, then Islamic theory from the earliest period demonstrates similar concerns. However, indigenous concepts of civil society from within Islamic culture are more innocent concepts, value free and without a hidden agenda. They are more consistent and less opposed than the ingredients of civil society projected from Western culture onto Islamic societies in a misguided attempt to replicate the Western model. The key Islamic ingredients for civil society require less oppositional tension between institutions because in Islam there are no kings or popes, no kingdoms and no churches. Instead we begin with the following salient concepts.

The first is the *umma,* which means a nation without boundaries, a community of believers. Islam views all human beings to be ontologically members of the same family, the same umma. And today, even though humankind is fractured into different moral communities (*umam*), Islam upholds the essential similarities that link all human beings with mutual obligations of respect and decent behavior.

All Muslims everywhere are members of the Islamic umma, this ideal community irrespective of geography. And yet Islam acknowledges that human identities are never monolithic, but varied and sometimes crosscutting. So even though Islam posits the moral primacy of membership in the single community of Muslim believers, it also accepts the reality of other societies and nations, sometimes existing within the Muslim umma and at other times including non-Muslims as well.

Groups that may or may not connote a religious basis include *qabila,* or tribe; *ta'ifa,* which means an intimate group dedicated to a cause; *milla,* which means a religious community or sect; and *nas,* which could mean either a group of people or the whole human race. All refer to different sizes of human groups.

Related concepts refer to place or abode, such as *madina,* a town or city;

qariya, a village; and *wadi,* a populated valley or low-lying area. The important point about these terms is that they refer to inhabitants, not just to place.

Another set of concepts refers to specifically religious groups apart from the Muslim community. The most important such concept is that of *ahl al-kitab,* or "people of the Book," namely Jews and Christians who share with Muslims the revelation of Abraham. The word *ahl* suggests a common family or parenthood. Jews, Nazarenes, and Sabeans all form communities of believers equal to Muslims. They are groups for positive action and common cause.

Some categories refer to social classes, such as rich and poor, the deprived, and the homeless. Others relate to political categories, such as princes and other wielders of power; to religious authorities, such as priests and rabbis; to gender categories, such as male and female. Finally, there are a number of concepts related to the core institution of the family, which establish the rights and duties connecting fathers, mothers, sons, daughters, parents, neighbors, and friends.

The above list may read as an agglomeration of unrelated terms. In fact, the concepts and the groupings outlined above are intrinsically related to one another because they combine to form an integrated whole that is Islam's conception of human society. Islam certainly puts primacy on the rights and obligations incumbent upon Muslims as members of the same religious community. But it does not renounce the possibility of the affiliation of Muslims to nonreligious identities and groups, nor does it obviate the rights and obligations that emerge from such membership. A Muslim man, for example, may marry a woman from the ahl al-kitab, thereby becoming a member of a non-Muslim extended family, with all the attendant privileges and duties such an alliance entails. Similarly, a Muslim ruler who contracts with non-Muslim communities residing within the Islamic state incurs obligations toward these communities while retaining the prerogatives of sovereignty.

In short, Islamic theory and practice sustain a number of legitimate human groupings existing between the state and the individual. These groupings are endowed with their own sphere of autonomy free from government intrusion, which made Islamic societies historically far less monolithic and undifferentiated than some Western stereotypes of a theocratic society allow.

Islamic theory also provides a number of institutions that serve to operationalize the concept of civil society. Medieval theorists posited a tension between the wielder of power (variously termed the *imam,* the *khalifa,* or the *sultan*) and the *'ulama,* namely the intellectuals and legal scholars who were most familiar with the shari'a. The latter are the guarantors of the shari'a's proper interpretation. They are in theory independent from political authority, thus maintaining the system of checks and balances in society—similar to the role of the mass media in modern societies.

The judges are also independent from the political authority. They judge according to the law, which is just as binding on the ruler as it is on a common person. The high judge, similar to the supreme court, is appointed by the ruler, but he cannot be removed by him. In case the ruler does not abide by the law, the high judge can lead a revolution against him.[3]

Islamic theory provides for a number of other subsidiary institutions that bridge the executive power of the imam and the judicial authority of the ʿulama. One key concept is that of *hisba*, which means the supervision of the application of the law in society, especially in the marketplace, against treachery, mishandling, monopoly, usury, exaggerated profits, and the like. The person performing this function (*muhtasib*) serves as the eye of the law on both state and society.

Furthermore, there is the *diwan al-mazalim*, which served in ways analogous to both a small claims court as well as a court of popular appeal. The *mazalim* court was a tribunal to which every Muslim could go and complain against any form of injustice done to him directly by the ruler or the ruler's agent. It allowed a direct appeal to the highest institutions of the state when the institutions of either the state or society failed to defend a common person's legal rights.

Awqaf, or religious endowments similar to scientific, literary, and academic foundations for the development of art and science, are another key autonomous institution in medieval Islamic societies. Individuals could endow awqaf so that scholarships, schools, universities, and publications were all supported by the institution without government interference. Likewise, mystical orders (the Sufi *tariqas*) were able to recruit members and form religious autonomous societies that existed largely independently from state control and played extremely important mediating roles between families or tribes and the state in which they lived.

All of these institutions played roles analogous to those of institutions we today identify with civil society. Of course, the relative weight and independence of all these institutions varied according to time and location. What is important to emphasize is that Islamic theory contains within it the idea of an integrated politico-religious community, but with power dispersed among its constituent elements. As modern Muslim states began to emerge in the early-twentieth century, it is no surprise that one of the first targets of their secular, nationalist state-building enterprise was traditional Islamic institutions. The Egyptian state placed awqaf under the control of a government ministry at the beginning of the Egyptian revolution. It is directed now in the spirit of doing business and making profit. Similarly, the Sufi tariqas were among the first social institutions to be affected (and dissolved) when Mustafa Kemal Ataturk began his nationalist project in

Turkey. And yet despite all attempts to co-opt or crush them, Sufi orders remain a very important autonomous force in such Muslim societies as Morocco, Sudan, Turkey, Eastern Europe, and Central Asia.

SOCIETY

The Islamic ideal of the umma is grounded in the concept of unity. The unity of God (*tawhid*) reflects itself in the unity of the umma. The unity of God is not a simple, closed dogma or a reified abstraction, but a whole worldview that affects the individual, society, and history. The individual is one, which means that his powers and energies are one. His internal powers of cognition, feeling, and thinking are one. His thoughts should express what he feels, and what he feels can be rationally demonstrated. Hypocrisy is to think something without feeling it. Fear is to feel something without thinking on it.

Man's external powers of action are also one. His words should be related to his acts; what he says, he should do, and what he does, he should say. Incapacity is to say something without doing it. Automation is to do something without saying it. The unity between the inside world—feeling and thinking—and the external world—saying and doing—makes the human personality one, free of fear, double-talk, double-face; it creates a free individual. To believe is to attest. To declare is to testify. This is the meaning and the significance of *shahada,* the first pillar of Islam, the solemn declaration that there are no other gods except the only God, Omniscient, Omnipresent, and Omnipotent.

All human beings are equal before this Universal Principal, equal in birth and death, equal in life and worth. There is no human genealogy stemming out of royal families, of caste systems, or of social classes. All human beings are the sons and daughters of Adam and Eve. Every human being has a body and a soul, a reason to distinguish good from evil, and a free will to choose the good, not the evil. They are all created from one soul.

Society is a unity of equal individuals. No distinction exists between human beings according to color, language, tribe, or state. All societies, peoples, tribes, classes, and the like, are also equals. They all have the same rights and the same duties. The right to differ is a legal right. Diversity of language, social customs, and manners is part of people's rights. All ought to be treated according to the same international law without any double standard in practice. Peaceful coexistence between peoples is guaranteed by treaties of nonaggression and mutual respect. There is no elected people or chosen tribe or best umma except through the good deed and ethical standards. Election is offered to all, to every individual, according to perfection acquired through ethical performance.[4]

To realize this principle of equality in society, Islam enshrines the notion of the brotherhood of all believers. Given the natural differences among individuals in aptitudes and talents, which yield different incomes and generate social classes, brotherhood intervenes to bring back equality to its early stand. Those who have give to those who have not. Those who have more give to those who have less. This is not the conventional idea of charity or altruism on the part of the rich toward the poor. In Islamic society, the poor have a vested right in the wealth of the rich, not only through *zakat,* the tax on surplus wealth that is another pillar of the faith, but also through other measures to be taken by the ruler, such as nationalization of public services and confiscation of exploitative monopolized means of production. Public goods, such as water, salt, and mineral resources lying deep below the surface—including oil—cannot be claimed as private property because they touch the lives of all members of society. Even so-called private property is only a deposit or a trust granted conditionally, because absolute ownership can be properly assigned only to the Creator. Property is granted to the individual to use, not to misuse; to invest, not to accumulate; to spend, not to withhold and hoard.

Faith in the unity of God and the unity of His Creation helps to unify Islamic societies, despite their great social, cultural, and economic diversity. While Islamic civil society is differentiated and contains many organizations and subgroups, it forms a coherent society by virtue of a shared commitment to faith and brotherhood. One senses this unity immediately while traveling in Muslim countries, whether it is in Mauretania or Turkey or Malaysia. The universal umma ideal may have little political significance today, but it is alive at the ethical and spiritual level, which unites individuals into a greater whole transcending their own often unrepresentative states. And it does have obvious importance within specific countries, where Islamic values of community pressure elites toward certain policies or even fuel popular resistance to corrupt regimes.[5]

But what is the status of non-Muslim groups? Are they excluded from Islamic conceptions of civil society? On the contrary, Islam has a long tradition of recognizing and accommodating non-Muslim communities. Indeed, the tradition originates from the earliest period of Islam's existence as a coherent society in Medina. In this society, established by the prophet Muhammad, Jews and Christians were granted a status that placed them on equal terms with the Muslims. Every community was accorded autonomy in language, costumes, manners, laws, and the like, within the larger community. The Islamic umma is not composed exclusively of Muslims, but it is a confederal umma composed of many communities bound together by a treaty of nonbelligerence and mutual respect. The millet system practiced by the Ottoman Empire into the twentieth century was de jure an Islamic system. This system acknowledged the right of each religious community to live within the confederated umma and exercise self-rule in many areas of communal life, while it prevented modern ethnic and religious cleansing.[6]

Today, this concept of Jews and Christians as *dhimmi* has acquired in public opinion a derogatory meaning, that of second-class citizenship. However, the etymological sense of this term is moral commitment. *Ahl al-dhimma* means those with whom a moral commitment is made to protect and defend them against all forms of injustices and aggression, as allies and brothers. In the old law, they have to pay an extra tax (*jizya*) in return for defense and protection, since they are exempted from military service. They have their own courts, and they are judged according to their own law. They have their own customs and manners, their languages, and their cults. But as members of the larger Islamic society, they have their claims to the social welfare provided by the state. They are entitled like all other members of the community to all the rights and privileges of the citizens on an equal basis: education, work, public services, and so forth.

Unfortunately, this earlier Islamic tradition of religious tolerance and inclusiveness is now under threat. In modern times and within contemporary nation-states many false images of the old law have been circulating that view Jews and Christians as second-class citizens, living in isolation from the broader Muslim population and yet subject to Islamic law, especially the penal code. This view is especially current in fundamentalist circles.

These false images need some clarification. The old law was conceived when religious identity was equated to political identity. Now national identity is taking over. All citizens of a nation are equal before the law by virtue of their citizenship and irrespective of their religious affiliations. In the past, Jews and Christians often preferred to take their own disputes to Muslim courts rather than to their proper courts because Islamic law is an objective law based on the idea of impartial justice. The actual civil code in much of the Muslim world today is based on secular, mainly European sources. The exception to this generalization remains family law, but this area is also under revision to cope with modern circumstances. Jews, Christians, and Muslims are equal in front of the civil law and the constitution. The fact that many otherwise secular states declare Islam to be the state religion, and that the head of state must be Muslim, does not mean there are any practical distinctions between ordinary Muslims and non-Muslims. In societies that are overwhelmingly Muslim in numerical terms, it is only natural that the population would want some acknowledgment of the role of Islamic values in their national life. Moreover, given the Muslim majority, it is likely that the head of state would be a Muslim. However, these positive expressions of Islamic values as undergirding national politics should not negatively affect the equality of all citizens before the law and the right of all citizens to participate and contribute to national life. Islamic values applied properly in politics promote not a communal culture favoring the Muslim population, but a pluralistic, "national" culture to which Muslims and non-Muslims belong.

In addition, the penal code in Islam—which fundamentalists are so eager to impose upon Muslims and non-Muslims—ought to be applied only to Muslims. Jews and Christians are liable under their own laws. Indeed, the severest penalties of the Islamic penal code are rarely applied even to the Muslims. The severity of some punishments is a motivation for the judge and for society as a whole to look for the causes of crimes in order to ameliorate them, to mitigate the chances for the crimes at their roots. The moral purport of Islamic punishments is not so much to punish the crime a posteriori but to prevent it a priori.

Thus, Islamic theory in its general outline does not view Jews, Christians, and others as necessarily or typically second-class citizens within Islamic societies. Indeed, non-Muslims are assured a remarkable degree of communal autonomy aimed at preventing their independent identities and cultures from being overwhelmed by the Muslim majority. In their communal life, they are autonomous from state regulation so long as they acknowledge the sovereignty of the Islamic state and the predominance of Islamic law as the regulatory mechanism across communities. At the same time, they are essential components of the broader, what may be termed quasi-federal, "national" structures. In other words, the Islamic conception embraces a number of limited civil societies with the hope that each will promote the greater civil society of all.

The generally positive picture presented thus far must of course be tempered with some caveats. Certainly, there have been some Muslim scholars who have argued for inequality of treatment and there have been some Muslim rulers who oppressed non-Muslim minorities within their realms. In some countries of the Muslim world today, religion is used to legitimize a political regime that lacks democratic legitimation. Religion is here only a cover for dictatorship. The sectarian clashes occurring in the Muslim world from time to time are not really due to sectarianism but to backward societies that suffer from marginalization of large numbers of people. The clashes are everywhere between poor and rich, between the state and the workers, between the government and the opposition, between the secularists and the fundamentalists. Since the state lacks legitimacy, democratic institutions, and legal opposition parties, apparently sectarian clashes are in reality driven by the economic-political struggle to seize the state, or at least to show its vulnerability and to destabilize the oppressive regimes. These are most often at root political clashes between the disenfranchised and the elites, not religious clashes between the Muslim majority and non-Muslim minorities arising out of a desire to exclude or marginalize non-Muslims because of their faith.

But we should end this section by emphasizing that there are numerous examples where Islamic conceptions of a peaceful, cooperative, pluralistic society are being realized. To cite but one example, Coptic Christians in Egypt (about 10 percent of the population) are equal citizens. They are very active in the political, social, and economic life of the country. They have their own schools, communal institutions, and intellectual presence. They are ministers in the government, generals in the army, and several rank among the eminent leaders of the Egyptian national movement in recent history. The positive facts throughout Islamic history are much more numerous than the negative incidents.[7]

Values

Individual human beings cannot live alone. They are drawn naturally toward social solidarity. The importance of civil society derives from the need to balance the desires and needs of the individual with the will and needs of society. Where civil society is present, an individual is a part of the body, joined to other members to form an organic whole, as the medieval philosopher al-Farabi describes in his virtuous city.

In Islam, civil society protects the rights of its members by anchoring these rights in a conception of universally binding duties or obligations that resemble Western conceptions of natural law. Within an Islamic framework, the ultimate author of these laws is God, but there is a long tradition in Islamic philosophy which argues that natural law is an objective law that human reason can discern. I shall pursue this line of thinking in outlining what I consider the principal values promoted by this law, which in turn foster civil society. Each of the values discussed below may be said to exist in a cyclical relationship with civil society, reinforcing it and being reinforced by it.

The first value must be the protection of life against all threats bringing death. Life is an absolute value. Genocide, assassination, murder, and even capital punishment are against life as an absolute value. God gives life and God takes it. As the Qur'an says in affirmation of biblical scripture, Whoever kills one person is as if he killed all mankind. But the commandment to preserve life—found in all moral systems—contains both positive as well as negative implications. It is not enough simply to abstain from killing; one cannot stand by passively while thousands, sometimes millions die even though society has the means to save them. The struggle against hunger, drought, disease, malnutrition, starvation, and nakedness is a struggle for human survival and welfare. It is a struggle intimately connected with the struggle for responsive and effective government and a tolerant, responsive society.

Reason is another absolute value, which translates into the right to know against withholding information for commercial monopoly and maximizing power. Ignorance and illiteracy are against the function of reason. Maleducation, misinformation through commercial or government propaganda, and blind imitation are all forms of antireason. Through reason man can prove that God exists, the world is created, and the soul is immortal. Reason is the very foundation of faith. Reason is not only deductive but also inductive. It deduces the causes of human behavior from the textual sources as it induces them from human actions. Reason is also the glue that binds individuals into a whole. If reason is not the common standard between human beings in communicating and understanding, the will to power takes over. Might will be substituted for right. Islam opens all avenues toward the promotion of reason and blocks all paths toward antireason. Open scientific and spiritual inquiry is one of the hallmarks of classical Islamic civilization. The consumption of alcohol, on the other hand, is prohibited because drunkenness is against reason.

The defense of human honor and dignity is another of the pillars of civil society. Human honor includes all the principles stipulated in the Universal Declaration of Human Rights, including freedom of speech, belief, and movement; the right to privacy; and the respect of the human body against nakedness and torture. Human dignity is not confined to the individual, but applies also to whole communities, requiring for its realization the right for autodetermination and self-rule, the right for independence and respect.

Last comes the preservation of wealth against usurpation, pollution, or waste as the material basis for life. Wealth here does not mean only individual earnings, but national wealth as well, which must be safeguarded against corruption, profligate spending, negligence, and speculation. It has to be spent for development. Public servants including the ruler himself have to set a high example of honesty and integrity.

Private property is one of the Western individualistic human rights that may be incompatible with the communitarian concept of human rights in Islam. It was included in the Universal Declaration of Human Rights in 1948 because of opposition to the socialist regimes emerging after the Second World War and in the context of the cold war. Yet I would question whether it ought to be ranked among essential human rights. It is not, I would suggest, on the same level as the right to live, to survive, to believe, to think, to express, to work, to move, to choose, and to self-rule. Accordingly, in Islamic ethics the right to private property is decidedly lower in importance than the duty to ensure social justice. We noted earlier the positive mechanisms that Islam instituted for the distribution of wealth, including a tax on surplus wealth (zakat) that is collected by the state. In addition, in case of misuse, monopolization, or exploitation, the political authority has the right to confiscate and to nationalize this private property to become a public one.

But the social justice aims of Islamic ethics are not confined to state action. Indeed, the state is merely an agent of Muslim society in the realization of distributive justice goals. It is the society that bears the obligation to promote these values within itself, even if the state does not or cannot do so. We see how this obligation is taken up by society in many Muslim countries today, where a myriad of nongovernmental organizations, such as mosques, Sufi orders, and charitable organizations, perform social welfare tasks in the name of Islam while the state remains oblivious to its population's problems. This is where Islamic civil society is most active and most visible, though these manifestations of civil society receive scant attention among Western students.

All of the values discussed above are values shared—in varying degrees of emphasis—by all cultures. This convergence alone permits us to generalize the concept of civil society (adjusted according to many confluents) and to avoid taking the Western concept as a yardstick according to which all other concepts stemming out of other cultures are judged. The only difference among cultures is in scope and practice. Many in the West suggest that reason, truth, and honor are relative concepts, changing from one society to another. If life and wealth are absolute values, they are applicable within the geographical borders of the West, not outside them. In Islam the objective values of "natural" law are absolute and universal. They do not change from one society to another, nor are they to be applied in one area not in another. These values, according to the Islamic approach, must be rooted in social consciousness, and they must be implemented foremost by society. If these values are not upheld by civil society, then they can hardly be expected to be enforced by the state.

RESPONSIBILITY

Many individuals and institutions are responsible for the good management of civil society and the promotion of its values: the individual, the family, the state, and nongovernmental institutions. They are inseparable given the importance and the commitment of all to the common cause.

The individual is responsible for himself as well as for others. He cannot shirk his social responsibilties, because Islam enjoins upon all believers ordering the right and preventing the wrong (*al-amr bi'l-ma'ruf wa al-nahy 'an al-munkar*). A simple and wise counsel is: "Religion is the advice." Some conditions attend to the fulfillment of this responsibility. The advice should be dispensed when it may be best received. Thus, the person advising should consider the mood, the readiness, and so forth, of the person being admonished. The advice has to be in private, not in public, so that the advised should not be blamed publicly. No harm should result out of advising. It is better to accept a smaller harm before advising than to cause a bigger one after. Advising is not criticism from one individual to another, but mutual action for a common cause. It is not a personal matter but a collective work, a reminder for the common good and public welfare.

The family has a large role in maintaining the rights and the duties of individuals in civil society. The family is a microcosm of the larger society, and thus a harmonious family serves a crucial educational function in preparing its members to participate in a harmonious and well-balanced society.

The state is not an oppressive institution but a guarantor of human rights and responsibilities. Political power is wielded by representatives freely chosen by the people, as suggested by the old expression *ahl al-hall wa'l-'aqd* (literally, "those who loosen and bind"), namely, those who speak on behalf of the people. Political power is based on a contract between the ruler and the representatives of the people. The people must obey the chosen ruler as long as he is applying the law. If not, the first remedy is to admonish the errant ruler through public statements in mosques, schools, centers of learning, and even in the markets. If the ruler is still recalcitrant, disobeying the law, he has to be brought to court. If the high judge sentences him to obey the law and the ruler still disobeys, he becomes in contempt of the law and is no longer worthy of obedience. Now and then a revolt against him becomes the last resort and is directed by the *ahl al-hall wa'l-'aqd*. The unjust ruler cannot be obeyed.

Finally, nongovernmental organizations have an eminent role in assuming major responsibilities in the civil society. They are the neighbors, the relatives, the friends, and the comrades of work without institutional forms. Others are more institutional, such as workers' and students' unions, bar associations, press corps, literary and academic societies, university clubs, religious associations for public services such as burial, wedding, health care, social security, tutorship, and the like. They are quicker and more efficient than the state apparatus in dealing with national disasters such as earthquakes or floods. Mosques play extremely prominent social roles. They are not only houses of worship but community centers offering public services. Social annexes to the larger community mosques are more populated than the mosques themselves. Religion and society are intertwined. Helping the needy has more value than praying in the mosque.

FREEDOMS AND RISKS

As stated earlier, civil society is not a panacea for all the problems of state and society. If civil society is present and functioning properly, it fosters a distribution of power in the polity and a balance among the constituent elements of society. That balance allows group autonomy while preserving a wide scope for individual freedom. Nevertheless, maintaining the balance is always a precarious enterprise, and within an Islamic framework the following risks are particularly relevant.

If the state is strong and the power of the ruler becomes absolute, the whole system risks sliding toward theocracy because theoretically the purpose of the state is to apply divine law. The ruler, in order to consolidate his power, gain legitimacy, and tame the opposition, pretends that he is the representative of God on earth, the follower of the Prophet, the guarantor of the application of the law, the right interpreter of religion, and the guardian of public morality and public welfare. He is the custodian of law and order. Any opposition to his power is tantamount to a revolt against God. In this perverted approach, God chooses the ruler, not the people. He nominates him, not the community. Carried to extremes, this ruler sometimes claims that he is even mentioned in the religious text, if not by name, then at least by description, if not explicitly, then at least implicitly.

We find many examples of this theocratic authoritarianism in Islamic history. In this case, there is no difference between Sunnis and Shi'is. Even now many regimes, such as Morocco and Saudi Arabia, are based on religion as a legitimizing device. The rulers in these countries are considered to be following the model of the Prophet, or even to be descended from the Prophet's family. Any protest against them is treated as a violation of the shari'a.

Of course, the balance may tilt the other way, toward the strengthening of societal elements in the face of the loss of state power. This risk is particularly relevant to the Islamic case because of the strongly communitarian bent of Islamic social ethics. An individual's freedom and welfare may be just as jeopardized—perhaps even more so—by a society or smaller social groups convinced of their divine mission as they are by a state with similar ideological convictions.

One subset of Muslim society has historically been particularly vulnerable to overbearing societal pressures: women. Islamic family law is frequently mentioned as violating some values in modern civil society through its sanctioning of polygamy and discrimination against women in divorce, inheritance, witnessing, leadership, and the like. All of these legal limitations can be seen in their historical perspective. The purpose of Islamic laws relating specifically to women was to change gradually the gender situation in Arabia without setback, with the maximum of success and the minimum of loss. Before Islam, polygamy was unlimited, not to mention the taking of concubines and captives of war. In order to abolish this custom, Islam made it limited to four wives *in exceptional cases,* paving the way to monogamy, which conforms to human nature, physically and emotionally. The exceptional cases are sterility or some other physical handicap, or when the number of females exceeds the number of males, such as following war. Moreover, many restrictions have been put in the old law, such as separate apartments for each wife, the requirement of the first wife's permission, financial capacity, and so forth. All of these restrictions promote monogamy as the Islamic ideal.

Before Islam, women did not have the right of inheritance from their parents' property. On the contrary, women were inherited. Islam gave a woman a half share in order to change the status quo in a society where a female baby was buried alive for fear of shame. The share must be seen in the context of the shareholder's position, namely, as a member of a family. When the woman marries with a half share to a husband with a full share, the outcome is one and one-half shares in the new family. These minimum share requirements notwithstanding, during their lives either parent can distribute their wealth equally among their children regardless of gender, as many pious Muslims do.

Before Islam, women had no legal status. They were not recognized as autonomous characters. They could not buy and sell, witness, or participate in the political process. Islam made a woman a half witness for the same reason as in inheritance, to change her status gradually. In practice, the testimony of an educated woman was preferred to that of an uneducated man.

Women cannot be the head of state in the old law, since the head of the state is also the head of the army, which requires fatigue and hard work unsuitable for pregnant women. Veiling is an old custom in certain parts of Arabia. A simple head cover protects male and female alike from the heat of the desert. All limitations on women in Islam can be so conceived, in their historical perspective, as a gradual social change to be followed by other steps, since history does not stop.

Indeed, many Muslim states have realized that the dictates of the medieval Islamic law must be revised in light of the changed conditions and needs of twentieth-century Muslim societies. Family law has been the last area of the shari'a to be enforced, and wherever reform has been attempted, it has always been met with great controversy. Nevertheless, serious legal changes have been implemented in most Muslim countries that dramatically broaden women's rights and move them toward greater equality with men.

But it is one thing for the state to legislate women's rights and another thing for women to realize these rights. As numerous human rights organizations have documented, Muslim women lag significantly behind Muslim men in many states in key indicators of material and emotional well-being, such as infant mortality, literacy, life expectancy, age at marriage, and jobs. The problem stems often from government indifference toward enforcement of rights enshrined in constitutions and statutes. But an even greater obstacle is societal resistance to change in an area that so many view as an essential aspect of their tradition and faith. Women's status for many traditional Muslims falls into that broad area of privacy that their understanding of Islam throws around the family. Within the confines of the family, the state may not intrude. And for most Muslim societies that are heavily rooted in patriarchy, even those rights that the medieval law guarantees women are frequently flouted in the name of social mores and tradition. In this area, the protected, private space occupied by the family, which all civil society rightly fosters, can become an oppressive well of custom and convention.[8]

CONCLUSION: REFLECTIONS ON THE PROSPECTS FOR ISLAMIC CIVIL SOCIETY

There are some risks to civil society stemming from Muslim societies that are related not to Islamic conceptions of civil society per se, but to the historical moment Muslim societies are living nowadays, a moment that can be characterized as conservatism dominating the Muslim world for over a millennium. Muslim societies in the first four centuries were pluralistic societies with many philosophical, theological, mystical, and legal trends. No single school of thought equated itself with Islam. In the fifth Islamic century, the great thinker al-Ghazali launched a conservative revolution that stifled this pluralism and transformed Islamic culture and society according to an absolute and state-enforced doctrine: Ash'arism in theology and Shafi'ism in law. All other schools of thought were marginalized, criticized, or anathematized.

Over the last century reformers have tried to revitalize Islamic pluralism again. These efforts have been threatened over the past fifty years or so as secular military revolutions erupted or new traditional kingdoms were institutionalized. Conservatism and unilateralism generated dogmatism and fanaticism that spread in the mass media and in the educational system from the smallest schools up to the university campuses. Muslim societies, which the reformers in the last century wanted to liberalize, and which the military regimes in this century wanted to revolutionize, persisted in their traditional culture. Both efforts failed because the reformers had Western enlightenment as a model, which tended toward Westernization and thus alienation of the masses from the elites.[9] The military, on the other hand, was interested merely in the infrastructure, not in the superstructure.

The failure of both modernist Islam and secular nationalism has in recent decades played into the hands of the fundamentalists. "Authentic" Islam according to these groups is equated with traditional conservatism, and this narrow interpretation is used as a whip against all liberals who continue the work of the reformers of the last century. Since Islamic movements were not legalized as legitimate elements of civil society and indeed have been suppressed by states, they tried to control the mass media, labor unions, professional associations, and to infiltrate other NGOs.

Elements that are not allowed to compete for popular support within civil society will inevitably become as averse to the values of civil society as those who suppress them. It is hardly surprising therefore that fundamentalist groups employ the traditional accusation of anathema, false innovation, and heresy against artists, thinkers, writers, professors—all methods to obstruct any alternative interpretation of Islam. They wage their battles in the mass media to sway public opinion. Sometimes they go to court to sue their opponents in the name of hisba, that is, in the name of the "public good." Sometimes conservative judges rule for them and declare the thinker accused to be an apostate who should suffer penalties including divorce from his wife because a Muslim woman cannot be legally married to an apostate. Such a ruling actually occurred in the famous case of Nasr Hamid Abu Zaid, a professor of literature at Cairo University, because of his studies in the Qur'an and Islamic law.

But acts of intimidation often do not stop with media campaigns or lawsuits. Zealous and ignorant followers of these conservative groups are willing even to murder the declared apostates or "enemies" of Islam, as they did successfully in the case of the journalist Faraj Fouda or unsuccessfully in the case of the Nobel laureate Naguib Mahfouz.

The zealots' call for an Islamic state means essentially the application of the penal code and the replacement of secular elites with religious men like themselves. Once this occurs, religion and politics will be united, they claim. Indeed, religion in Islam is a political system, an economic theory, and a social structure. But this does not mean the imposition by the state on society of any one interpretation of Islam. It means only that Islamic values cannot be divorced from the business of the state, and the foremost values are the free election of the political power, the defense of common interests and public welfare, and the maintenance of a social order exempt from huge differences between classes.

The struggle between fundamentalism and secularism to the point of civil war as in Algeria would completely destroy civil society. In both cases, whether religious groups take power or the secular state survives, human freedom is violated. The oppression is the same, in the name of the army or in the name of Islamic opposition. The major risk for the future is that Muslim societies will be offered only the fundamentalist/secularist alternatives. Unless Muslim advocates of a middle course resume the serious task of developing and implementing pluralistic and representative conceptions of state and society from within the Islamic tradition, Islam will offer no alternative conception of civil society.

As I have argued throughout this essay, such an alternative is possible. In constructing this alternative Islam can learn from the West, and the West can learn from Islam. Traditional Islamic culture may be based on the idea of duties rather than on the idea of rights (duties of man and rights of God), while modern Western culture is essentially based on the idea of rights rather than duties (rights of man and maybe duties of God). In both cultures, there is a certain imbalance between rights and duties. Muslim societies may have duties without rights while Western societies may have rights without responsibilities. Islam needs a universal declaration of human rights beside the traditional Islamic declaration of human duties. The West needs also a universal declaration of human duties to complete the Universal Declaration of Human Rights.

Pessimism in the short run leads to optimism in the long run. Islamic culture is still strongly bound to conservatism inherited over a millennium. Reformism is a recent phenomenon dating only to the last century. Modernism may have a better chance in the future, as Muslim consciousness achieves a more equal historical presence of both traditionalism and modernism so that a healthy dialogue between the two major schools results. In this progress, the lead must be taken by Muslim intellectuals and modernist scholars practicing ijtihad, creatively linking ageless concepts of a just and virtuous society with modern ideals of civil society. As the Islamic aphorism says, The scholars are the heirs of the prophets.

FURTHER READING

Leonard Binder. *Islamic Liberalism: A Critique of Development Ideologies.* Chicago: University of Chicago Press, 1988.

John L. Esposito and John O. Voll. *Islam and Democracy.* New York: Oxford University Press, 1996.

Albert Hourani. *Arabic Thought in the Liberal Age, 1789–1939.* Cambridge: Cambridge University Press, 1983.

Charles Kurzman, ed. *Liberal Islam: A Sourcebook.* New York: Oxford University Press, 1998.

Abdullahi Ahmed an-Naim, *Toward an Islamic Reformation: Civil Liberties, Human Rights, and International Law.* Syracuse, N.Y.: Syracuse University Press, 1990.

Augustus Richard Norton, ed. *Civil Society in the Middle East.* Leiden: E. J. Brill, 1995–96.

Jillian Schwedler. Introduction to *Toward Civil Society in the Middle East? A Primer,* edited by Jillian Schwedler. Boulder, Colo.: Lynne Rienner, 1995.

NOTES

1. A survey of the prospects for civil society in different Muslim states is available in Augustus Richard Norton, ed., *Civil Society in the Middle East* (Leiden: E. J. Brill, 1995–96).

2. Many of the ideas presented in this essay are elaborated in Hasan Hanafi, *Al-din wa'l-thaqafa wa'l-siyasa fi'l-watan al-'arabi* (Cairo: Dar Qiba, 1998).

3. For succinct treatments of Islamic political theory, see H. A. R. Gibb, "Constitutional Organization," in *Law in the Middle East*, ed. Majid Khadduri and Herbert J. Liebesny (Washington, D.C.: Middle East Institute, 1955), pp. 3–27; and Ann K. S. Lambton, *State and Government in Medieval Islam* (Oxford: Oxford University Press, 1981).

4. The Qur'an is very clear on this point: "Those who believe, the Jews, the Christians, and the Sabaeans—whosoever believe in God and the Last Day and do good deeds, they shall have their reward from their Lord, shall have nothing to fear, nor shall they come to grief" (2:62; see also 2:111–12, 4:124–25, 5:69, 18:30, 21:94). "But God is free of all wants, and it is you [Muslims] who are needy. If you turn back [from the path of Islam] He will substitute in your place another people. Then they would not be like you!" (47:38).

5. On modern understandings of *umma*, see Abdullah al-Ahsan, *Ummah or Nation? Identity Crisis in Contemporary Muslim Society* (Leicester, U.K.: Islamic Foundation, 1992).

6. Leading studies of the status of non-Muslims in Islamic societies include: Antoine Fattal, *Le Statut Légal de Non-Musulmans dans le Pays d'Islam* (Beirut: Imprimerie Catholique, 1958); A. S. Tritton, *The Caliphs and Their Non-Muslim Subjects* (London: Frank Cass and Co., 1970); Bat Ye'or, *The Dhimmi: Jews and Christians under Islam* (London: Associated University Presses, 1985).

7. For a more developed argument regarding the place of non-Muslims in Islamic society, see Hasan Hanafi, *Religious Dialogue and Revolution: Essays on Judaism, Christianity, and Islam* (Cairo: Anglo-Egyptian Bookshop, 1977).

8. Three particularly useful discussions of the status of women in Islamic morality and law are: John Esposito, *Women in Muslim Family Law* (Syracuse, N.Y.: Syracuse University Press, 1982); Leila Ahmed, *Women and Gender in Islam: Historical Roots of a Modern Debate* (New Haven: Yale University Press, 1992); and Amina Wadud, *Qur'an and Woman: Rereading the Sacred Text from a Woman's Perspective*, 2nd ed. (New York: Oxford University Press, 1999).

9. A penetrating critique of the modernist agenda is available in Fazlur Rahman, *Islam and Modernity: Transformation of an Intellectual Tradition* (Chicago: University of Chicago Press, 1982).

CHAPTER 10

Confucian Conceptions of Civil Society

Richard Madsen

CLASSICAL CHINESE INTELLECTUAL traditions (which were not confined to China proper, but had enormous influence throughout East Asia, particularly in Japan, Korea, and Vietnam) did not even have words for *civil society,* much less a theory of it. In Chinese, for instance, the word for *society* (*shehui*) is a neologism from the West, introduced into China via Japan in the late-nineteenth century.[1] Though based on classical Chinese characters, it was a new combination of characters, used in a new sense, to name a modern phenomenon—the development in Treaty Port cities of a separate societal sphere of life that could be at least analytically distinguished from separate economic and political spheres, which were also denoted by words new to the Chinese lexicon. The term *civil* is even newer, and less well established in modern Asian lexicons. In contemporary Chinese, for example, there are no fewer than four words that are used to translate the *civil* in *civil society.*[2] Alternatively, Chinese intellectuals today call civil society *shimin shehui,* which literally means "city-people's society"; or *gongmin shehui,* "citizens' society"; or *minjian shehui,* "people-based society"; or *wenming shehui,* "civilized society." These are all attempts to name phenomena and to articulate aspirations that have arisen in an urbanizing East Asia linked to a global market economy. In this confusing, transitional context, many intellectuals are feeling the need to develop new theories of civil society and new ways of developing such a society, even if they are not completely sure what to call it and how to link it—if it can be linked at all—with their cultural traditions.

Those traditions are complex, pluralistic, and full of conflicting and contradictory ideas about how to live a good life in a well-ordered world. Major strands include the Daoist celebration of natural, virtually anarchistic spontaneity, the Legalist pursuit of centralized political order through carefully controlled allocation of rewards and punishments—and the "thinking of the scholars," to which Western Sinologists in the nineteenth century gave the name "Confucianism." Systematized by great philosophers such as Zhu Xi into a comprehensive framework of ideas during the late Song Dynasty in the eleventh and twelfth centuries C.E., the "Neo-Confucian" tradition blended some metaphysical ideas from Buddhism with the moral teachings of Confucius (551–478 B.C.E.) and his disciples (particularly Mencius, 390–305 B.C.E.), which advocated a middle way between Daoist anarchism and Legalist authoritarianism.[3]

Unlike the Daoists, the Confucians searched for a stable political order. But unlike the Legalists, they insisted that such order had to be based on moral principles, not simply on power. Scholars in this tradition had vigorous disagreements about how people could know these principles and learn to apply them. On one side of these debates were what Wm. Theodore de Bary has called a relatively "liberal" interpretation, which would be consistent with many of the standards for human rights advocated by modern Western liberals—or at least "liberal communitarians."[4] But there were also authoritarian interpretations of the Neo-Confucian traditions. In East Asia today, apologists for authoritarian governments like that of Singapore invoke the Confucian tradition to suppress much of what would be considered part of civil society in the West. At the same time, prominent Asian intellectuals like Tu Wei-ming invoke more "liberal" strands of Confucianism to build a base for relative openness in East Asian societies.[5]

If there is to be a meaningful dialogue between modern proponents of Confucian thought, on the one hand, and theories of civil society that derive from the Western Enlightenment, on the other, it will, in my view, have to draw upon those relatively liberal strands of the Neo-Confucian tradition. These are the strands that I will emphasize in this chapter.

INGREDIENTS: WHO, AND WHAT, DOES CIVIL SOCIETY INCLUDE?

This question seems to envision a social framework that can gather together certain individual parts while excluding others. If this is so, the question fails to make sense in a Confucian context. Confucian thought does not conceive the world in terms of delimited parts.[6] The great social anthropologist Fei Xiaotong has given the following vivid account of the difference between Confucian and Western ways of thinking about the configuration of relationships that constitute a society.

> In some ways Western society bears a resemblance to the way we bundle kindling wood in the fields. A few rice stalks are bound together to make a handful, several handfuls are bound together to make a small bundle, several small bundles are bound together to make a larger bundle, and several larger bundles are bound together to make a stack to carry on a pole. Every single stalk in the entire stack belongs to one specific large bundle, one specific small bundle, and one specific handful. Similar stalks are assembled together, clearly classified, and then bound together. In a society these units are groups. . . . The group has a definite demarcation line."[7]

The configuration of Chinese society, on the other hand, is "like the rings of successive ripples that are propelled outward on the surface when you throw a stone into water. Each individual is the center of the rings emanating from his social influence. Wherever the ripples reach, affiliations occur."[8]

The ripples can eventually reach everywhere. The Neo-Confucian vision was thus holistic. As Tu Wei-ming characterizes it, "[S]elf, community, nature, and Heaven are integrated in an anthropocosmic vision."[9] Insofar as discourse is driven by this holistic imagination, it is difficult to make the distinctions that are the staple of Western secular civil society discourse: between public and private, and voluntary and involuntary forms of association.

There are words in Chinese—*gong* and *si*—that translate as "public" and "private," but in the logic of Confucian discourse the distinction between them is completely relative. Once again, according to Fei Xiaotong:

> Sacrificing one's family for oneself, sacrificing one's clan for one's family—this formula is an actual fact. Under such a formula what would someone say if you called him *si* [acting in his private interest]? He would not be able to see it that way, because when he sacrificed his clan, he might have done it for his family, and the way he looks at it, his family is *gong* [the public interest]. When he sacrificed the nation for the benefit of his small group in the struggle for power, he was also doing it for the public interest [*gong*], the public interest of his small group. . . . *Gong* and *si* are relative terms; anything within the circle in which one is standing can be called *gong*.[10]

Likewise, the distinction between voluntary and involuntary forms of association is blurry. In the West the family is the prototypical involuntary association; one does not choose one's parents. But in the Asian traditions there is a different way of thinking about the family. Fei Xiaotong again: If a friend in England or America writes a letter saying he is going to "bring his family" to visit, the recipient knows very well who will be coming. But "in China, although we frequently see the phrase, 'Your entire family is invited,' very few people could say exactly which persons should be included under 'family.'" A person can choose to include distant relatives or even friends as part of broadly conceived family. The involuntary relationships that make up the kinship group are expanded in indeterminate ways by voluntary affiliation.[11]

A traditional discourse centered on a holistic "anthropocosmic vision" and unable to make fixed distinctions between public and private, voluntary and involuntary forms of association—this would not seem a very promising basis for developing a coherent theory of civil society. Contemporary Chinese and other Asians are faced with social realities that cannot readily be encompassed by this vision. One of the words for civil society, it will be noted, is *shimin shehui*, "urban society." In modern metropolises like Hong Kong, Shanghai, Taipei, Tokyo, or Seoul, the Asian intellectual has to contend with extreme social fragmentation, industrial or postindustrial divisions of labor, populations influenced by global media and demanding opportunities for free, individualistic self-expression, and a powerful, globalized market economy—all of which put complex demands on the state.

There are those, of course, who think that the only way to confront these new challenges is through "all-out Westernization," rather than through any appropriation of the Confucian legacy. But others believe that it is neither possible nor desirable to discard that legacy.[12] When those who consider the reappropriation of the Confucian legacy consider the issue of civil society, they look to the intermediate associations between the nuclear family and the state. The logic of Confucianism makes it difficult to make sharp distinctions between the various elements in this intermediate realm. Instead of seeing different kinds of associations as independent entities, like so many separate sticks within a bundle of firewood, each with its own purposes and each at least potentially in competition with each other, they tend to think of the different elements as fluidly interpenetrating each other, like the ripples on a pond. When they use the word *minjian shuhui*—"people-based society"—to translate civil society, they do not usually connote popular groups acting independently of the state. They assume that people-based groups cannot properly exist without the general permission, guidance, and supervision of the government.

At one extreme, those envisioning such people-based groups from top to bottom might see them simply as a "transmission belt" between the state and the lowest realms of the society. (Ideologues in Mainland China and some apologists for the Singapore regime would fall into this category.) Public purposes infuse what we in the West would think of as private matters. At the other extreme, those envisioning people-based groups from bottom to the top are likely to blend what Westerners consider private matters with public affairs. They may think of groups like the family as legitimately being able to influence affairs of state. (Into this category might fall some of those who celebrate familistic, "guanxi capitalism," in which business deals are regulated by particularistic connections between relatives and friends rather than impersonally applied laws.) But most intellectuals working within the Confucian tradition fall between these extremes. For instance, they recognize the necessity for intermediate associations to maintain a large degree of autonomy from the state. Yet because of the difficulty that Confucian discourse has of offering a principled justification for such autonomy, they advocate it more on pragmatic grounds. An institutional embodiment of this stance is perhaps seen on contemporary Taiwan, which in many ways is witnessing a "springtime of civil society," with a tremendous proliferation of intermediate associations—religious, ethnic, commercial, environmentalist, feminist. To have a legitimate standing in Taiwanese society, all of these groups must be duly registered with an appropriate government ministry, and thus in principle accept government supervision. But there are now so many of these groups that the government could not regulate them, even it wanted to. For all intents and purposes these groups function as autonomous, voluntary associations. Members of such groups definitely seem to want this practical autonomy. But most seem reluctant to undertake the effort that would be necessary to establish a principled basis for it.[13]

SOCIETY: WHAT MAKES CIVIL SOCIETY A SOCIETY AND NOT A SIMPLE AGGREGATE?

The Confucian vision is radically social. As Herbert Fingarette puts it: "For Confucius, unless there are at least two human beings, there are no human beings."[14] The relationships that define the conditions for human flourishing were given a classic formulation by Mencius:

> Between parent and child there is to be affection
> Between ruler and minister, rightness
> Between husband and wife, [gender] distinctions
> Between older and younger, [siblings] an order of precedence
> Between friends, trustworthiness[15]

This formulation assumes that human persons flourish through performing different, mutually complementary roles. Some roles should take priority over others—for instance, the role of parent is more important than the role of friend. But this formulation does not justify a top-down, authoritarian system in which it is the prerogative of superior people to give orders and the duty of inferiors blindly to obey.

There is another formulation of the basic Confucian relationships that does justify authoritarianism. That is the doctrine of the "three bonds," between ruler/minister, father/son, and husband/wife. Today, in common discourse, the core of Confucian teaching is indeed understood in terms of these authoritarian three bonds. According to Wm. Theodore de Bary, however, the three bonds "have no place in the Confucian classics, and were only codified later in [first century C.E.] Han texts."[16] They are of Legalist providence, products of an age when Confucianism became the ideology of the imperial state. Apologists for Asian authoritarian regimes like to stress the importance of the three bonds. But Zhu Xi and most Neo-Confucians rarely mention them.[17] And when Tu Wei-ming and other modern Confucian intellectuals try to press Confucianism into the service of creating a democratic civil society, they claim that the Mencian vision of mutuality is the most authentic expression of Confucianism.[18]

Even if one tries to build a vision of civil society around the five relationships of Mencius, it would be difficult to avoid making moral distinctions between men and women and older and younger people that would be unacceptable to Western liberals. However, in theory at least, these distinctions would lead not to inferiority but to complementary reciprocity. The emphasis in the parent/child and husband/wife relationship would be on mutual affection and love, expressed energetically and creatively on all sides. The parent should instruct the child, but the child should also admonish the parent if the parent is doing something wrong. In the *Classic of Filial Piety,* the disciple of Confucius asks the Master, "[I]f a child follows all of his parents' commands, can this be called filiality? The Master replied, 'What kind of talk is this! . . . If a father even had one son to remonstrate with him, he still would not fall into evil ways. In the face of whatever is not right, the son cannot but remonstrate with his father.'"[19] In the *Classic of Filial Piety for Women,* "The women said, 'We dare to ask whether we follow all our husbands' commands we could be called virtuous?' Her Ladyship answered, 'What kind of talk is this! . . . If a husband has a remonstrating wife then he won't fall into evil ways. Therefore if a husband transgresses against the Way, you must correct him. How could it be that to obey your husband in everything would make you a virtuous person?'"[20]

A civil society grounded in such notions of creative reciprocity would discourage configurations of power that would prevent weaker members from acting as moral agents in the reciprocal exchanges that bind the society together. It would protect from retaliation members who exercised their duty to remonstrate with those in power. It would encourage everyone to receive the kind of education that would enable him or her properly to fulfill their responsibilities. It was in this spirit that the seventeenth-century Neo-Confucian scholar Huang Zongxi proposes, according to de Bary, "a constitutional program resembling, in some important respects, the constitutional system of the modern West."[21] There are two main elements in his proposal for institutional innovation. First is a Confucian justification for a rule of law that would place limitations on the ruler's power. Second is a proposal to strengthen schools and learned academies so that they could increase the numbers of civil servants and prepare them to perform an expanded range of functions in civil government—and could become strong centers for the expression of educated public opinion.[22] Huang's "scholarly forum was to be a well-defined, state-supported, fully accredited, and legal function of a duly constituted order, and yet as independent as possible in a society that lacked a middle class, popular press, church, legal profession or other supporting infrastructure independent of the state."[23]

Huang was recognized as one of the most learned men of his time, and his ideas resonated with other leading Confucian scholars during the early Qing dynasty. His ideas were not implemented during the Qing, but Chinese revolutionaries and reformers in the twentieth century have drawn upon them in the effort to create a Chinese version of Western constitutionalism. Although the actually existing structure of the imperial Chinese state and society was alien to Western notions of a civil society, the writing of scholars like Huang Zongxi demonstrates that there are intellectual resources within the Confucian tradition for imagining such a society—one based on a constitutionally limited state and on an array of mediating institutions, especially educational institutions.

Values: How Is Civil Society Important? What Particular Values Does It Offer Its Members That Might Be Unobtainable in Its Absence?

In the Confucian vision, as noted above, human flourishing can occur only if social relations have a proper moral basis. This means that people have to learn to discern what is the right way to behave and that for the most part they voluntarily act accordingly. A community based on force and fear cannot be a good community. But neither can a community based on an amoral clash of competing interest groups, even when this leads to a stable, peaceful balance of power and many opportunities for individuals to choose between rival versions of the good life. The Confucian project requires moral cultivation at all levels of the society.

This cultivation is to develop the mind-and-heart, an inextricable combination of mental and emotional faculties. The goal of this cultivation, as Tu Wei-ming puts it, "is not an idea of abstract universalism but a dynamic process of self-transcendence, not a departure from one's source but a broadening and deepening of one's sensitivity without losing sight of one's rootedness in the body, family, community, society, and the world."[24] This cultivation must begin within the family, and it is sustained at the most fundamental level by the rituals of family life. For most people in imperial China it stayed within the (extended) family. However, the more advanced levels of moral cultivation—the kind required to set oneself on the path to becoming a "gentleman," capable of responsible political leadership—required a plentitude of intermediary institutions: in the words of Tu Wei-ming, "community schools, community compacts, local temples, theater groups, clan associations, guilds, festivals, and a variety of ritual-centered activities."[25] Each of these institutions had its own integrity—its core practices were seen as ends in themselves, not just means to some larger, universal ends. But Confucian self-cultivation aimed to see these institutions in the widest possible context. With proper self-cultivation, a Confucian could see how a strong commitment to one's family would not be in conflict with commitment to one's community; and commitment to one's local community was not in conflict with commitment to the state. The more intimate commitments indeed should train one to engage properly in the broader commitments.

The challenges of creating stable societies with a common moral basis in the modern urban environments of contemporary Asia are far greater than the challenges facing Confucian thinkers in the predominantly agrarian societies of imperial China. The realization of the Confucian project under modern conditions would require more self-cultivation of more people, especially more of the cultivation that would enable people to place their family and local community commitments in the broadest possible context. This would require an even richer array of intermediary institutions than there were in imperial China. To fulfill the purposes of self-cultivation, these institutions would have to be seen as educational, in the broadest sense of the word. They would have to be based on humanistic principles, not just the pursuit of money and power for their own sakes. Their organizational structure would have to encourage the kind of give and take necessary for effective learning.

It is through such groups that Asian societies could become *wenming shehui*, "civilized societies," societies full of the values of civility. In the Confucian context, however, civility does not simply mean tolerance for rivals in a world of competitive coexistence—as Michael Walzer interprets the idea in the context of the liberal-egalitarian vision of civil society. It means the eventual achievement of a kind of social consensus. The attitude of Huang Zongxi was characteristic of even the most "liberal" Confucian scholars. Huang advocated open discussion of public questions in the enhanced schools and academies that he proposed. "At the same time," as de Bary puts it, "it must be noted that by open discussion of public questions, Huang did not mean complete freedom of expression in all matters. As a Confucian he believed the upholding of strict moral standards was necessary to the social and political order; thus he was prepared to ban, on the local level, forms of moral impropriety and social corruption."[26]

Today, even citizens in relatively liberal East Asian regimes like Taiwan give general support to laws that ban breaches of filial piety. For instance, family law in Taiwan as well as in most East Asian countries mandates that children must take care of their aged parents—something that in Western liberal democracy is generally regarded as a private matter, no matter how desirable such a mandate might be. There is also a fair amount of social consensus in favor of laws formally banning the kind of pornography that would be protected by the First Amendment in the United States (even though in practice there are plenty of pornographic materials available in most East Asian countries). Finally, there is considerable support for government restriction of "irresponsible" (sensationalistic, scandalous) journalism, although intellectuals in the more open East Asian regimes are also concerned about how to protect legitimate criticism of people in power.

This concern for achieving social consensus is also reflected in the ordering of educational systems throughout contemporary East Asia. The assumption is that schools are supposed to develop not just technical skills but proper values and that the state should play an active role in ensuring that the proper values are indeed taught. There are ambiguities within traditional Confucian epistemology about how learning of proper values takes place. One school of thought stresses the need for the learner to absorb proper information. Another—with roots in the ideas of Mencius—sees learning as the unfolding of knowledge that is immanent in the learner. Depending on what side of the tradition one emphasizes, learning can involve greater degrees of indoctrination, on the one hand, and education, on the other. The Maoist government in China, obviously, emphasized indoctrination. From research academies and universities at the top to the "small groups" that honeycombed all levels of society and carried out "study sessions" throughout the grass roots, participants were expected to learn the proper political line and encourage one another, through criticism and self-criticism, to conform to it. In contemporary Taiwan, in sharp contrast, there is extremely lively and open intellectual discussion in universities and research institutes and in the media. (At the primary- and secondary-school levels, on the other hand, there is more of an emphasis on conformity than there would be in the United States.) Throughout all levels of society, a vast assortment of associations and community organizations try to develop and propagate their various visions about cultural, political, and economic issues. Other East Asian societies, like Singapore, Japan, and South Korea, fall somewhere between these two extremes of emphasizing indoctrination versus education. And they differ similarly with respect to government and unofficial public opinion about how much social consensus is required and how it should be achieved. But even in Taiwan, which currently is probably the most open society in East Asia, there is less principled support for moral pluralism and more of a tendency to equate civility with social consensus than there would be in the classic liberal or the liberal egalitarian visions.

RISKS: WHAT RISKS AND LIABILITIES, IF ANY, DOES CIVIL SOCIETY
   POSE FOR ITS MEMBERS?

Perhaps the main risk to the Neo-Confucian project over the centuries has been its excessive idealism, its unrealistic assessment of the demands of ensuring social order in a large and complex society. As Tu Wei-ming notes,

[B]y addressing, in a fundamentally humanist way, the meaning of politics, Neo-Confucian intellectuals not only developed their own distinctive style of political participation but also formulated the ritual of exercising power in East Asian politics. To be sure, it is easy to criticize the Neo-Confucian insistence on the inseparability of morality and politics as a failure to understand the political process as an independent arena of human activity. It was perhaps constitutive to their intention to moralize politics that they inevitably experience alienation from the center of power. The interjection of the category of "self-cultivation" into the discourse of *realpolitic* may seem naïve. Indeed, this has been widely interpreted by modern scholars as characteristic of the Confucian predicament: inner spiritual self-cultivation does not at all lead to positive social and political consequence.[27]

However, Tu argues that if seen from the proper perspective, the Neo-Confucian position does not have to be naïve. Indeed, Tu might argue that from a Confucian perspective it is Western liberalism that seems naïve, in its notion that political order can be maintained through technically expert management upon a citizenry divided by extreme ethical pluralism and predominantly focused on private pleasures rather than public duties. "The cliché that virtually all Confucian scholar-officials were actively involved in purifying the ethos and revitalizing the spirit of the community suggests that, as self-styled ministers of the moral order, their commitment to social transformation was, in their view, the calling of their political engagement."[28] Historically, Tu argues, the Confucians were extremely successful in their calling. "[I]t was in the shaping of the habits of the heart of the East Asian people that the Confucian persuasion exerted its enduring influence. The pervasiveness of the Confucian life-orientation was such that Confucian ethics manifested itself in morality books, peasant rebellions, entertainment, religious movements, and popular literature. . . . The learning of the heart and mind, with emphasis on human nature and feeling, became a grammar of action in East Asian social praxis not necessarily because of its impeccable logic in moral reasoning; its reasonableness in the practical living of ordinary people accounted for much of its persuasive power."[29]

Throughout the centuries, however, powerful Asian rulers themselves have thought that Neo-Confucianism was naïve about the dictates of power. When faced with the task of holding together a large and diverse empire, and especially when faced with the dangers of internal rebellion and external invasion, they often resorted to the hard-headed realpolitik of Legalism. In the twentieth century, the problems arising from increased population, increased fragmentation, civil war, and outside aggression have, of course, risen exponentially. It has often seemed to successful political leaders that they could not afford the humaneness of Confucianism. The last political campaign of Mao Zedong's regime, for example, was aimed at condemning Confucius (which was meant as a veiled criticism of

Zhou Enlai) and praising the Legalists, whose vision inspired Mao's own form of dictatorship.[30] East Asian regimes that suppress dissent and engage in large-scale state-led mobilization are acting very much in the Legalist tradition, which is what remains if the Confucian vision proves itself to be insufficiently robust.

To succeed on their own terms in setting the political agenda in the contemporary world and thus in avoiding the slide into Legalist authoritarianism, Confucians need to find new ways of shaping the "habits of the heart" of the East Asian people. The greatest challenge to doing this, perhaps, is that posed by the development of mass society, atomized by widespread social mobility, distracted from public affairs by a globalized consumer culture, and vulnerable to manipulation by mass media. Confucian self-cultivation requires slow, hard work, difficult to sustain in a frenetic market economy. It requires the development of moral discipline, difficult to accomplish in the face of the self-gratifications promised by consumer culture. Classic Confucian education aimed to produce some "superior persons" whose authority would be respected and accepted by ordinary people—an elitist notion that goes against populist instincts encouraged by mass media and global popular culture, and against the notion of a *gongmin shehui,* a "citizens' society," in which each citizen has an equal right to participate in the polity. Without creative adaptation, the Confucian vision may fail to be attractive to modern mass societies, and be unable to inspire a civil society possessed of enough civility to sustain orderly forms of democracy. If that happens, perhaps the only viable path toward political democracy would be an adaptation of Western liberal visions. Failing that, the probable outcome might be forms of authoritarianism arising out of indigenous East Asian traditions.

RESPONSIBILITY: HOW IS RESPONSIBILITY FOR HUMAN WELL-BEING PROPERLY SHARED BY, OR DISTRIBUTED AMONG, THE INDIVIDUAL, THE FAMILY, THE STATE, AND PRIVATE ASSOCIATIONS?

As noted above, in the Neo-Confucian vision social order is based on the proper performance of interdependent social roles. If everyone plays his or her roles properly—that is, if parents are good parents and children are good children, if rulers are good rulers and subjects good subjects, and so forth—then there will be peace all under Heaven. Sometimes it may appear that the roles one occupies in one sphere of life come into conflict with roles in other spheres. For instance one's role as a parent might seem to conflict with one's role as a loyal citizen or political subject. The Confucian position is that if one cultivates oneself fully enough and thus understands the responsibilities implicit in these roles deeply enough, one will find that there is ultimately no contradiction.

The roles and their attendant responsibilities are determined by cosmic Principle (*Li*). This Principle is an objective reality, and insofar as the moral life is to conform to such an objective reality, Confucian thought is like the Western natural law tradition. But there is an important difference. In the natural law tradition, people can know through reason the laws to which they should conform, and then it is the task of moral cultivation to achieve this conformity. But in the Confucian tradition, one cannot simply know the Principle through reason. This requires learning of the mind-and-heart, an embodied form of knowledge that is at least as affective as cognitive. It is the task of the Confucian to cultivate the moral sensibility that would enable him or her to apprehend this fundamental Principle. One becomes moral not by following external rules, but by struggling to develop the self.

The place for such self-cultivation is in the midst of the world. The Confucians, as Tu Wei-ming puts it, were "action intellectuals." It was their responsibility to be immersed in all the political and social conflicts of their time. But unlike the liberal who learns to live with conflict by tolerating it, the Confucian aspired to learn through conflict so as to overcome it by changing the rules of the game, so that the exercise of power would be subordinated to moral commitments, rather than vice versa.

In the midst of the world, Confucian self-cultivation involves some combination of academic study of classic literature, sincere participation in family, community, and political rituals, and meditative introspection. There is no pope of Confucianism to define correct interpretation of such things, only an ever-evolving consensus forged through discussion among whose who sincerely follow the Confucian Way. There is something almost existential about this, and it helps keep Confucianism from the dogmatism into which the natural law tradition can sometimes fall.

In general, though, the Confucian sense of social responsibility is biased toward the fulfillment of roles at the most fundamental levels of society. The opening statement of *The Great Learning,* the best known and most influential of all the Confucian classics, offers this summary of the Confucian moral and political program:

The ancients who wished to illuminate "illuminating virtue" all under Heaven first governed their states. Wishing to govern their states, they first regulated their families. Wishing to regulate their families, they first cultivated their personal lives. Wishing to cultivate their personal lives, they first rectify their hearts and minds. Wishing to rectify their hearts and minds, they made their intentions sincere. Wishing to make their intentions sincere, they first extended their knowledge. The extension of knowledge lay in the investigation of things. For only when things are investigated is knowledge extended; only when knowledge is extended are intentions sincere; only when intentions are sincere are hearts and minds rectified; only when hearts and minds are rectified are personal lives cultivated; only when personal lives are cultivated are families regulated; only when families are regulated are states governed; only when states are governed is there peace all under Heaven. Therefore, from the Son of Heaven to the common people, all, without exception, must take self-cultivation as the root.[31]

This is a vision of rippling waves of interdependent, mutual responsibility extending through all the levels of the world. But the waves emanate from a center—the self. The cultivation of the self is an end in itself, not simply (as in the Western civic republican tradition, which otherwise has important affinities with Confucianism) a means to achieve a well-ordered polity. Self-cultivation cannot be done alone, however. It requires in the first instance a strong family, cultivation of which is also an end in itself. Eventually, it also requires a well-ordered state. One's most basic responsibilities, however, are to those closest to oneself—family and local community. Before there can be proper governance of the state, there must be proper self-cultivation leading to proper regulation of the family. A wise government, therefore, will support the individual, family, and local community in their work of mutual cultivation, but it will not attempt to preempt these functions.

FREEDOM: WHAT IS THE APPROPRIATE BALANCE BETWEEN INDIVIDUAL AUTONOMY AND CONSTRAINTS IMPOSED BY NONGOVERNMENTAL GROUPS?

For the Neo-Confucian, freedom is not the "freedom to choose." The fundamental building blocks of a civil society are nonoptional institutions. The foundation of the Confucian project was expanding family virtues beyond the confines of the home. The point of departure is the most nonvoluntary of human institutions, the family. For the Western liberal, even the family becomes like a voluntary association, whose members have easy exit and the ability to affiliate or not if they so please. For the Confucian, on the other hand, even voluntary associations, like learned societies or guilds, should be like families—their members should be bound by loyalties that make exit difficult. In the Neo-Confucian perspective, then, freedom does not consist in choosing which groups one will belong to. It consists in creatively contextualizing those commitments which fate has assigned. It involves more deeply understanding the meaning of one's roles as parent/child, ruler/minister, husband/wife, older sibling/younger sibling, and friend—so that one can flexibly, even playfully, reconcile these with each other and with all the other confusing roles that one must play in an evolving modern world. This task can provide wide latitude for action and immense challenges for personal creativity, and it can lead to a plethora of individualized responses to particular situations. Under the right circumstances, it can encourage vigorous entrepreneurial initiative. In practice, well-cultivated Confucians would have a great deal of freedom to choose. But in principle, their choices would be directed toward a larger goal, a dynamic, open process of spiritual development leading toward a truly *wen-ming shehui*, a civilized society of *gongmin*, or public citizens, rich in *min-jian*, or people-based associations, within the conurbinations of *shimin*, city people in the modern world.

FUTURE READING

Donald Munro, ed. *Individualism and Holism: Studies in Confucian and Taoist Values*. Ann Arbor: Center for Chinese Studies, University of Michigan, 1985. Essays on connections between self and society in Chinese philosophical traditions.

Wm. Theodore de Bary, *The Liberal Tradition in China*. New York: Columbia University Press, 1983; and Wm. Theodore de Bary. *Asian Values and Human Rights: A Confucian Communitarian Perspective*. Cambridge: Harvard University Press, 1998. Essays by one of America's leading Sinologists on the relevance of Confucian tradition to Western cultural and political concerns.

Tu Wei-Ming. "Confucianism." In *Our Religions*, ed. Arvind Sharma. San Francisco: HarperSanFrancisco, 1993. Authoritative introduction to the Confucian tradition by a prominent proponent of Confucian humanism.

David Hall and Roger Ames. *Thinking through Confucius*. Albany: State University of New York Press, 1987. Introduction to Confucian ethics.

NOTES

1. Lydia H. Liu, *Translingual Practice: Literature, National Culture, and Translated Modernity—China, 1900–1937* (Stanford, Calif.: Stanford University Press, 1995), p. 336.

2. William T. Rowe, "The Problem of 'Civil Society' in Late Imperial China," *Modern China* 19, no. 2 (April 1993): 142.

3. For a comprehensive summary of the tradition see Tu Wei-ming, "Confucianism," in *Our Religions*, ed. Arvind Sharma (San Francisco: HarperSanFrancisco, 1995), pp. 141–227.

4. Wm. Theodore de Bary, *The Liberal Tradition in China* (Hong Kong: Chinese University Press of Hong Kong, 1983); and *Asian Values and Human Rights: A Confucian Communitarian Perspective* (Cambridge: Harvard University Press, 1998).

5. Tu Wei-ming, "Cultural China: The Periphery as the Center," *The Living Tree: The Changing Meaning of Being Chinese Today*, special issue of *Daedalus* 120, no. 2 (Spring 1991): 1–32.

6. See Donald J. Munro, introduction to *Individualism and Holism: Studies in Confucian and Taoist Values*, ed. Donald Munro (Ann Arbor: Center for Chinese Studies, University of Michigan, 1985), pp. 1–30; see also the other essays in this volume, passim.

7. Fei Xiaotong, "Chinese Social Structure and Its Values," in *Changing China: Readings in the History of China from the Opium War to the Present,* ed. J. Mason Gentzler (New York: Praeger, 1977), p. 211. Originally published as *Xiangtu Zhongguo* (Shanghai, 1948).

8. Fei Xiaotong, "Chinese Social Structure and Its Values."

9. Tu Wei-ming, "Heart, Human Nature, and Feeling: Implications for the Neo-Confucian Idea of Civil Society," Reischauer Lecture, Harvard University; paper presented at the Ethikon Conference, Redondo Beach, Calif., July 10–12, 1998, p. 27.

10. Fei Xiaotong, "Chinese Social Structure and Its Values," p. 213.

11. Fei Xiaotong, "Chinese Social Structure and Its Values," p. 211.

12. See the controversy over the 1988 Chinese television series *Heshang,* which was seen by many as advocating "all-out Westernization." Su Xiaokang and Wang Luxiang, *Deathsong of the River: A Reader's Guide to the Chinese TV Series "Heshang,"* trans. and ed. Richard W. Bodman and Pin P. Wan (Ithaca: Cornell East Asia Series, 1991).

13. Hsin-huang Michael Hsiao, "The Development and Organization of Foundations in Taiwan: An Expression of Cultural Vigor in a Newly Born Society," in *Quiet Revolutions on Taiwan, Republic of China,* ed. Jason C. Hu (Taipei: Kwang Hwa, 1994), pp. 386–419; and Makito Noda, *Emerging Civil Society in the Asia Pacific Community: Nongovernmental Underpinnings of the Emerging Asia Pacific Regional Community,* ed. Tadashi Yamamoto (Singapore: Institute of Southeast Asian Studies; and Tokyo: Japan Centre for International Exchange, 1995).

14. Herbert Fingarette, *Confucius—The Secular as Sacred* (New York: Harper and Row, 1972), as quoted by Henry Rosemont, "Reply to Nosco," in paper presented at the Ethikon Conference, Santa Fe, N.M., January 15–17, 1999.

15. Mencius 3A:4, quoted in de Bary, *Asian Values and Human Rights,* p. 17.

16. de Bary, *Asian Values and Human Rights,* p. 124.

17. de Bary, *Asian Values and Human Rights,* pp. 124–25.

18. Tu Wei-ming, "Confucianism," pp. 186–94.

19. *Classic of Filial Piety,* as quoted in de Bary, *Asian Values and Human Rights,* p. 126.

20. *Classic of Filial Piety for Women,* as quoted in de Bary, *Asian Values and Human Rights,* p. 128.

21. de Bary, *Asian Values and Human Rights,* p. 102.

22. de Bary, *Asian Values and Human Rights,* pp. 100–109.

23. de Bary, *Asian Values and Human Rights,* p. 106.

24. Tu Wei-ming, "Heart, Human Nature, and Feeling," p. 22.

25. Tu Wei-ming, "Heart, Human Nature, and Feeling," p. 18.

26. de Bary, *Asian Values and Human Rights,* p. 107.

27. Tu Wei-ming, "Heart, Human Nature, and Feeling," p. 20.

28. Tu Wei-ming, "Heart, Human Nature, and Feeling," p. 23.

29. Tu Wei-ming, "Heart, Human Nature, and Feeling," p. 23.

30. Jun Jing, *The Temple of Memories: History, Power, and Morality in a Chinese Village* (Stanford, Calif.: Stanford University Press, 1996), pp. 53–54.

31. *The Great Learning,* in *Sources of the Chinese Tradition,* vol. 1, comp. Wm. Theodore de Bary, Wing-Tsit Chan, and Burton Watson (New York: Columbia University Press, 1963), p. 115.

PART V

CHAPTER 11

Conclusion

Are Civil Societies the Transmission Belts of Ethical Tradition?

Michael A. Mosher

THESE DAUNTING ESSAYS combine reflections on civil society with an analysis of a fair sample of the world's ethical traditions. Each stands alone as a guide for the inquisitive about the character of its respective tradition. More importantly for our purposes, the juxtaposition of these distinct outlooks provides a deep sense of the rivalry that persists over the nature of ethical commitment. They also occasionally show how opposed traditions mutually inform one another.

Several of the contributors spotted a source for the current interest in civil society in the revolution that swept across Europe in 1989, when communist governments collapsed in the face of pressure brought to bear upon them by large numbers of citizen activists. Writers within a Western "civic republican" tradition were at the same time renewing the notion of civil society in works that expressed fear for the survival of a vigorous associational life in the Western democracies. The locus classicus of this literature was probably Robert Putnam's *Making Democracy Work.*[1] As it now appears that the strength of the civic virtues in the former communist bloc countries has been exaggerated, observers might conclude that civil society, understood as a sine qua non for democracy, was withering on the vine everywhere.

Given these heightened anxieties, one valuable exercise in these essays was directed to casting suspicion on the notion of there always being a positive link between civil society and democracy. There have been instead good and bad forms of civil society. German and Italian civic life once sponsored Nazi and fascist movements. In America one has the spectacle of violent "patriot" organizations. Postcommunist societies seem prone to nationalist passions and gangster capitalism. There was also vigorous disagreement about capitalism itself. Was commercial enterprise an ingredient in a good civil society or were the dolorous effects of such commerce instead prime examples of what associational life should try to correct? Liberal egalitarian Michael Walzer, in agreement (and not for the only time) with libertarian and classical liberal Loren Lomasky, saw no reason to exclude commercial organizations from civil society. On the other side, critical theorist Simone Chambers and Islamic spokesperson Hasan Hanafi rehearsed the anxieties that often seem to accompany capitalist endeavors and asked whether these were not sufficient to exclude private profit-seeking firms from a civil society that they think represents more elevated ethical ideals.

In thinking about these essays, I asked how many authors recognized the significance of the following choice in models of civil society. Either you want civil society because it is a transmission belt for the dominant republican values (or for Confucian, classically liberal, critical theoretical values, if these are dominant); or you want civil society because it entrenches diverse values and is consequently a barrier against concentrations of power. Either civil society lacks legitimacy unless it reflects the values of the state; or civil society entrenches diverse values that would otherwise be absorbed in or swept away by the state. The first picture of associational life suggests it be always congruent with the prevailing norms. Where these are liberal democratic, all associations ought to be minidemocracies. Private clubs that encourage "hierarchical" relationships will come under pressure to conform. Naturally, if the dominant norms are, say, Islamic or Christian, associational life will mirror the relevant theological tenets. The second picture suggests that associations serve their own purposes, which are diverse and separate from any direct civic function. Their ability to entrench values different from the dominant norms not only helps minority cultures to preserve their own way of life; these associations indirectly become a source of a healthy resistance to national institutions that have become tyrannical. For instance, communists populated European anti-Nazi resistance movements. Thus, illiberal groups served a liberal cause. But things can go the other way, too. By making their norms popular, undemocratic groups sometimes threaten liberal democratic regimes. In addition, associations are not always constant in their allegiance to ideals. The very chorale groups that Robert Putnam claims sustain democratic life in Italy were in the previous regime singing Mussolini's tunes.[2] We do not evidently know which groups will be schools for democracy when the illiberal virtues of communist groups can transform its members into fighters for democratic dignity while the republican virtues of Italian civic life were effectively put to use in support of a totalitarian regime.

I offer a preliminary observation to which we will return in concluding. Though it may have been an artifact of how the question was posed (what does civil society look like from within your ethical tradition?), many of the contributors seemed overly committed to the view of civil society as a transmission belt for dominant values. Though all gave ritual or rhetorical affirmation to the importance of diversity and the independence of associations, this was often qualified by a larger commitment to the transmission belt model.

The Strategy of Redrawing Civil Society: Critical Theory and Natural Law

Simone Chambers's suggestive and useful account of the development of critical theory led this reader to an admittedly unconventional comparison. Perhaps critical theory, exemplified in Jürgen Habermas, could be viewed as an extension of the natural law claims that Michael Pakaluk sets out with precision and economy. Thus, when Chambers appeals to our "intuition," embedded in U.S. tax law, that there is a fundamental moral difference between the nonprofit activities of "churches, universities, unions, associations, and political parties" and the for-profit activities of incorporated firms and parterships, she is making a type of argument parallel to that of Pakaluk when he similarly appeals to intuition in saying, "[I]t is impossible for a person of good character, buying a good book at a bookstore, to look upon a person of bad character, who buys pornography in an 'adult' bookstore, as engaged in something analogous."

Both want to draw a censorious line around activities that have strayed too far beyond any intent, as Pakaluk expresses it, "to foster some aspect of the human good," a good discovered by unbiased reflection upon the nature and purposes of human endeavor. It is germane to the force of these examples, but irrelevant to the larger distinctions being made, to say to Pakaluk that "bad" books can be bought now in any "good" American bookstore (e.g., Borders or Barnes and Noble); or to remind Chambers of the many morally dubious activities in which nonprofit associations might be engaged, which might easily outweigh the alleged wrong of innocently making money, as Samuel Johnson once put it. Michael Pakakluk could reply that bad books in good stores exemplify what's wrong with America or civil society or both. His argument could link up with that of Chambers by drawing the conclusion that bookstores forget about the good they serve when they are motivated solely by the demands of the bottom line. Simone Chambers could reply that making money, innocently or not, is beside the point in the light of the macrotransformations that occur behind the backs, so to speak, of the moneymakers, who are unwittingly destroying the very activities that in other respects they cherish. Making money is now an activity carried on in ways that remove its practitioners from the associational contexts that sponsor human good.

Pakaluk's and Chambers's arguments contain empirical premises that may or may not prove adequate. My intent is only to draw attention to the parallels in their common indictment of much that goes on in contemporary society. This indictment is accompanied by a terminological effort to relocate civil society so that it stands only upon the sanctified ground of a stipulated understanding of human good. Redrawing the map of human decency permits one to excoriate any liberalism that would indulge its taste for forbidden fruit on the other side of these boundaries.

In drawing this parallel between two critiques of the liberal enterprise, it is important to remember their differences as well. Unlike natural law, critical theory stands on the modern side of an immensely important divide. The latter is a self-consciously post-Kantian enterprise. For the natural lawyers, however, Kant is only a misleading blip on the radar screen of intellectual history. I take Kant to affirm the rights of subjectivity, which were already apparent in the social contract tradition that inspires classical liberalism. Subjective freedom is arguably the very terrain of a civil society that accommodates a wide range of ethical disagreement under the auspices of a none-too-demanding legal framework. The natural lawyer seeks to narrow the legitimacy of permissible activities within this framework by appealing to a sense of tradition that, from antiquity, has stressed the analogies between human and natural activity. Yet Habermas's notion of a "lifeworld" constitutes a similar appeal to tradition. Like every other self-conscious highlighting of tradition, the lifeworld is understood to be fragile and exposed to forces both untraditional and predatory.

The parallel is not perfect, however. Critical theory would presumably accommodate a post-Kantian sense that a life may be permissibly self-fabricated, so long as the fabrication entailed no exploitative intent. Within the natural law tradition, there is also choice, but more typically it is between being a good or a bad character. There are few inventions here and little innovation, no making or unmaking of cultures, for all these require the latitude of legitimated subjective choices and not just the longitude of good and bad ways of living.

CHRISTIANITY: FABRICATOR AND CRITIC OF WESTERN LIBERALISM

Christianity was the crucible, Michael Banner indicates, within which Western liberal societies arose. Christian doctrines were paradoxically a source for both the rise of Western liberalism and for some of the most trenchant criticisms of it. I grant both of these points. Banner elaborates them well. I am inclined to think, however, that Augustine was the more central figure in these developments.

The account of society that classical liberals presuppose did not have to await the secularization of Christian notions. It was there from the beginning in Augustine's two cities metaphor. Augustine took from the earthly city the whole Greek and Roman philosophical heritage, which celebrated the human origins of communitarian virtue, and transferred it to the heavenly city, the true Church whose members were united in love of God. The earthly city now stood alone, denuded of transcendental aspirations and guidance. Its inhabitants were motivated solely by self-love and, for the ambitious among them, the lust for domination. For the first time since Aristotle and his successors had tried to prove the opposite, neither human nature nor society could claim any distinctive self-organizing principle. The earthly city of Augustine was not only secular; it approximated the condition that a millennium later in Hobbes grounded the claims of the state whose power transcended this strife to provide external order for egoistic competitors. Oliver O'Donovan's account of Augustine's earthly city (cited by Banner) is not surprisingly a purely Hobbist picture of secular society lacking political order: "a fragile and shifting convergence of human wills with respect to limited categories of earthly goods in a sea of moral disorder, of personal and group hostilities." For Augustine this was the city "of the devil" (*Enchiridion* 29). This became *the* task for the early-modern liberal: to provide legislation, as Kant put it, for a "nation of devils" that would re-create the good effects of those virtues that could no longer be supposed were in some Aristotelian sense natural to human beings. To be sure, Hobbes's formulation of rules for Augustine's secular society could appear only when the epistemological anarchy in the notion of Christians united in a love of God was exposed. No such stable union was possible. The Protestant schisms and debilitating religious warfare that followed eventually disabused Christians of any expectation of a divinely ordered convergence of Christian hearts on earth.

Not every Christian followed Augustine. As Banner shows, the Thomist-Aristotelian synthesis that represents mainstream thinking in Catholic and, increasingly, Protestant circles rejected the Augustinian separation of two cities. It replaced Augustine's story with an account of a single organically interconnected society in which the natural virtues of human fellowship still existed, though they were supplemented by revelation and consequently fell under a divine order that resanctified human life outside the church. Since Aquinas synthesized two virtue-laden accounts of the teleological goals of human ethical striving, classical pagan and Christian, it became for evident reasons one of the prime Christian sources of criticism of liberalism's characteristic skepticism about allying the state with "thick" ethical goals.

Augustine's two cities metaphor also points to a pervasive tension that suggests a distinctly different set of protoliberal consequences. Beginning with the crucifixion of Jesus under Roman authority, Banner observes, Christians have been deeply suspicious of political rule. But this almost liberal sense of the corruption of power was accompanied by something else even more propitious: a faith in the spontaneous ability of hearts rightly oriented to achieve fellowship without being tainted by power. This is the democratic and even anarchist proclivity at the heart of both Christian and liberal dispositions. It gives priority to the resources of "spirit" (in the Christian understanding, "Holy Spirit" infused in human spirit) over any mere external order whose legal power disciplined recalcitrant bodies. To be sure, the problems of power were never far away, whether for an Augustine beset by heretical interpretations of Christian creed or later by liberal skeptics troubled by any satisfactory way of resolving multiplying interpretations of the human spirit. With respect to the latter dilemma, observe how Habermas's strategy shadows the old Christian effort to detach oneself from the corruption of power. He indefinitely defers the resort to coercive authority by counting on a conversation/conversion that ever expectantly converges on elusive moral consensus.

Whether or not liberal societies are in some unintended sense the product of Christian dispositions, this does not lessen the ethical hostility many Christians feel when they contemplate practices sanctioned by liberalism. The one programmatic criticism that Banner rehearses, the denial of natural human solidarity in both socialism and liberalism, is best made out as following from the mainstream Thomist-Aristotelian tradition. One might, however, lodge a complaint about this particular pretension of Thomist thought. In supposing that it was an adequate correction for a market society that ignored human solidarity, it overlooked how from the eighteenth century on a secular debate about the origins of solidarity was putting religious claims on the defensive. In Montesquieu's *Spirit of Laws,* for instance, commerce does more work than religion in fostering a tolerant and civic-oriented sociability. Commercial sociability was an adequate replacement for religious solidarities that were on this account thought of as neither tolerant nor civic.

Banner's Thomist synthesis raises a question about who decides. His defense of a principle of subsidiarity privileges the autonomous human spirit. It does so not by making individuals autonomous, but by seeking greater independence for the local communities within which the human spirit is expressed. Subsidiarity is the religious moderate's way of conceding the original devolutional heresy, Luther's "Here I stand, I can do no other." But subsidiarity takes back the autonomy it appears to grant when religious communities seek to legitimize activities forbidden under prevailing understandings of orthodoxy—for example, abortion, euthanasia, divorce, women priests, married priests, or same-sex love. Then all deference to local authority dissipates.

The dilemmas of subsidiarity are apparent in another domain as well: market relations. Is the capacity of cooperating individuals to make and own or to exchange and invest a sign of the autonomous powers of the human spirit? If so, subsidiarity will sanction capitalist social relationships. But what if this compromises other (and higher) values? Such a discussion mirrors the debate among the contributors about whether capitalist firms fall into or out of the sanctified spheres of a genuinely civil society. One interpretation of the subsidiarity principle would leave it to individuals and their local communities to worry about the weight of other values, but the typical Christian interpretation would seem to call for an authoritative creedal solution from on high. On every issue, the subsidiarity principle has no principled way to say how much autonomy is enough except by acts that deny its operative value altogether: a voice from on high simply says no.

This leads us to the "no" that evidently issues from some contemporary and distinctly antinomian Protestant understandings. Without the Thomist-Aristotelian resources of a belief in natural order, they lack any grounding for social criticism except in endlessly variable interpretations of the inscrutable will of God. In societies that are open and liberal, such interpretations will multiply harmlessly as will the ever-new Protestant sects organized around these views. It is another matter in societies with anything resembling a church establishment. In this respect, dissenting German Lutherans deserve our admiration in accepting Karl Barth's Barmen Declaration of 1934 as it corrected doctrinal deficiencies that, by conceding too much to secular authority, inclined German bishops not to oppose Hitler's totalitarianism. But the gloss that Banner places upon this doctrinal correction, that the command of God is "totalitarian" and tolerates no autonomy, would seem to imitate rather than to oppose Hitler. Indeed, it suggests a source for contemporary fundamentalist intolerance. If this account is faithful to the beliefs of Christians, what can we expect after the defeat of one totalitarianism but a (certain kind of) Christian expectation of establishing another, God's "totalitarian" order or, failing that, bitter resentment at the liberal society that frustrated God's will?

Perhaps, however, *totalitarian* is an ill-chosen term. One might refer to the absolute will of God, meaning simply what liberals mean when they make claims for the necessity of sovereign authority. The fact that some body or institution must have the last word, and is thus sovereign, is not inconsistent with the idea that the sovereign consults with others who therefore possess some degree of autonomy. Sovereignty is not totalitarian; neither is the will of God as interpreted by the faithful in a consultative environment that manages to preserve plural understandings. Banner brings this out in his discussion of Calvinism and its incarnation in the colonial New England congregation. Because it worried about the corruption of political order, it had a liberal suspicion of the state and accommodated (limited) disagreements among believers that (eventually) resulted in a pluralist society. Because it acknowledged God infused in the human spirit, it had the confidence to celebrate voice in congregational practices of self-rule. However limited the voice, it planted the seeds for democracy and a more extensive civil society. New England congregations carved out a sphere of collaboration that, Banner concludes, was civil society as it was "classically conceived."

Yet one has only to think of New England's greatest critic of these arrangements, Nathaniel Hawthorne, to understand the risks entailed in not acknowledging the moral imperfections of such Christian perfectionism. For Hawthorne, New England Calvinist associations did not so much resist the state as provide it with theocratic and authoritarian underpinnings. In addition, Christian cruelty and hypocrisy were such that the only redeeming grace of puritan society was the quiet rebellion it provoked, majestically exemplified by Hester Prynne in *The Scarlet Letter*. Her needlework elaboration on the letter *A*, which for her sins she was required to wear, turned adultery into a commentary on the transcendent possibilities of the human spirit. Banner sees in avowals of virginity a paradigm example of Christian freedom to resist the "authorities for the sake of yet a higher authority." Hawthorne settles upon a version of the same resistant freedom to celebrate something very nearly the opposite, outlawed sexual intimacy understood as an expression of the human spirit in justified rebellion against the yoke of Christian authority.

CLASSICAL LIBERALISM: FRAMEWORK FOR OR DISSOLVANT OF ETHICAL TRADITIONS?

Loren Lomasky's classical liberal state has the intent and possibly the capacity to become the container for all the other ethical traditions. Its very abnegation about the good life would seem to make it a suitable vehicle for the friendly or unfriendly jostling and rivalry of each of the other ethical traditions within it. The one condition imposed upon this framework for rivalry is that none of the other ethical traditions can ever win. No ethical tradition can advance to the goalpost of state power. Even a majoritarian consensus could be frustrated by rights that are intended to protect dissent from consensus and to privilege the efforts of those willing to put their property and time into resistance. Thus, without overthrowing this state, none can ever substitute its good for what looks like the abstention from the good that prevails in the liberal state. Possibly for this reason, few of the spokespersons for the other traditions represented in this book sound overwhelmingly grateful for the presence of the liberal state.

A common response of rival traditions to this (allegedly) universal framework is to feel demeaned and diminished. Few want to admit to having only particular hopes for particular people in particular places. Almost every tradition wishes for what liberalism has almost succeeded in achieving for itself: universal empire. Classical liberalism asserts a priority for its good, peace, along with the procedural justice and tolerance this requires. These are not inconsiderable civic accomplishments, even if they remain on the "thin" side of the ledger of moral goals. Nevertheless, while the thin liberal good accommodates the pressure of other traditions, it subtly demotes their more expansive aims. Demanding more egalitarian, or women friendly, or Christian, or lifeworld nourishing goods is always possible within the liberal framework, but only within an acknowledgment of liberal authority, which sometimes seems to its rivals set up to frustrate its ethical demands. Much of what Loren Lomasky says about the self-abstention and modesty of liberal authority should deflect some of this criticism, but I suspect it is not enough. The essays in this book have been unusually instructive in showing how shallow the appeal of a framework of liberal accommodation is to someone for whom other goods loom larger.

Besides having to deal with rivals in other ethical traditions, liberals have internal debates as well. "Exit" from demanding or suffocating relationships with unchosen communities is only half the story of the liberal state. The other half to the story is claimants in civil society who want "voice," not exit. They want the state to hear them, because they want it to change the terms of its relationship, with them and with all citizens. The challenge of democracy for the classical liberal is nowhere more evident than in those groups who want the state to redistribute market gains. Lomasky's strategy is to construct a fire wall between them and the state. Thus, Lomasky is only formally right to stress that "a liberal order affords maximum latitude to voluntary association." Though he accuses social democratic rivals of expanding the state and thereby diminishing "the space within which civil society can flourish," Lomasky nevertheless admits that classical liberalism has a profound ambivalence about civil society. All those pesky little redistributionist groups would, if they got their way, undermine the foundation of a "regime of rights." He aims to show how the very constitution of such a state prohibits any such amendments. If so, what the classical liberal offers to civil society with one hand, the right to organize for rent control or minimum wage, he takes away with the other, the right occasionally to succeed. This is bound to have a chilling effect on group formation.

Let us agree that overbearing voices from civil society can threaten rights. But where can we find the once and for all time set of rights that ought not to be violated? Reading and rereading Locke? There are often real conflicts among rights. The wager that the classical liberal makes is that there will be necessarily only one such rational solution to the problem of protecting human dignity and autonomy. If there is more than one solution, there is no settled doctrine of rights and no easy way to defeat redistributionist arguments, which may now claim to rest on alternative schedules of rights, upheld or denied. There will then be no way to settle on one set of rights without either an appeal to empirically contingent utilities or to the constraints suggested by other ethical traditions.

JEWISH TRADITION, ETHICAL LIFE, AND THE "FACT OF PLURALISM"

Suzanne Stone identifies in the Jewish tradition a moral anxiety common to many of the other ethical traditions, a feeling of disgust or bewilderment at alternatives to itself. This feeling inhibits each from coming to terms with value conflicts in civil society. Jewish tradition teaches, she says, that there is no morality beyond its boundaries, but only "a state of moral chaos." When Jewish tradition confronts the liberal state and its freedoms, anxiety takes the form of feelings of "self-isolation and estrangement." These expressions of dread indict societies given over to principles of individual choice. The latter undermine a sense of the given quality of observance and community.

It might be useful to compare this dread of liberal modernity with a similar anxiety that one finds in a classic text of political philosophy, *The Philosophy of Right*. In civil society, Hegel argues, the self-chosen are "just there." In just being there, such individuals feel no necessity to justify themselves by their family background, their history, or their citizen identity—all things that Hegel insists are still important. Not caring in their state of just being there about any of these things, they are forms of "particularity" who know only how "to develop and express themselves" in all directions. They accommodate themselves to others by a kind of experimental morality. They try out universal principles. Kant's categorical imperative would be an example, but so would Mill's later principle for restrictions on liberty. The point is to see whether their own sphere of self-chosen activities can be rendered consistent in an abstract and formal way with a like choice offered to others. In such a way, individuals lacking all sense of either ethical origins or destiny negotiate a juridically possible life with others by testing different formulas for consistency and comprehensiveness.

Hegel's attitude toward these innovative self-fabrications is wholly negative. It is, he says, "ethical order split into its extremes and lost."[3] Though secular, this judgment is a version of the sense of "moral chaos" Stone says was a characteristic reaction of traditional Jewish culture to modernity and liberal principles. Hegel may well have expressed an objection common to most of the traditions: an ethical life stands in contrast to individualistic negotiating and fabricating. Hegel seems to have thought that where there was no bedrock of history or community upon which to found a way of life, the principles that might organize our now separate lives were just too numerous. Moreover, he thought there was an "objective" way of perceiving human lives issuing from a historical and ethical *Geist,* or spirit, much as the other ethical traditions make similar claims today for moral perception. A well-educated "universal class" of bureaucrats was to be the instrument for reminding the wildly individualistic agents of civil society of their ethical duties.

Why is the classical liberal's riposte to this not apt? The "ethical" state is just as likely to be arbitrary and inventive about its "ethics" as are liberals in acting according to self-chosen moralities. Like many representatives of the ethical traditions in this volume, Hegel counted rather too heavily on the fact that he had a coherent account of a tradition from which "objective" duties could be read. But coherence is not truth. There are too many merely coherent stories. One of them, Hegel's *Phenomenology of Spirit,* begins the project of transforming philosophy into a kind of didactic remembrance of who "we" are that is then put into the service of collective identity. When countless imitators followed this first magnificent example of "identity" politics, the alleged "objectivity" of *Geist* fell victim to the same fate that Hegel thought was in store for the endless variety of liberal principles. There were simply too many such historical spirits for anyone who contemplated the spectacle to believe one of them counted as objective.

I rehearse this paradigmatic example of an effort to recover objective ethical duty from the multiplying interpretations of it because it succinctly spells out the problem in the way the traditions are represented in this volume. Each tradition on its own would present itself as "objective," as that without which a given people lose their bearings. But when we bring them together, as we must in this final chapter and as civil society ordinarily does, it is an assembly of the incongruous. The sense of "moral chaos" Stone detects in Jewish tradition becomes a recognizable anxiety across every tradition. Though Stone acknowledges that this reaction must be overcome if we are to tolerate civil society, even she worries whether it is possible for civil society to accommodate both community informed by ethical tradition and the voluntarism made possible by the alternatives to tradition. It may be an illusion of civil society to suppose unchosen community and self-chosen identity can coexist.

Despite these misgivings, Stone does not succumb to the temptation to fill up civil society with only her kind of ethical tradition. Civil society must remain a space where many such traditions rub up against one another. Walzer and Stone both cite the authority of John Rawls. For Walzer, Rawls's "fact of pluralism" explains why the question cannot be, What would civil society look like if everyone shared our faith or ideology? Stone agrees, but goes further in defending her views against those of Walzer. For her the "fact of pluralism" is not acknowledged if Walzer's egalitarians interfere with religious education when such schooling curtails citizens' material life chances. Holding out against egalitarian integration, she claims that the Jewish tradition would seek "to avoid a comprehensive liberalism." With this phrase, she invokes the newly discovered self-abnegation of John Rawls's *Political Liberalism.* For Rawls, the "fact of pluralism" leads to necessary vigilance against "the fact of oppression" that can be detected in every effort to secure society-wide consensus by appealing to "a comprehensive philosophical and moral doctrine."[4] By this demanding standard, most of the portraits of civil society in this volume are "oppressive," or in denial about the inevitability of plural moral understandings.

Stone turns her back on Walzer's egalitarian liberalism and embraces Lomasky's more libertarian understanding of these issues. Though the reasoning for this tactical maneuver is clear enough, the result is ironic. On behalf of a deep sense of tradition, an alliance is joined with the ideology the standard criticism of which is that it dissolves all traditions. For Stone, the survival of Jewish tradition in the modern world requires more pluralism, not more equality.

Stone and Walzer have come to terms with having only limited success. The egalitarianism on whose behalf Walzer speaks does not "imagine that progress toward that goal will be uncontested or that the partial successes will bring an ethically unified society." Again Stone goes further. For the Jewish tradition, "universal order is potentially dangerous." Stone admits that this very lack of universality poses a conceptual problem for Israel in finding a way to extend equal citizenship rights to non-Jews. Despite this issue, she finds in the Jewish tradition's respect for particularity a cautious modesty that avoids many worse problems.

The Boundary Disputes of Civil Society

While Michael Walzer presses the case for greater overall equality, Anne Phillips advocates the specific feminist case for greater equality as well as for more women-friendly policies and attitudes. Regarding the central organizational activities of civil society, both are content to leave it pretty much as it is, an instrument sometimes useful, sometimes not, for making oneself heard. Civil society is the not quite always serviceable platform from which to represent goods to fellow citizens and to obtain satisfaction from the state, satisfaction that will result in new policies, new funding for worthwhile projects, or both.

If not reformist about the content of civil society, both Phillips and Walzer have interesting things to say about its conventionally understood boundaries, which distinguish it from family, domestic, or private life on the one hand and the state or government on the other. Feminism has always been ambivalent about the segregation of the private from the public, often seeing in it not the provision of a sanctuary for private right, but a sanctuary for hidden and abusive male power. Even when women are treated fairly in the private sphere, the divide between private and public becomes all too often a barrier designed to keep them in the home and out of the public. Liberal egalitarians are made nervous by the conventional distinction between the political and the social, at least where this permits one to speak about political equality and its alleged compatibility with social inequality. Egalitarians worry that social inequality could undermine political equality. In any event, for egalitarians social inequality is bad in itself.

Phillips and Walzer sometimes work at cross-purposes. One of the advantages of "voluntary associations," she claims, is that "they belong to nobody but their members." Without outside pressure from a censorious establishment, they can become centers for quite radical innovations. For instance, churches often accept the ordination of women because they are independent of establishment pressure. But the general independence of voluntary associations is exactly what Walzer denies is the case. A great many such associations enjoy and depend upon "subsidies and subventions, 'matching grants' and low-interest loans, [and other] services provided by the state." If the state penetrates the associations of civil society to such an extent, would not some combination of regulatory services and funding temptations have a chilling effect on what Phillips seems to think of as their robust independence? Whatever cultural experimentation takes place is likely to be not too far in advance of the proclivities of the party in power or the culture of state regulators. Walzer's view directs reformers' attention away from the dependent associations of civil society and toward the task of conquering the state or, more modestly, of having an impact on its policies.

Phillips sometimes appreciates civil society because of its encouragement of cultural experiment, which would establish a civil society in rebellious counterpoint to state order. Yet at the same time she demands from this state firm policies that would impose more order on everyone. On the one hand, she enthusiastically cites Nancy Fraser's portrait of civil society as containing "a multiplicity of 'subaltern counterpublics' in which subordinated social groups can 'invent and circulate' their counter-discourses." On the other hand, like Lomasky's classical liberal, she sees how anarchic cultures unstructured by rights can become sites for manipulation, principally of women who are browbeaten into "volunteering" their unpaid time. In addition, like Walzer's egalitarian, she acknowledges that a "patchy network of voluntary associations [is] a poor substitute for universal provision by the state." But if the state is to provide these services, it will not do to have too many recalcitrant subaltern publics subverting its order.

Phillips raises an important feminist issue that concerns the linkage between equality on the job and inequality of effort in the household. She concludes that without equality in family life, women are unfairly burdened. She poses the further issue of what we should do about the man who tries to "extricate himself from pressure to do an equal part of the housework by buying a dishwasher or employing a cleaner." My response is that here is someone who is making an efficient use of his time in a market-savvy way. My next thought is that this man is an identifiable part of a vast "subaltern" counterpublic that anarchically resists the politically correct action. For Phillips, however, he is someone whose defective understanding of equality stands in dire need of a little juridical discipline. There ought to be a law against his evasion of duty.

Her juridical solution, an across-the-board equal-hours law encompassing household and public workplace, raises a fundamental problem. If civil society should prove to be so open and transparent to the state, so amenable to its being shaped and reshaped by its officials, is there any sense in which it exists as an independent entity apart from the state? There are two ways of characterizing Phillips's thirty-hours proposal. First, it might be another progressive triumph in the achievement of civil rights for everyone in an inclusive society. Second, juridically mandated equality according to the model one size fits all might be a characteristic top-down reform by rationalists who ignore all the cultural issues that would make a mess of any such reform.

Phillips herself highlights the way cultural issues undermine clear egalitarian reforms. "Feminism has recently moved into alliance with multiculturalism," she says, and adds regretfully "that this mutes some of its criticism of sexual subordination and inequality." Here is a (belated) recognition that the feminist label should not be denied to women who, representing other cultures, question Western feminist interpretations of equality. But in this context, one wonders how a thirty-hours law would accommodate immigrant Pakistanis who run family grocery stores in Britain? In order for these families to survive and to save for the future, these stores remain open for long hours. This would make them among the first targets of any such legislation.

Phillips describes her encounter with multiculturalism as a kind of threat: "it can lead to a loss of nerve in the face of inequality and inability to act." Would it be fair then to construe the demands, in this case presumably of Caribbean and Asian women in Britain, as an obstacle to the domination of a single principle, equality for all? Prior to this multicultural encounter, society was a transparent pane of glass through which a uniform and persistent inequity was visible, namely, gender inequality between men and women. A clear solution was available, giving priority to legislation and education that would sweep away obstacles to greater equality. Only a group that held a prior or competing dignity could arrest this impulse to transform competing claims into mere obstacles. Today it appears that only the dignity of a rival "culture" stands in the way of what Michael Walzer once referred to as the tyranny of "simple equality," which is to say, the application of a single principle across the domains of multiple complexities.[5]

The "Other" Civil Societies

In turning to the countries of Islam and Confucian East Asia, we gaze at territory in which, since Edward Said's *Orientalism,* Western commentators stand forewarned that their sentiments and instincts may be false. In a book devoted to a concept whose origins are European or Western, this effort at giving "civil society" a global reach by bringing in these two great ethical systems of the East could be construed as a gesture of respect. On the other hand, it could come across as an artificial supplement to the main story. The latter conclusion is premature, however. It would artificially separate out the entwined history of Islam from that of its transcendental partners, Judaism and Christianity. As Hasan Hanafi reminds readers, Islamic civilizations were hosts for considerable scientific and scholarly traditions, which contributed much to the development of Europe.

Compared to the world of Islam, however, Confucian China was until relatively recently far less connected to the West. Even Said's book betrays this fact. Under the title of *Orientalism*, there are relatively few references to the Confucian cultural zone.[6] That is not to say there is no history of Western contact with these regions that would not fall under the opprobrium of illustrating "orientalist" attitudes. But it is to suggest that Europeans had wholly different attitudes and complexes about regions closer to them, the Islamic countries, than they did to more remote places, at least before the nineteenth century. There is not one "Orient," but several.

Nevertheless, East Asia has increasing relevance to the West. This goes beyond the expectations for a Pacific trading zone. As Richard Madsen amply illustrates, Confucian East Asia is a rich source of ethical models of evidently worthy conduct that Western communitarians can invoke to excoriate what they regard as excessive individualism in the United States and elsewhere. Adding to the force of these arguments is a sense that the torch of progress has been handed to Asia. The economic crisis of 1997 may have dampened this particular enthusiasm for some, but many are still persuaded that Hegel's *Geist*, having passed out of Europe and across America, is about to take up long residence in the Confucian cultural zone.

The ideological uses of East Asia are an extraordinary development and stand in contrast to the fact that in recent times almost no one in the West, except (some) Muslim immigrants and, interestingly, American black Muslims, takes Islam as a relevant utopian ideal. There is a sense in discussions of Islam of nostalgia for past glories, but of anguish about present difficulties. Few Westerners use Islam as a mirror for self-criticism. Why are Western communitarians willing to listen to Confucius but not to Mohammed? In Hanafi's mildly reformist gestures toward feminism, he uneasily puts his finger on a possible answer: the treatment accorded to women in Islam.[7] The relative absence of a public life for most ordinary women (Benazir Bhuttos aside) and their relatively greater subordination within the household makes it almost impossible for Western societies to uphold Islam as a model. Confucian culture is also hard on women, but it has benefited in recent years from some remarkable reinterpretation and reappropriation by, among others, Tu Wei-Ming and Richard Madsen, not to mention the modest transformations in gender relations that have taken place in many societies thought to be nominally Confucian.

Though "veiled" and housebound women were a common enough feature in the history of Western societies, European thinkers from about the Enlightenment on began to take (what they understood as) the Islamic case as a foil and negative example. This helped to establish a new Western norm. Sequestering women was wrong. Furthermore, the wrong of sequestering was connected to the rightness of creating an "open" society that requires a civility only a gendered public life confers.

Global emigration is another reason why Islamic and Confucian cultures require treatment in a book devoted mostly to Western civil societies. Large numbers of Muslim- and Confucian-instructed families, whose ancestors were born in the Middle East, Southeast Asia, or East Asia, find they are now living in Western democratic and pluralist societies where they are distinct minorities.

Islamic and Confucian countries are not marginal to these analyses for another reason. They may well serve as future sites of civic heroism. There is a danger in any such effort. Nevertheless, such conflict was unavoidable in the West. Is it possible that much of the work of constructing or growing civil society is left to do in Islamic and Confucian cultures? Sometimes the state is too powerful, sometimes too weak. Only when the Chinese state ceases to fear "intermediary bodies" like the Falun Gong and only when the Islamic state can assert itself enough to tame or deflect the tyranny of the fundamentalists will we know whether civil society has taken root in these two regions.

Islam: Civil Society without Pluralism?

Hasan Hanafi carefully weaves a middle path between two extreme models about what Islamic society could become. The fact that one of these extremes is simply the Western model suggests part of the difficulty. There must be a distinctly Islamic path to civil society, since anything else would look like servile conformity to the West and would subsequently play into the hands of Hanafi's rivals, fundamentalists of several descriptions who represent the opposing model. In this context, Hanafi is a moderate reformer. Even as a moderate, he runs some risk. Recall his reference to the case of Cairo University professor Nasr Hamid Abu Zaid, who was hauled before a religious court for a modest reinterpretation of Islam and declared an apostate. When fundamentalist judges compelled him to divorce his wife (because she could not remain married to an apostate), they simultaneously struck the classic totalitarian posture of seeking to eradicate all resistance to uniformity of belief and presented a dramatic example of a "lifeworld" turning upon and consuming itself. Religious beliefs designed to reinforce family life were now used to destroy it.

The above example suggests the problem. A polarized civil society that contains groups even more repressive than the illiberal state that presides over Egyptian society paralyzes any effort to weave a middle way. Hanafi's explanation of the behavior of these groups shares something in common with Walzer's suggestion that unless one addresses the "weakness" of the groups involved in an "identity" politics, one will not be able to dampen down the conflicts they generate. Hanafi claims that Islamic groups are repressive and intolerant because they are proscribed by a repressive state: "elements that are not allowed to compete for popular support within civil society will inevitably become as averse to the values of civil society as those who suppress them." But how quickly will groups change when their "weakness" is addressed? As the Algerian, Northern Irish, and Yugoslavian cases point out, there may well be long delays before newly empowered groups unlearn the habits of repression.

Is Islamic culture compatible with pluralism? Hanafi answers yes, but this pluralism flourished only in the remote past. "Muslim societies in the first four centuries were pluralistic societies," which "the great thinker al-Ghazali" destroyed a millennium ago. Hanafi's regretful reflections on the role of this particular Islamic intellectual in politics provide an ironic counterpoint to the overall confidence he has in such intellectuals. To be sure, he says there is no alternative within the tradition. The sole pluralistic alternative to the sovereignty of the prince (the *iman* or sultan) comes from the intellectual authority of cleric-judges, the *ulama,* who in interpreting and appropriating sacred scripture have the right to call the *iman* to account and even to call for revolt against him. He cites only one other historical source of pluralism, lodged in the privately funded *awqaf,* or religious endowments and foundations, but these, too, are filled with scholars. This intellectual authority can be abused, he admits. In some Muslim countries religion is used "as a cover for dictatorship." Nevertheless, Hanafi is not deterred from asserting that in any reform movement, "the lead must be taken by Muslim intellectuals and modernist scholars."

When intellectuals alone bear the responsibility for voicing the concerns of society, whom does this leave out of account? We have not far to go for an answer when we learn that "private property" is not a fundamental human right. With this move, the intellectual's natural rival, the merchant, has been, so to speak, conceptually eliminated and the grounds for a pluralist Islam have been undermined. To be sure, one ought to be sensitive to the danger of converting the benefits of private property into unjustified political power over others. One may accordingly call for public regulation of private property sufficient to avoid such misfortune. But arguments which assure us that property and market exchange have no rightful legitimacy go further than even contemporary socialist or social democratic discourse would allow. Michael Walzer has best adduced the reasons. He worries constantly about how those involved in "free exchange" might go beyond their "sphere" of legitimate endeavor, but he never doubts that free exchange and private property constitute a legitimate sphere of human endeavor. Without acknowledging the multiple and conflicting spheres of human endeavor, the search for justice and "simple equality" risks ending in "tyranny."[8]

It could nevertheless be claimed that on Walzer's own grounds, Hanafi wins the point. Since Walzer adopts culture as the basis of justification, if Hanafi is right in claiming that pluralism disappeared from Islamic culture a thousand years ago, then there would be no grounds for justifying pluralism within Islamic culture. But that still leaves Walzer's judgment about all nonpluralist contexts, that they are "tyrannical," hanging in midair like the Cheshire cat's smile. Hanafi might not disagree with the judgment, since he, too, seems to be searching for a new pluralism.

If so, I would urge him to reconsider his disapprobation of private property. The defense of pluralism is made easier in societies in which there exist alternative sources of power. Private property (in its appropriate sphere) is one such source. For some this argument is less telling in countries whose pluralism is alternatively provided, say, by distinct cultural traditions. But I fail to see how distinct cultural traditions can be protected, especially minority cultures, if the property held by adherents of a given culture can be appropriated or taxed into oblivion by the state. Walzer spells out the prevailing and, he thinks, justified consensus on these issues: "Private property is [to be] safe against arbitrary taxation and confiscation, and state officials cannot interfere with free exchange and gift giving within the sphere of money and commodities, once that sphere has been properly marked off."[9] On Hanafi's own evidence, the pluralism in the countries he considers is thin or nonexistent. By eliminating the merchant class and therefore a moral perspective predictably different from that of an Islamic intellectual, we have abandoned not only an alternative source of initiative and energy for Muslim countries, but the only moral and secular rivals to Islamic intellectuals.

To the extent the other ethical traditions in this book also presuppose the need for authoritative intellectual interpretation, they too run the risk of seeming to invoke a will to power by the intellectual. There can be a Christian as well as an Islamic society, but neither of them will count as "civil societies" so long as the dominant mores, Christian or Muslim, close off all avenues to alternative interpretations and perspectives.

CONFORMITY AND REMONSTRANCE: CONFUCIAN CIVILITIES

It is possible to agree with Richard Madsen that in many East Asian societies one sees evidence of the survival of communitarian habits and sentiments that, much to the regret of their Western advocates, have become weaker and more attenuated in places like the United States. In naming this communitarian spirit "Confucian," those associated with this effort offer East Asians an all-encompassing ideological framework. It serves several purposes simultaneously. Invoking Confucian culture permits each society to look to the future with a sense of being anchored in the past. By not seeming too dependent on the West, Confucian civil society solves the legitimacy problems that plague Islamic variants. In place of the dissolving communist idea in China, Confucianism offers new social cement. It presents itself as a cultural resource for the Singapore experiment. In affirming once again the centrality of the Sino-cultural sphere in East Asia, these interpreters consolidate the pride of the Chinese and extend a palm branch of reconciliation to the Koreans and Japanese, who are included as members of the broader community. *Confucian culture* is meant to function much as the term *Christendom* once did before Europe and America substituted for it the more secular geographical reference, *the West*. This is ambition enough for a recently reformulated set of cultural themes. But do these add up to a coherent tradition?

One can claim that Chinese Confucian culture extends, say, to Korea, but this begs the question of how the tradition changes when it crosses national boundaries. The issue of the differential impact of ideas across national or other boundaries plagues all the other descriptions of ethical traditions in this book, too. In assessing the quality of Confucian belief, one must also identify its dialogue partners. In China, the ruling communist party is sometimes said to have exhausted its ideological hold on its adherents, but it nevertheless is the final arbiter of norms and settler of disputes in the country. Do reminders of a Confucian heritage help cadres, newly confused about the nature of the communist authority they wield, reconcile themselves to the temptations of a capitalist economy? In all likelihood it could, though whether it does or not in the minds of the relevant Chinese is an empirical question.

In its latest incarnation, Confucian culture presents itself as a synthesizer and conciliator. But for it to function in a civil society that presupposes conflict (as the cases of Tiananmen Square and the Falun Gong suggest), we also need to know whether there is anything in it that can justify opposition and conflict, as opposed to the harmony that it usually commends and indeed commands. In this respect the most useful part of Madsen's discussion is his stress on the ancient Confucian practice of scholars who remonstrate, often at great personal cost, with authority. The right and capacity to remonstrate is a prerequisite to any civil society.

Given the identification of Confucian morality with being Chinese, one may look askance at the idea that Japan is Confucian. For Hiroshi Watanabe, "Japanese society has been a poor disciple of the Confucian sages."[10] The new wave of Confucian studies may gesture toward a united Asia, but it is on Chinese terms. Of course, maybe Japan is Confucian and China is not! China was subject to colonization, civil war, invasion, revolution, and communist restructuring. Japan avoided colonization, civil war, and communist revolution, and was occupied for only a short while by a foreign power content to leave much alone. Thus, Japan, not China, is an ancien régime, perhaps the last surviving Confucian culture. Whatever the case, being Confucian is evidently an idea so general that it loses any explanatory value faced with such different societies as China and Japan.

Until recently the conclusion that Japan was Confucian would have been taken as naming the magic elixir that had made Japan rapidly so wealthy and powerful. But times change. Now one can ask not only, Is Japan Confucian? but also, Is this a good thing? For one reviewer of a book extolling the communitarian virtues of a Confucian Japan, the worst part of the Confucian heritage is that one comes to believe "it is not polite to protest, or to argue with those above you."[11] If remonstrance is the key theme in bringing a Confucian into civil society, one prepared for public dialogue with authority, it would appear on this account that in Japan this art has died out. Not only is it impolite to protest; potential dissenters must constantly worry about the humiliation or lost face of those exposed to protest. This suggests a comparison to Islamic civil society, for there, too, according to Hasan Hanafi, "advice [to superiors] has to be in private not in public so that the advised should not be blamed publicly." Whatever civil society may be in either an Islamic or a Confucian culture, it is not yet public dialogue.

For Madsen, Taiwan is "probably the most open society in East Asia." But the openness is less a toleration for "moral pluralism" than a respect for "civility" in search of "social consensus." Madsen's distinction suggests two legitimate modalities for achieving social order: a liberal mode, which tolerates pluralism, and a communitarian mode, which presupposes that pluralism must be subordinated to a common ethical heritage. But in practice, does a shared heritage mean anything more than a thin official morality that pretends it is thick while averting its eyes from the exceptions that effectively spell out the reality of moral pluralism?

Should Civil Society Become Transparent or Remain Opaque?

Most of the ethical traditions surveyed in this volume would offer some sort of reform of civil society. Even Lomasky's generous acceptance of its possibilities is qualified by a wish to restrict by a stipulated agenda of rights what might be constitutionally allowable. Let us then raise the issue that is prompted by the presence of so many self-confident espousers of ethical reform. If the reformer is always right or rational, the intermediary organizations possess no legitimate independence. These associations become the accommodating transmission belts of reforms invented elsewhere. Transmission belts neither add nor subtract from what is transmitted. To alter the image, associations are transparent and open to the surveillance of enlightened officials. Opaque associations, which do not transmit light, are mere obstacles. An "obstacle" has no prior or persisting dignity. It names unjust or irrational action, which fully deserves the fate of being swept away.

No doubt there are occasions in which a reformer may legitimately be glad for associations that simply transmit new ideas. The reformer may also legitimately find satisfaction in reducing recalcitrant "bodies" to impotence. But if the reformer should find that all intermediary bodies are simply friends or foes, allies to be counted on or enemies to be dispersed, there is no need for civil society. There is only the need for a political calculation of who is a friend or not of a singular vision of what society, all of it, could become. By contrast, the landscape of a civil society is strewn with people and organizations situated in the middle, neither particularly your friend nor especially your foe. These groups have identities and dignities each to their own, and concerned with their own, however much each group's activities may unintentionally or intentionally frustrate grand designs from elsewhere.

Let us conclude with the questions about civil society to which the authors responded. (1) What are its ingredients? (2) How is society defined? What (3) values, (4) risks, (5) senses of responsibility, and (6) freedom are in play in these conceptual worlds? The "fact of pluralism" looms large in my responses to these questions. I cannot shake the conviction that many of the authors had a hard time coming to terms with it. As I said at the outset, this may have been a result of answering only the question How should civil society be reformed in the light of a given ethical tradition? But if there is anything constitutive about either the theory or practice of civil society, it is that it represents a space where rival understandings of the good life either jostle one another constantly or remain quietly opaque one to the other. Suzanne Stone, Loren Lomasky, and Michael Walzer (representing the Jewish, classically liberal, and egalitarian liberal traditions, respectively) generously acknowledged this. Indeed, Stone took Walzer to task for not sufficiently insisting upon it. The other contributors drifted in the direction of viewing civil society as a transmission belt for singular ethical traditions.

What are the ingredients and definitions of civil society? On the first model, civil society consists of groups who are transparent to one another and to the state. The "ingredients" are groups who try to perfect themselves in the light of the norms of a specific ethical tradition that, it must be assumed, has captured the state or defines the culture of state officials. On the second model, the ingredients of a civil society consist of groups who embody plural and, within limits, incompatible values. Both theories of civil society require a lawful state—otherwise these are just descriptions of anarchy. In one account, the state is strong enough to impose its values or to persuade others of their importance. On the other account, it is strong enough to preside over a society where there is no or only a minimal social consensus. Accordingly, the values of civil society will differ as well. On one account, they vary narrowly within parameters defined by the dominant mores. On another account, these values are protean, except for one exception. There will be a general recognition that each way of life embodied by a value requires a prior deference to a lawful sovereign.

To turn to the risks, once again they come on two accounts. The risks of the transmission belt theory of civil society is that it may justify a little too fully the never failing "rightness" of dominant mores (whether represented in the "virtuous" state or in "virtuous" groups). As a consequence, citizens will not know how to oppose the state or groups when its officials or members do wrong while acting in the name of official values. This is as much to say that where some see civic virtue, others see undue or unreflective conformity. Nor will transmission belt advocates understand the moral limits of being right. In identifying this as risk, I appeal to the complexity of moral judgments that often require balancing among conflicting values, not all of which are satisfactorily acknowledged within any ethical tradition. As for the risks of the entrenchment model, groups that benefit from it may have too little cognizance of their duties to others and even too little understanding of the advantages that lawful authority confers upon them. This blindness could be dangerous for themselves as well as for others.

As for responsibility, it comes in several shapes. On the transmission belt view, every citizen must remain attentive to a core of substantive agreements, however distracted he or she becomes by the endless temptations of complex societies. This may prove to be impossible. If so, the responsibility of officials and citizens alike is to recognize this impossibility and not to resort to a frenzy of intolerance and repression when some groups for perfectly good reasons of their own interpret their core commitments in ways that stray from official ideology. In other words, upholders of civic morality have a responsibility to avoid the intellectual self-deception that made cruelty so much easier in Hawthorne's New England or in the religious courts of Islamic Egypt. The entrenchment account avoids the intellectual vices to which those who believe in a thick social consensus are prone. But it may indulge in purely moral vices. Entrenched groups can become self-absorbed, narcissistic, selfish, and indifferent to the fate of others, and this is quite apart from the self-serving values legitimated by market societies.

Since these are recognized as vices (intellectual and moral) on almost every account of the ethical traditions, perhaps we should take this as affirmation of the relevance of an expanded understanding of natural law. My problem with Michael Pakaluk's natural law or Michael Banner's Thomist Aristotelian tradition and as well with Simone Chambers's progressive critical theory to which (I claim) they are related is that each is tempted to curtail too many freedoms for which there are legitimate constituencies in alternative ethical traditions. However overloaded the term may have become, freedom—"subjective freedom"—is both the most characteristic feature of every actually existing civil society and the element of it that most frightens the ethical traditions. They tend to see in it immoral innovations rather than an invitation to find a niche where, under acknowledgment of lawful authority, they may practice their own "subjective" versions of being free.

NOTES

The Institute for Advanced Study Princeton 1998–99 and Yale University 1999–2000 were congenial settings for considering these issues. I am grateful to Simone Chambers, Will Kymlicka, the anonymous readers, and to my colleague John Bowlin at the University of Tulsa for pointing the way to revisions.

1. Robert D. Putnam, with Robert Leonardi and Raffaella Y. Nanetti, *Making Democracy Work: Civic Traditions in Modern Italy* (Princeton: Princeton University Press, 1993).

2. "Civic is the adjective that best captures the nature of the activities . . . of the various Veronese fascist organizations . . . where chorale singing was a favored activity. . . . [A]ll of Italy engaged in public acts of chorale singing during the fascist period." Mabel Berezin, *Making the Fascist Self: The Political Culture of Interwar Italy* (Ithaca: Cornell University Press, 1997).

3. G. W. F. Hegel, *Philosophy of Right,* trans. T. M. Knox (1952; reprint, Oxford: Oxford University Press, 1967), p. 123, par. 184.

4. John Rawls, *Political Liberalism,* (New York: Columbia University Press, 1993), pp. 36–37.

5. Michael Walzer, *Spheres of Justice: A Defense of Pluralism and Equality* (New York: Basic Books, 1983), pp. 13–17.

6. It would be unmanageable to include much beyond the Islamic realm, Said not unreasonably insists, but he also offers a more substantial reason: Europeans considered Islam a bigger threat. Edward Said, *Orientalism* (New York: Random House, 1978), pp. 16, 73.

7. For comments on women in Islam by a Muslim woman scholar, see Fatima Mernissi, *Beyond the Veil: Male-Female Dynamics in Modern Muslim Society* (1975; reprint, Bloomington: Indiana University Press, 1987). I thank anthropologist Kamran Ali for discussing this with me.

8. Walzer, *Spheres of Justice,* pp. 3–26.

9. Walzer, *Spheres of Justice,* p. 283.

10. Hiroshi Watanabe, "They Are Almost the Same as the Ancient Three Dy-

nasties": The West as Seen through Confucian Eyes in Nineteenth-Century Japan," in *Confucian Traditions in East Asian Modernity: Moral Education and Economic Culture in Japan and the Four Mini-Dragons,* ed. Tu Wei-ming (Cambridge: Cambridge University Press, 1996), p. 120.

11. Frank Gibney, "The Real Asian Miracle: Exploring the Values That Underpin Modern Confucian Societies," *New York Times Book Review,* July 11, 1999, p. 27.

Contributors

MICHAEL BANNER is the F. D. Maurice professor of moral and social theology at King's College, University of London, formerly Bampton research fellow at St. Peter's College, Oxford, and director of studies in philosophy and theology at Peterhouse, Cambridge. His books include *The Justification of Science and the Rationality of Religious Belief.* He has written on the nature of Christian Ethics and its relevance to a number of contemporary issues. Some of these essays appear in *Christian Ethics and Contemporary Moral Problems.*

SIMONE CHAMBERS is associate professor of political science at the University of Colorado at Boulder. She is the author of *Reasonable Democracy: Jürgen Habermas and the Politics of Discourse,* for which she received the award for the Best First Book in Political Theory from the American Political Science Association. She has also published a number of articles on deliberative democracy, and she is currently working on democratic models of constitutional reform.

HASAN HANAFI is professor of philosophy at Cairo University. He has served as secretary-general of the Egyptian Philosophical Society as well as vice president of the Arab Philosophical Society. His publications include more than fourteen books, three critical editions, and four translations. His most recent books are *Islam in the Modern World* (2 vols.) and *The Anguish of the Scholar and the Citizen* (2 vols.) He has been a visiting professor at major universities in the United States, Japan, Morocco, and Germany.

WILL KYMLICKA is professor of philosophy at Queen's University. He is the author of *Liberalism, Community, and Culture; Contemporary Political Philosophy; Multicultural Citizenship* for which he received the Macpherson Prize from the Canadian Political Science Association and the Bunche Award from the American Political Science Association; and most recently of *Politics in the Vernacular: Nationalism, Multiculturalism, and Citizenship.* He is also the editor of *Justice in Political Philosophy; The Rights of Minority Cultures;* coeditor (with Ian Shapiro) of *Ethnicity and Group Rights;* and coeditor (with Wayne Norman) of *Citizenship in Diverse Societies.*

LOREN E. LOMASKY is professor of philosophy at Bowling Green State University and contributing editor to *Reason* and *Liberty* magazines. He is the author of *Persons, Rights and the Moral Community,* for which he received the 1990 Machette Prize. His most recent book, coauthored with Geoffrey Brennan, is *Democracy and Decision: The Pure Theory of Electoral Preference.* He also coedited (with G. Brennan) *Politics and Process: New Essays in Democratic Theory.*

RICHARD MADSEN is professor of sociology at the University of California, San Diego and a co-author (with Robert Bellah, William Sullivan, Ann Swidler, and Steven Tipton) of *The Good Society* and *Habits of the Heart,* which received the *Los*

Angeles Times Book Award and was jury nominated for the Pulitzer Prize. A former Maryknoll missionary, he has authored or coauthored five books on China, including *Morality and Power in a Chinese Village*, for which he received the C. Wright Mills Award; *China's Catholics: Tragedy and Hope in an Emerging Civil Society*; and *China and the American Dream*. His most recent book is *Meaning and Modernity: Religion, Polity, Self*, coedited with William Sullivan, Ann Swidler, and Steven Tipton.

MICHAEL A. MOSHER is chair of the political science department at the University of Tulsa. A contributor to the *American Political Science Review, Political Studies,* and *Political Theory,* he recently co-authored *Montesquieu's Science of Politics: Essays on the Spirit of Laws.* A recipient of two Fulbrights to Japan, the most recent at Tokyo University, he was in 1998–99 a fellow at the Institute for Advanced Study in Princeton, and in 1999–2000 a visiting professor of political science at Yale.

MICHAEL PAKALUK is associate professor of philosophy at Clark University, director of the Boston Area Colloquium in Ancient Philosophy, and a founding member of the American Public Philosophy Institute. His scholarly work has focused on the philosophical analysis of friendship and community, the philosophy of logic, and early analytic philosophy. He is the author of a Clarendon Aristotle volume on Nicomachean Ethics.

ANNE PHILLIPS is professor of gender theory at the London School of Economics. Her books include *Engendering Democracy, Destabilizing Theory: Contemporary Feminist Debates* (coedited by Michele Barret); *Democracy and Difference; The Politics of Presence; Feminism and Politics;* and *Which Equalities Matter?* She is currently working on tensions between sexual and cultural equality.

ADAM B. SELIGMAN is professor of religion and research associate at the Institute for Economic Culture at Boston University. He has taught in the United States, Israel, and Hungary, where he was a Fulbright Scholar from 1990 to 1992. His books include *The Idea of Civil Society; Innerworldly Individualism: Charismatic Community and Its Institutionalization; The Problem of Trust; Modernity's Wager: Authority, the Self and Transcendence;* and *Market and Community: The Bases of Social Order, Revolution and Relegitimation* (coauthored with Mark Lichbach). He is currently working on issues of authority and toleration.

SUZANNE LAST STONE is professor of law at Cardozo Law School, Yeshiva University. Her publications include articles on Jewish law in the *Harvard Law Review, Commentary,* and *Cardozo Studies in Law and Literature.* She is also a contributor to the Yale University Press Series on the Jewish Political Tradition. Her special interests include connections between the Jewish legal model and contemporary American legal theory; justice, mercy, and gender in rabbinic thought; and legal pluralism in Jewish law.

MICHAEL WALZER is a permanent member of the School of Social Science at the Institute for Advanced Study in Princeton. He is coeditor of *Dissent* and a contributing editor of the *New Republic.* He is the author of *The Revolution of the Saints; The Company of Critics; Just and Unjust Wars; Spheres of Justice; Interpretation and Social Criticism; On Toleration;* and other books as well as many articles.

Index